SIMON ILLINGWORTH

One man's stand against police corruption and Melbourne's gangland war

Published by Fontaine Press, Australia
P.O. Box 948, Fremantle, Western Australia, 6959
www.fontainepress.com

Copyright © Simon Illingworth 2006

National Library of Australia Cataloguing-in-Publication
Author: Illingworth, Simon.
Title: Filthy Rat : One man's stand against police corruption and
               Melbourne's gangland war / Simon Illingworth.
Edition: 3rd ed. (International)
Publisher: Fremantle, W.A. : Fontaine Press, 2008.
ISBN: 9780980417043 (pbk.)
Subjects: Illingworth, Simon.
               Victoria Police--Corrupt practices.
               Police--Victoria--Biography.
               Police corruption--Victoria.
               Gangs--Victoria.
               Organized crime--Victoria.

Dewey Number: 364.132309945

No part of this publication may be translated, reproduced, or transmitted in any form or by any means, in whole or in part, electronic or mechanical including photocopying, recording, or by any information storage or retrieval system without prior permission in writing from the publisher.

DEDICATION

To my former colleagues, honestly slogging it out against the odds, twenty-four hours a day, picking up the pieces of shattered lives and wrestling through an impossible system of justice while trying to keep their own integrity intact. And to the truly brave whistleblowers, witnesses and their families, who, like me, have risked their lives in the fight against organised crime and corruption. A sickly culture refers to these people as 'rats', but they are heroes.

CONTENTS

Foreword	1
Introduction	3
Prologue	11
1 From patriotic panache to penniless poachers	17
2 Baptism of fire	28
3 Caging crims: early days	38
4 In the giggle	46
5 The rat trap	57
6 Organised and disorganised crime	70
7 Hooray for Collingwood	83
8 The courage of a coward	92
9 Homicide Squad	102
10 Professional practices	116
11 Ethical standards	127
12 Pot luck	140
13 Change of heart	156
14 Collecting the mail	171
15 Just the birthday present I wanted	188
Appendix 1: Glossary	201
Appendix 2	205
Appendix 3	207
Appendix 4	217

FOREWORD

Those of us fortunate enough to know of Simon Illingworth realise that this brave man certainly has a story to tell. Many of us were touched by his *Australian Story* program in 2004. If you haven't seen it — get a copy. Meeting and working with him has been one of the proudest experiences of my life. Anyone who has ever been a whistleblower knows how difficult your life can be. I was the deputy general manager of finance at HIH Insurance. In 1999 and in the following year, I went to the authorities to alert them to the company's problems. It was a difficult decision to make, and I guess you could say I wasn't too popular. Anyhow, the authorities did not listen to me, and as a result, the company went broke in 2001 with estimated debts of $5.3 billion.

When Simon first blew the whistle he was in his early twenties and from this time on he became a marked man. No one would have begrudged him if he'd quit, but he didn't; he stuck at it.

Being a whistleblower in the HIH tragedy was hard; many people were affected by the collapse, including me, but in Simon's case the danger to him personally was magnified many times. His story brings home how bad things can get.

This is a remarkable book of one man's courage in a sleazy underworld very few people ever see. Simon wants to change our culture, and for everyone's sake I hope he achieves his ambition.

Jeff Simpson

INTRODUCTION

Our community expects so much from our police officers. Sometimes they just can't deliver; no police budget will ever satisfy everyone. But police integrity stands alone. It is not part of a community wish list; it is absolutely non-negotiable.

This book will take you into the underworld, a stinking dog-eat-dog environment that left Melbourne reeling from a spate of killings and rampant police corruption. The last of the murders attributed to the Melbourne gangland wars took place in February 2006. Most people clearly thought it was all over in May 2004, but history tells us it is not because it never is. Crime and corruption will never end, not ever. At best we can control it and minimise it. At worst it will consume the spirit of the good people and entrench itself in our culture.

We were warned decades ago that if our mobsters were left to operate unchecked they would infiltrate legitimate business: that has happened. Now, if Australia's mateocracy stays loyal to the real rats — the bent cops and underworld crooks who prey on our most vulnerable people — a new Australian culture will be born, a culture of business chaos and corruption where our wealthiest people will undoubtedly also be the most corrupt.

I have studied organised crime and corruption internationally, and I have been up to my neck in this shit for a long time, and I warn you, we are dangerously poised for yet another era of gangland violence with cunning bent cops and crooks the likes of which we've never seen before.

I know, I've watched it escalating; it's never been as bad as it is now. No one seems willing to admit it — society has been blindfolded. Well, enough is enough; it's time someone told the truth. Albert Einstein was right when he said, 'The world is a dangerous place, not because of those who do evil but because of those who look on and do nothing.'

Today the people who stand against evil are persecuted. But despite the hardship they face, they know what they stand for. Criminals, on the other hand, live a slimy existence, they pretend to be legitimate, some have flash cars and houses, but they are never satisfied.

A large portion of our community is made up of spineless jellyfish. Those poor insipid souls never know who they are, or what they stand for, they live life in a perpetual vacuum. They tumble down the road like a foam cup in the breeze — they just go with the flow. Meanwhile, morally, our community degenerates to the lowest common denominator.

When parts of cities become overcrowded slums, approximately 5 per cent of the residents develop a lifestyle based on crime. In the 1950s US scientist John Christian studied the overcrowding of non-aggressive animals. He found that some overcrowded deer literally gave up and died. But perhaps more important for this book are the findings of researcher John Calhoun who, according to Colin Wilson in his book *True Crime*, studied the overcrowding of a more aggressive species — the rat. Calhoun found that the rat's response to overcrowding was violence, including rape and cannibalism. In the late 1980s, another young man unwittingly began studying the effects of overcrowding in the poorer areas of Melbourne, but his research was based on the human species. That young man was me.

I am thirty-eight years old and too young to be writing an autobiography. But every time I look in the mirror I am reminded of the seventeen-year war I've waged with the true rats of our society. I don't feel thirty-eight. I feel much older.

You might think that criminals have no values, principles or skills, but they do. Their values are just different to those of most people. Most criminals understand and like greed, deception, blind loyalty, rape, blackmail, extortion and frenzied, unrelenting violence. But most of all, criminal behaviour is about power. The egotistical swagger along a crowded city street in the best suit money can buy may be just as lawless as an open display of brutal violence.

There are many kinds of power. There is the power of blackmail: the intimidation of hard-working civilians, combined with the fear of financial or physical repercussions, creates a business environment in which a gangster cannot lose. The power of invincibility and lawlessness, the solidarity of men with little if any self-control, provides a criminal with the ability to make someone an offer they can't refuse. And last, there is the power of cultural knowledge, in which a criminal group preys on their own expatriated folk. For these people crime knows no boundaries and immigrants are easy picking no matter where they settle. Interestingly, many gangsters are likely to be first or second-generation immigrants themselves.

Traditionally, policing agencies obey geographical boundaries, but organised criminals and extortionists don't; this is the cold, hard reality for some of Australia's most vulnerable people.

Most gangsters delight in displaying the power of their wealth. Recently, a Melbourne gangster and reputed hitman was buried in a gold-plated casket. The sickening and often tacky display of ill-gotten gain demonstrates two significant things about mobsters: the police either can't or won't catch them, and they're proficient at what they do.

I've endured intimidation and fear in many different ways and for many reasons. I am neither a deer nor a rat (although some may dispute the latter). I am human, the same flesh and blood as we all are, yet I'm different to most because I've fought the criminal underworld in many forms and I'm still here to tell the tale. I'm sure I need to write this more than you need to read it.

My inadvertent experiment is almost over now and so I should describe to you who I am. I am a solidly built bloke, 1.8 metres (six feet) tall, with fair hair and blue eyes. I scrub up OK despite some telltale scars on my head, face, hands and knuckles. I suffer bouts of insomnia and stress and probably unhealthy doses of paranoia. I trust very few people.

I've risked my life many times. My friends and relatives have also risked theirs, not because they wanted a Russian roulette gamble, but simply because they know me.

Unwittingly, I've been searching for my Holy Grail in life: the key to a good ethical community. In trying to find this end, I've lived a lifestyle that I now believe is unachievable for one person to endure long term, either mentally or physically. I've hit the wall; I can't do it any more.

I've been called a 'give-up', a 'lagger', a 'rat from the filth', a 'filthy rat' and many other things, some of which are unprintable. Effectively, I've been a crime and corruption investigator, having previously been a whistleblower. I've been a member of the 'police police', Internal Affairs. When I speak of corruption in this book sometimes it's in general terms; at other times I nominate the specific offences, but you need to understand that corruption takes many different forms in many different contexts.

Generally, most international anti-corruption bodies deal with, or attempt to deal with, the receipt of bribes (graft), extortion, shady dealings, cover-ups or fraud by public officials. Public officials include police, council workers and politicians. A number of Australian anti-corruption agencies also consider that acts performed by private firms working for public officials come under their umbrella of public corruption. Many countries take this view, but not all. When I use the word 'corruption' I take in all these definitions, not any particular one. I write of corruption holistically.

I also suspect that, when I mention my lifestyle, I mean something different from what you may be familiar with. My lifestyle has involved security doors, sensors, video surveillance, revolvers and security fences. The taxpayer has funded the large percentage of these necessary expenses. Tragically, this security I have at home is the 'reward' that the taxpayer gives people like me for our dedication, honesty and courage in taking on corruption, being bashed and threatened and putting our necks on the line over a number of years. I know I am not the only one who has made personal sacrifices for the good of our community. There are many others.

Today's newspaper will probably have about ten pages devoted to our courageous sporting champions, some of whom donate their spare time visiting the sick and frail or helping worthwhile charities. These actions are worthy of praise, yet it is relatively easy to donate your time when you are paid excessively well and have television cameras ready to show the rest of us what a community-minded person you are.

Most people are like you and me. We have to work hard to make ends meet and, if we're one of the few with any spare time left to be community-minded, we receive little if any recognition for our charitable work. In the same way, a cop's charitable work is rarely warm and fuzzy — it's a hard slog that often involves blood, violence and a personal war with your conscience. No one can claim to be perfect in a world of cops and robbers.

A helicopter hovering above a sports star's head provides an unusual camera angle for the viewers at home; a helicopter hovering over my head for the last seventeen years usually meant someone had been murdered, raped or mugged. It's not easy to forget the thud of the police helicopter's rotor blades.

Most people think a hero is somebody who acts courageously in white-hot moments, but to me there is far greater courage in making an ethical decision when detrimental consequences are known. It is far tougher than taking a risky gamble. I know because I've done both many times. During my career as a detective I've seen plenty of unsung heroes, people performing selfless and courageous acts for the good of our community. Most have received nothing in the way of recognition. In some cases, they've actually suffered for standing up for what is right. These people haven't chosen to be involved in life-changing events. They just happened to have been there and seen, heard or known something and have chosen to do the right thing. People achieve incredible things when they are encouraged and supported; indeed, the lack of support for these heroes just makes their courage all the more precious.

A friend once quoted to me that 'Reasonable people change themselves to suit the world, unreasonable people change the world to suit themselves'. Only the unreasonable person can change the world. Given the right circumstances, I can be one of the most unreasonable people you'll meet. But I don't necessarily want to change the world — it's just that I can't accept the disgraceful treatment of some of Australia's true heroes. Australians need to change.

Like other honest cops, I've worked for you, assessing facts and evidence, doggedly tracking down and incarcerating the underworld people you fear. Most of us are tough and we try to do the job as ethically as possible, not just within the rules.

It isn't easy dealing with notorious criminals or corrupt cops in real life. You're lucky, you just read about them in the newspapers or see versions of them on TV or in the movies. This is the kind of crime that most people see.

People's craving to be given a head on a stick when a heinous offence occurs is always satisfied in fictional television shows. Many TV programs have a rogue cop character, someone who, much to the delight of the audience, bends a few rules to get the job done. That's OK on TV, but this behaviour cannot be tolerated on the street. In real life, police misconduct has lasting effects. This type of corruption is counterproductive to lasting and effective policing. In essence it's tackling wrong with wrong, and nobody wins. Most people think movies show them what it's like working within the underworld. They don't. Being a cop tracking the worst of the worst is a hard slog. For a detective to play by the rules, while investigating underworld gangsters or corrupt police who clearly don't, isn't easy. Add to this the public's cultural acceptance of police cutting corners, as they have seen on television, and the Australian culture of blind mateship, and you'll see why we have big problems.

Cops often turn a blind eye to colleagues who cheat or take short cuts and this has led to many large voids and grey areas in policing. But the perception that a detective who acts unethically is somehow more effective in cleaning up crime is wrong. When Clint Eastwood played the fictional detective Dirty Harry Callahan he carried a monstrous handgun called a 44 auto–mag. Harry often reminded cowering crims of its power, 'When this is used properly it doesn't leave fingerprints …', but the simplistic idea of meeting fire with fire in the real underworld creates an inferno, not peace. Corrupt detectives are the ones who cut corners, disregard rules and rely predominantly upon information from informers. These are the same police who often become willing to cut shady deals with criminal informers to get another easy pinch, and later to make a quick buck for themselves. These detectives rarely put in the hard slog. Most of them couldn't track a bleeding elephant through the snow, but they can track down a freebie, a part timer or an 'earn' very well.

Some police have tacitly allowed informers to take part in the same crime as that of the criminals they inform on. This of course is counterproductive but makes the detectives' arrest rate look impressive. The net result is that you, the community, gain nothing from the so-called successful arrest. Worse still, the community loses; as one crook gets a red light another is given a green. I've never met an underworld crook who has wanted to help me in some way without wanting something in return.

It's very tempting to run an informer and get easy pinches, but resisting the insidious compromise makes the true ethical champion and, indeed, the best detective. My investigations speak for themselves. I've been responsible for incarcerating criminals for combined sentences of well over 100 years. Very few of my arrests have relied solely upon informers. It's too dangerous; information is a good start to an investigation.

This autobiography is my life's story, the way I heard it, saw it, smelt it and lived it. I've changed many names to protect the innocent, some not-so-innocent and others I don't want to name for legal, personal or safety reasons. This book is about the big picture, although I expect some of the intricate detail will blow the lid off some of the spin that you've been fed over recent years. All is not well in this country.

I've done a great deal of research to ensure that any of the events not personally witnessed by me or by other reliable sources are corroborated with evidence or are based on court convictions, news reports or facts. Otherwise the event doesn't appear in this book, despite the temptation.

I respect the law of defamation and the rights of others, so I've edited out a tragedy or two from what I'd originally written. I've done this to protect other people, not myself. I've never shied away from being a completely fallible human being, as we all are. Like you, I've made mistakes and done some stupid things, so if you've purchased this book with the intention of reading the story of a shining white knight — stop reading, wrap it up and give it to a relative for Christmas. Hopefully, he or she likes true stories, not fiction.

It should come as no surprise that some don't want the system fixed: they'll say it's OK the way it is. Clearly, I don't agree, but that's my opinion

— and, as Dirty Harry Callahan says, 'Opinions are like arseholes, we've all got one', so I'll leave it to you to make up your own mind.

I would like to thank my loving wife Sarah, as well as Milly, Mum, Chris, Bin, Poss, Ross, Caitte, the old man, Gran, Jim, Merilyn, Lee Flanagan, Sandy Robertson, Bill, Dawn, Con and the lads, Steve, Sharon, Damien Morgan, Dave Goodrich, Dan, Lauren, Darren, Dr D. Morrell, Dr D. Barkley, Jeff Simpson, Robert Doyle, Kim Wells, the Liberal Party of Victoria, Neil, Toni O'Sullivan, Billy, Mick and Pete, Nick and Jo, Old Scotch Football Club, Port Campbell Community, Scotch College, Simon, Graeme, St James Ethics Centre.

Belinda Hawkins and ABC's *Australian Story*, radio stations 4BC and 3AW, journalists on the *Australian, Herald Sun, Age, Ballarat Courier*, Neil Mitchell, Padraic Murphy, Katie Lapthorn, Nick McKenzie, Brian Hansen, Jeremy Kelly.

And 97 per cent of the Victorian Police Force.

Simon Illingworth
Melbourne 2006

PROLOGUE

I ran to the shed and fumbled with the well-used lock. On my tail was an old foe, his face red with fury; despite being almost out of breath he kept telling me I was a goner. I quickly opened the shed door, entered and managed to lock it, just as my enemy slammed against it. I was safe, but only temporarily — the lock was sure to give way. Then I grabbed the gun resting behind an old war chest next to a dusty World War II leather pilot's hat.

The gun was rusty but once I'd opened the lever and forced the spring action back I could see it still worked. This was to be the day I took a stand and won some respect. I donned the pilot's hat and loaded a small berry into the breach. I opened the door wearing the hat and pointed the gun at my enemy. My overweight older brother Rossco stared at me, a nervous smirk on his face, and began to use his negotiation skills to avoid being shot, but alas, to no avail. I pulled the trigger and the purple berry slammed into his stomach. Purple juice stained a star design on his favourite white T-shirt. He was mad, really, really mad.

Once I'd pulled the trigger and let my brother take the berry in the guts, I found my own negotiation skills developed quickly. Unfortunately, I hadn't created sufficient distance between my older brother and me at the time of impact. This was not a personal development course that I wanted to put myself through; it resulted directly from my inability to reload the gun fast enough. Rossco, stained with purple juice, was about 2 feet behind me as we ran around the backyard of our grandparents' house when, stupidly, I threw the gun away. Ross simply stopped, armed himself, found some camouflage among our grandmother's lush garden and waited for me to return. Despite the danger, this situation was a turning point, an early lesson in life: how to negotiate with a madman.

Ross was, and still is, one of the hardest people around to negotiate with, hence his success at stockbroking and his ability to make serious returns for his clients. I learnt that negotiation often requires the need to accept the inevitable, though one should allow room to finesse the finer points if possible. Once I had thrown away the gun I had to resign myself to the fact that I was going to be shot, so eventually, I stopped hiding and began negotiating with him on which body part he could shoot and the distance from the end of the gun to that body part. This worked, and after some intense negotiation, Ross shot me in the butt from a distance of about 6 metres. A berry travelling at speed into any part of the body hurts, but not as much as a shot into the guts from about a metre away, so I figured I'd had a win.

On 17 January 1995, eighteen years later, I negotiated with another gunman, but this one, though he was as angry as Rossco had been, was real. I was working at a nearby CIB in Melbourne at the time, and had heard the urgent police radio message: 'Man in his fifties firing shots from a residential house, one, possibly two, hostages . . . Any unit clear?'

My blood began to pump faster: I was nervous but I wanted to give my negotiation skills a go. This attitude was very distressing to Brad, my police partner, who made it very clear that he was quite happily seated in his bargain-priced $10 ex-Salvation Army recliner. 'It's not in our patch,' he told me.

I was desperate to go and convinced him that the local CIB would respond first, as well as promising that I would drive slowly and not radio in until they arrived. Not radioing ensured that police base didn't know we were out and about, and hence we wouldn't be called upon for any major role-playing (work). I promised that the locals would do the paperwork and all we needed to do was to prop around the corner and lend a bit of a hand. We knew we didn't have to go because it wasn't our region; as my partner delicately put it, 'Crikey, this dickhead could be there for fucking days!' But something draws police to these events and we were no different. Brad didn't take too much convincing. He and I were old heads when it came to violent incidents and both of us knew the value of experience in these situations.

I wanted my first big role as a detective. So I got my kit together and was fully armed and ready to go in a couple of minutes. Brad, on the other hand, walked so slowly to the gun safe that I actually thought he was moonwalking. He was a seasoned detective who had seen it all before. I had assured Brad that we would be so slow in getting out of the office that the scene would be swarming with coppers by the time we arrived. Of course we pulled up to find that we were the first crime unit there. Brad wasn't impressed.

The inspector at the scene began briefing us. The guy had a pistol. 'Do we have this bloke's phone number?' I asked. 'Yep, and his name's Sam,' the inspector told me. The boss handed me the phone number. At the time it seemed like a good idea to just dial this bloke up and try to talk him around. This is how the initial phone conversation went.

'Hello!' screamed a very angry Sam.

'Sam, my name is Simon. I am from the police and I would like to talk to you.'

'I don't want to talk to you!' Sam slammed the phone down.

Well, hot shot, nice try, I thought. Meanwhile, Brad was peeling off decisions and organising the uniform troops to cover the address; he loved all that, and he was an expert.

'How'd you go?' asked the inspector.

I explained that Sam had hung up and that I intended to call him back. I dialled the number again.

'Hello!' yelled Sam.

'Sam, these police mobile phones are shit! Sorry, mate, we must have been cut off last time . . . Anyway . . . my name's Simon. What's going on?'

A lengthy pause.

'That's all right, Simon,' said a more subdued Sam.

I knew that the more time I could spend on the telephone the easier it would be for the street to be cordoned off and the neighbours evacuated under Brad's instructions.

Soon the area immediately around the house was coated in plainclothes police, later assisted by the Special Operations Group. Cameras from channels 2 and 10 turned up, followed by smartly dressed news reporters nervously waiting for the live cross to the siege from the newsroom. *Age* and *Herald Sun* photographers arrived looking for action, as did Radio 3AW. The boss handled the media well.

I sat on the footpath with my mobile telephone to my ear and began a long phone call with a gunman. Sam had fired some shots, had a loaded gun and was holding his ex-girlfriend hostage. He was so stressed and upset that I felt the situation had the potential to end up as a murder–suicide. He was an Italian in his late fifties and, as the phone call began in earnest, I had to think of something to talk to him about. I took a punt and chose fishing.

As we talked a stranger walked over to me and handed me a foam cup of instant coffee, something I was used to drinking after ten years in the police force. I spoke to Sam for almost two hours before I felt confident the incident could be concluded safely. By then, we had come to an agreement that our shared passions for fishing and cooking were worth living for. (I left the cup on the pavement next to the car; litter was someone else's problem.)

Sam released his ex-girlfriend after I interrupted our cooking discussion with a simple request to let her go; I then explained how he could do this. Soon afterwards, Sam surrendered himself. No further shots were fired, the guns were seized and Sam was taken into custody by the Special Operations Group. I can't remember Sam's beer batter recipe now, but it sounded good over the phone. No matter how bad life gets, it's still worth living.

A number of police put their necks on the line that day. Brad had courageously evacuated the residents from the immediate area, the other detectives at the scene had made the arrest and taken the hostage to safety and, with no formal negotiation training, I had talked him into surrendering without the loss of life. We were all exhausted, none more so than me.

Some time later Brad and I received a congratulatory letter from the Deputy Commissioner of Operations for our work in what was a 'potentially life-threatening incident'. It was a form letter three and a half lines long. In the police culture reward and recognition just weren't seen as important to operational detectives and police so we received nothing else. There seemed to be plenty of certificates and other marks of recognition for the police who created policy, as distinct from those who risked their lives to keep the peace.

I

From patriotic panache to penniless poachers

I was born on 10 November 1967 at Geelong hospital, ten months after a notorious criminal named Ronald Ryan became the last man ever hanged in Victoria and a few weeks before Australian Prime Minister Harold Holt disappeared without a trace in swirling seas off Portsea.

My father, Adrian 'Horse' Illingworth, was good-looking, quick-witted and spoilt rotten by his wealthy parents. Dad reckoned he was called Horse because he kicked a bloke at school; he was a boarder at Geelong College from the age of ten. It's a good school but any boarding school would have been a tough place for a kid of that age. It should come as no surprise that Dad ended up a big drinker, a champion at handling a shotgun and a bloke's bloke. He spent excessive time with his mates and often enjoyed one too many pots of beer at the pub, but he also managed to snare my mother, Jenifer Searle.

Jenny Searle was a much sought-after young blonde with a slim sporting physique. She was an exceptional tennis player and swimmer and a real catch. Mum was the daughter of Bill Searle, a well-known bricklayer. Bill was one of ten, six boys and four girls, and his was a family you wouldn't want to mess with. He and four of his brothers fought in World War II; the sixth brother missed out for medical reasons. Bill's brother Lloyd was almost 2 metres tall (6'4" on the old scale) and built like a brick shithouse; like many other men in the family he was known for his bravery. But Lloyd was the toughest of the lot. He spent a great deal of time behind enemy lines during the war. One time a mortar landed between his legs as he slithered on his stomach. He heard and felt the thud, but kept moving without looking back. Luckily the explosive was a dud.

Lloyd's luck didn't end there. In Crete a bomb landed on the other side of a large rock next to him and exploded: all he got was a bruised leg. In Borneo, as he removed a tree over a Japanese-made track, he saw a glimmer of silver under his foot. Lloyd knew he was standing on a landmine. It was an antitank mine, not the conventional human variety. Lloyd had missed standing on the plunger and was able to slide his foot off safely. He was reported to have thanked the Lord. I imagine that what he actually said was a fraction more colourful, knowing the Searles.

Lloyd and my grandpa Bill lost one of their brothers during the war, and obviously thought about him all the time; they knew, of course, that they were lucky to be alive, and taught me that we should never take our freedom for granted. When I was a kid, the incinerator that Bill used to burn leaves in the backyard was actually an old sea mine with the bomb part removed. The war was always part of Grandpa's life.

Mum and Dad married in Geelong in the mid sixties and Mum soon gave birth to my older brother Ross, whom I affectionately call 'Junior'. Two years later, I followed.

Ross and I were snowy-haired kids who were always up to something. We spent our first few years in Geelong, which was a small town then. Most days we heard a constant knock, crack, knock coming from our neighbour's garage. We were told the noisy neighbour was practising batting. It was Ian Redpath, relentlessly hitting a cricket ball suspended from the garage roof in a nylon stocking. Not that my best mate Adrian and I cared that I was living next door to Australia's opening Test batsman; our focus was on collecting live spiders in the backyard and drowning them in the dog's water bowl.

Redpath wasn't the only highly successful neighbour we had; not far away lived an actor whose husband, also an actor, ended up winning an Oscar for his starring role in the movie *Shine*. He followed this up with a few more awards after that. I wasn't nosey about him: all I remembered was his name, Geoffrey something.

My brother's nickname Junior was much easier to remember; I'd created it when I outgrew him in our late teens. Unfortunately, the nickname backfired and now that's what many of my brother's friends and associates call me. This perpetual one-upmanship continues to this day: it must be more frustrating for him because he's one of Melbourne's stockbroking big hitters.

Rossco was always going to be a successful entrepreneur. When we were young kids playing in the sandpit at the back of our house, Ross divided the sandpit in half and took charge of all the toy trucks, graders, shovels and equipment, hiring the trucks and equipment to me on a bucket of sand per minute used basis. This process ensured that fifteen minutes later Ross had all the sand, trucks and equipment and I was left sitting on dirt; a good argument against dictatorship and monopolies, perhaps. It sounded fair when we divided up the pit — I had a fraction more sand on my side, and he got the trucks. I should have checked the fine print.

Our parents separated when Ross and I were three and five years old. After that, Dad only came to see Ross and me a couple of dozen times. I was twenty-seven years old when, on 24 November 1994, he died of cancer in the Royal Melbourne Hospital; he'd been living in a caravan park on the shore of Lake Mulwala in New South Wales.

Dad's drinking accelerated after the separation, as did his disrespect for the drink driving laws. He often pushed the limit of how much he should drink before getting behind the wheel. The number of times he was charged with drink driving gave no indication as to how many times he did it. In Dad's defence, drink driving was considered more of a social offence then, rather than the true menace it is on the roads — now we're all better educated about its pitfalls. This cultural change is a prime example of education and penalty working together to change a societal attitude.

Dad was a speculator, property developer and car salesman. He was a likeable fella who had a knack for getting things cheap. He spent quite a bit of time in pubs so I suppose he had plenty of mates who could get things even cheaper. He was also a light sleeper and often took his boat out for a spin in the early hours. It should come as no surprise that the boat engine he bought from a group of gypsies malfunctioned and Dad found himself in the Corio Bay shipping channel treading water in the midnight fog. As Dad was treading water in the foggy silence, he thought he was stuffed until he heard a boat coming towards him. Dad began calling out before realising it was his boat circling him with the gypsy engine stuck in low gear. After the boat did a number of laps around him Dad managed to climb back on board the moving boat and made it safely back to shore and eventually made his way back to bed. His girlfriend awoke next to him none the wiser, although she wondered why all his fishing clothes were wet. Dad saved the story for the boys back at the pub.

Dad was an entrepreneur of sorts; he once proudly showed us how he'd turned his garage into an illegal bar for old men. It even had a poker machine and beer taps in it. Dad said, 'It's my own RSL.' It looked more like 'Dad's Army' but they were all happy enough.

After the divorce Mum married the man who became our stepfather, Chris, and we moved from Geelong to Melbourne. Chris's parents, who were quite upper class, were a little suspicious that Chris was to marry a divorcee with two children, and I remember arriving at their address in Toorak and being shown, with Ross, into the backyard. Mum had dressed us like pansies and combed our hair before we arrived to be greeted with a glass of lemonade and a packet of fruit LifeSavers. Ross, aged seven, and I, aged five, amused ourselves in the backyard by changing our hairstyles from Mum's spit and comb-over to something more modern while Mum impressed her future mother- and father-in-law. This was quite a feat, as she had two young brats with new Mohawk hairstyles who were fighting over the last LifeSaver. Unfortunately, the packet contained an odd number. But she survived, she and Chris married soon after and Chris's parents shared a great relationship with us from this day on.

Chris's father Gideon was a very successful businessman, a legendary real estate agent, shoes that Chris found hard to fill, but he did it and showed how a university graduate could cut it in the real world. Chris had suffered polio as a child and with immense grit and determination became a Melbourne school sports champion. He took over the real estate business from his father and still writes many books on commercial real estate. He influenced the way I carved my future in policing. Some things were worth fighting for — he taught me that.

Ross and I were also budding entrepreneurs from an early age. We made our childhood fortunes diving in slimy larvae-infested water hazards on golf courses looking for lost balls, shining people's shoes, digging through an old rubbish tip for antique bottles and selling paintings we collected from discarded goods people put out during rubbish collections; we had little time for indoor activities. We were always covered in mud, grease, boot polish or slime.

Chris taught us a great deal about investing money, negotiation and real estate, but we found out the hard way that Chris's measure of discipline was drastically different from what we had been used to. He was a hard disciplinarian, necessary for two rogue lads like us, and something that stood us in good stead for any tough situations later in life. Ross and I had become accustomed to Mum's token wooden spoon on the rump for most of our serious misdemeanours, occasionally having our mouths washed out with Palmolive soap if we used unsavoury language or if other verbal offences crept into our vocabulary.

I preferred the taste of the cheaper no-name brand soap, but unfortunately, Mum always had Palmolive handy. These mouthwashing incidents inevitably ended in roaring laughter as Mum pretended to work the soap into our firmly shut mouths.

Chris had a different type of character adjustment that involved somewhat more pain. This was a blessing in disguise as I later found that physical and mental pain were regular features of my gainful employment with the Victoria Police. The only fundamental difference was that in the Victoria Police I received the physical beatings for doing the right thing. My lateral mind and self-discipline developed in the years with Chris. If I felt the urge to employ any questionable language or unruly behaviour, I made a mental note to assess the immediate geography around him, avoiding any large piece of sporting equipment that could be a handy instrument of pain. This ensured that the nearest apparatus was no more than a badminton racquet, but Ross was slow on the uptake in this regard and had a brittle hockey stick disintegrate on his well-rounded posterior before he caught on.

Very occasionally, Dad turned up at home to take us camping along the Murray River. Mum always gave Dad a not-so-subtle snapshot of what was, and was not, appropriate behaviour in front of two impressionable young boys. Needless to say once she was out of sight parental guidance became somewhat more relaxed. The car trip camping was always the same — a slow journey that involved Dad stopping for supplies at most major towns. The country publicans knew Dad well and they had his supplies ready: a fresh pot to cleanse the palate and two icy cold stubbies of beer to take away. Dad whipped down the pot with the locals and got the heads-up on the fishing spots and any traffic snags (police), then we made tracks. Each stop had a turnaround time of about twenty minutes.

I always had the worst car seat, cramped up in the back with Dad's shotgun at my feet and a couple of boxes of cartridges sliding around the floor. Ross was older, which had its privileges as he constantly reminded me, so he always got the front seat, despite my claims of carsickness. This situation changed after I once vomited down the back of Dad's neck.

Dad wasn't one to relieve the boredom in the car by playing kids' music or games such as 'I spy with my little eye'; he constantly reminded us to keep an eye out for toppies and woodies. Dad spent the city part of the drive drilling us on the specific characteristics of any native bird life that tasted good in a camp oven. From a young age I knew that toppies were a protected pigeon species and woodies were a species of duck, and that they both tasted good. Unfortunately, I also realised that neither species was smart enough to avoid the combination of two young boys' sharp eyes and Dad's trusty Winchester twelve-gauge.

So, en route to our camping spot, Dad exchanged his half-full stubby of beer for the shotty I'd load for him and he'd have an impromptu blat at some type of passing birdlife that Ross and I identified as a potential feed. More often than not, the old man's renowned skill with a gun would have us plucking birds for dinner, which was just as well; Dad never went overboard with the groceries apart from ice, gaspers and his favourite type of liquid gold.

At the campsite we met up with Allan, a mate of Dad's in his forties. Allan was thin, had flaming red hair and a perfect set of teeth; he was quite scruffy-looking. In hindsight I think his teeth were dentures. There was no time to sit around; Ross and I went straight to work helping Dad and Allan set their illegal gill nets and a few crayfish pots along the river. Dad's style of fishing took most of the luck out of it, and, especially for a young boy worried about getting busted, a great deal of the relaxation as well. These activities were recreational for the old man. Allan, on the other hand, was a poacher by occupation. Not that Ross and I knew what that really meant, although we gathered it wasn't necessarily an occupation one's mother would be happy with, nor one that would have involved the taxation department. So only a matter of hours after Ross and I had left the discipline of our inner-city household with Mum and Chris, we'd find ourselves sitting around the campfire eating a protected bird species, illegally caught fish and freshwater crays while Dad and his poacher mate drank cans of beer and smoked coffin nails.

Every time we camped, Allan and Dad talked about a staged horse race that took place at a country picnic race meeting. Apparently, they knew 'someone' who hatched a dodgy plan to win some cash. A city racehorse was sent to their mate's property for a spell before the Spring Carnival. But rather than rest the horse, he trained it for the local picnic races. They selected a name for it and picked a local female jockey for the ride. Allan said she was a tiny girl and had been given one instruction: 'Pull the horse up; don't let it win by too much.'

On the big day, the jockey did as instructed, but the horse pulled ahead early and bolted home by eight lengths despite the jockey doing her best to pull it up. Allan and Dad's mate panicked with the monumental win, so it was just as well the horse was back at the farm shortly after the race finished. Dad and Allan loved to brag about their horse race earn after a few cold ones in front of the campfire. Dad said there had been a late plunge and gave us a wink, adding, 'Someone must have made some good coin out of that race.' Allan and Dad rolled backwards and both had a huge belly laugh.

On our camping trips with Dad he always brought the aluminium fishing boat he called 'the tinny'. This was a leaking, unseaworthy boat equipped with one token life jacket, a corroded ten-year-old flare and an exhausted 25hp engine. Dad reckoned the boat had a few years left in it. Perhaps so, but I thought it was unlikely to take too many more rip crossings in heavy seas. The tinny did come in handy once when we were stopped on the highway by the traffic cops; the road was under 2 metres of water in some spots and the neighbouring market gardens were flooded. We sat in the car for a few minutes at the roadblock before Dad told us to get out and help him take the boat off.

'We're goin' vegie fishin',' the old man explained. 'It's a supermarket with no checkout.'

Shortly afterwards, Ross and I were hanging off the front of the boat as Dad put the boat engine through its paces over the flooded farms and highway. Before long, we had scooped up a boat full of fresh vegetables that had floated down from the flooded market gardens. Dad later swapped them for a couple of slabs of Victoria Bitter at the pub. Like most of Dad's deals, it was unlikely to have been a transaction the taxation department was ever privy to.

When our parents split up they agreed not to worry about child maintenance. Instead, Dad agreed that we would be sent to Scotch College in the leafy Melbourne suburb of Hawthorn, a school where many of the rich and famous send their boys. I have no doubt that the decision was quite an easy one for Dad because he wasn't going to pay; he was bailed out again by his parents.

Our education was paid for by my father's wealthy parents, Lancelot and Marjorie Illingworth. Dad didn't even buy us Christmas or birthday presents, nor did he ever call us on the phone and we often went years without seeing him. But I'm not going to go on about how this affected my childhood and development, because it didn't. I had plenty of male role models in the family, so catching up with the old man every few years was just a bonus. Not everyone is made for marriage and parenthood — we often forget that.

Lance Illingworth was a successful banker in his own right, as well as having very sound financial backing from his wife Marjorie. Her wealth came from her father Charles Herbert Smith, who invented a machine in the late 1800s that cleaned fleece without causing it any damage and enabled lanolin to be extracted from the wool. This invention mightn't sound overly technical these days, but at a time when Australia rode on the sheep's back it was a huge success. Charles Herbert Smith purchased an immaculate mansion named 'Edgecombe' in Skene Street, Geelong. The house still stands, renovated to its former glory. C.H. Smith also built one of the first beach houses in Torquay, now known for its world-famous Bells surf beach.

Lance, a lowly bank clerk from the small Victorian country town of Casterton, married Marjorie Smith on 14 April 1934. He co-founded Geelong's Apex business group and was a director of the Pyramid Building Society. Lance and his predecessors built Pyramid into a large organisation; it lasted many years after Lance had ceased to be involved in its operation, but, like many other people, he lost much of his life savings when Pyramid crashed. Lance and Marjorie had intended to pay for our education, but after Pyramid crashed they were left with virtually nothing.

The riches to rags in three generations saying rang true in this case, except that in my family the riches didn't quite last through the third generation. When Pyramid crashed Ross had one year of schooling to go and I had three. But we weren't taken out of Scotch College. Without prompting, an associate and former business colleague of my grandfather's stepped in and paid for our schooling until we finished. Our family had helped his family many years ago. (Ross and I knew nothing about this at the time.) My ancestors considered it bad taste that their philanthropy was ever made public. For better or worse, this is a principle that a few of us still like to follow.

Lance had a huge repertoire of stories, especially after Alzheimer's set in. He occasionally broke out of his nursing home and made his way back to the old ANZ Bank he had managed decades before. The pleasant bank staff allowed him to sit in the manager's seat while they contacted my brother to have him collected. Meanwhile, Lance could be heard giving the current manager some tasks to do.

Despite the ups and downs, Ross and I had a fairly privileged childhood. We went to a private school and lived comfortably and enjoyably with Mum, Chris and two younger half-sisters, Belinda and Anna, better known as Binny and Possy. The girls were two of my greatest supporters with things that counted and two of my greatest critics with things that didn't.

I can hardly remember my own age, let alone other people's, so let's just say Binny is seven or eight years younger than me, give or take a couple of years, and Possy is a year or two younger than that. Both my sisters are intelligent, hard-working women, although when they were babies they were often used as blank canvases for our art practice. The wooden spoon was drawn from Mum's kitchen scabbard whenever she saw her baby daughters sporting black Texta moustaches, black eyes and scars. The girls struck back a few years later with a home-made periscope that made it nearly impossible for Ross and me to get past first base with any of our young girlfriends. We found it quite disconcerting to have our sisters' periscope pop up from a garden bed in the middle of a passionate embrace with a young lass.

During my schooldays, I formed some great friendships with many of the lads at Scotch, and after hours I occasionally caught up with some of the girls from Lauriston, St Catherine's, Camberwell Girls' School, Merton Hall and other schools.

As a pubescent lad I partied hard, despite the discipline that awaited me back home. Mum didn't need an alarm clock to know when the clock struck one so I often caught the last tram home and sprinted up the street with seconds to spare. Ross and I were mischievous schoolboys who had many girlfriends, but if the truth be known, the girls were probably worse than we were. We had some fun: 'I know it looks bad, Mum, but I can honestly say I did not have sexual relations with that woman.' That was me, aged sixteen, well before a certain US president uttered very similar immortal words. They didn't work for me either: I was grounded for two weeks. But I did better than Clinton all the same, despite the nervousness caused by my sisters and their annoying periscope.

Although the perception is that private school boys are pretentious and snobby, my mates loved the adventure of surfing big waves more than anything else. Of course we played up, but quite often the wealthiest kids were the most understated, generous and loyal friends I had, particularly when things got tough.

Two of my friends were Michael and David Fox, the sons of the legendary trucking magnate Lindsay Fox. Both boys were terrific competitors on the football field; Michael was also a genius with figures. They were both talented, down-to-earth people, as well as really good fun. David and I were once caught by a railway inspector running across the main train subway at Richmond railway station after attending a cricket match at the Melbourne Cricket Ground. We insisted we were brothers and we gave the same fictitious last name, which happened to be that of the schoolmate we liked least. But once we were separated our story collapsed, the railway inspector observing that our parents probably hadn't christened us with identical first names as well. We were fined.

Although we were privileged to go to Scotch College we weren't lavished with gifts as kids. This didn't concern me, nor any of the other boys at Scotch, although I suspect that some of the boys wouldn't have used my cricket bat on Portsea back beach, let alone on a cricket field. But the bat worked well, and made no difference to my performance. I take pride in eventually having been selected in the First XI at Scotch and finishing the last three or four games with a batting average of 50 with my low-grade polycoated cricket bat. The sledging from the opposition players about my bat was good grounding for the storm of abuse I got later as a cop. But I never tired of seeing them fetch the cricket ball off the tennis courts or the roof of the grandstand after I'd clubbed it with my cheap bat.

I was no angel when it came to sledging. My fierce and unsportsmanlike competitive spirit on the sporting field often got me into trouble. As a batsman, my disapproval of an umpire's LBW decision during a cricket match against Xavier College led to me smashing all three stumps out of the pitch; I never made 'walking' a habit, even when I was clearly out. After the stump-smashing indiscretion, word filtered back to Scotch and I received a prompt two-week suspension from cricket for 'unprofessional and unsportsmanlike behaviour'. My suspension from cricket was a school first for me; I normally reserved such behaviour for the football field.

2

Baptism of fire

I attained my Year 12 Certificate in 1985, despite having attended classes in Year 10 with delicate names such as musical appreciation, special maths (fondly known as vegie maths) and special English. In reality, I studied seriously for the last two and half months of my final year and passed quite well; I had a knack of doing just enough to get through. This surprised some of my teachers, who had described me in school reports as, among other things, 'extremely disruptive'. My end-of-year score was testament to the quality of the teachers. I hadn't read any of the Year 12 English books, yet I passed all subjects, including English.

A few months later I found a nice cushy course doing a bachelor of business degree and set myself to cruise through university for a few years. By 27 March 1986, I had started at Melbourne College (now part of Melbourne University) the same way I finished school, happily drinking copious amounts of beer, surfing and enjoying the freedoms this country provides without straining in the slightest. But on this day, while I was having a few early cleansing ales with my new university mates, everything changed. I was sinking my forth or fifth pot of beer shortly after 1pm when a loud *boom* interrupted our meaningless conversation.

'That was a fuckin' bomb!' I said to the lads.

'Bullshit! You've spent too much time in Ireland,' was one smartarse response.

I'd never been to Ireland but we realised something bad had happened when the dust and smoke plumed up over the building tops and the air was filled with the sound of sirens. A horrific car bomb had exploded outside the Russell Street police station just a few hundred metres away. The evil bastards who set up the first bomb had set another to follow it. This is, I regret to say, standard practice. The first blast maims and kills, which attracts others to lend assistance, then the second bomb activates, ensuring large numbers of casualties. Fortunately, in this case, the second bomb failed to explode.

The initial blast injured twenty-two people and caused extensive damage to the facades of all of the nearby buildings. An innocent twenty-one-year-old policewoman named Angela Taylor died from her injuries. It was a crime that stopped Melbourne in its tracks.

Even though the bomb blast made me think about the meaning of life and how I took freedom for granted I didn't consider becoming a police officer until I went to the open day at the Glen Waverley Police Academy twelve months later. There I saw police abseiling down the side of buildings, dogs tracking people down and sniffing for drugs, leather-clad motorbike cops with reflector sunglasses on huge motorcycles, highway patrol police cars rumbling and scuba men diving into the swimming pool looking for a fake murder weapon.

Serious crime had fascinated me from the time I was small. I even kept the front page of the now-defunct *Herald* newspaper with photographs of villains who had escaped from jail. The whole idea of tracking down and convicting criminals engrossed me, the pleasure of incarcerating the people who take away the liberty of others and helping those whose only mistake was being in the wrong place at the wrong time was exciting. I thought it all looked terrific. It dawned on me that I'd finally found the job for me. Being a cop appealed to me for a range of macho reasons: I liked excitement, I liked adventure and I liked being outdoors, but most of all I liked the idea of being seen as the good guy, someone who helped the community and took responsibility for the freedoms I had taken for granted. This job was the ultimate win–win. I wanted to solve the hard and apparently unsolvable crimes that plagued the community.

A sign pointed to a recruitment tent. I headed over with just one question for the recruiting sergeant: 'Can I get out whenever I want to?'

'Yes,' he told me, 'this is the police force, not the army.'

I liked the idea of having an exit clause if it got too hard so I could go back to surfing and bumming around at university. But I was also a naive nineteen-year-old caught up in all the hype and excitement of the police show day. 'Wow! Where do I sign?'

I applied there and then in the recruitment tent and, because they were recruiting heavily at the time, the process was sped up. I did the tests required and before long I received a letter telling me I was starting in the academy in two weeks.

I got over the initial shock of it all and turned up at the academy with a number of other naive civilians. We were met by the drill sergeant who was loud and walked crisply, the metal caps on his boots clicking on the pavement. He looked angry; I figured he wasn't likely to be overly friendly so I decided to keep my head down and avoided eye contact where possible.

We were herded into a group for roll call. I kept my head down, but alas, the drill sergeant picked me out at random.

'What's your name, lad?' he demanded.

'Simon,' I mumbled.

'Simon *what*?'

'Simon Illingworth.'

'Simon Illingworth *what*?'

'Simon Illingworth, sir!' I yelled.

'I'm not inviting you to dinner!' he screamed. 'Your name is Illingworth, and I'm not a sir. I'm a sergeant.' So I had a new name, and had learnt two new rules. I ploughed my way back into the herd as the roll was called out, waiting for the sergeant to call my name — which was pretty pointless because everybody there had seen him belittle me and he knew what my name was. But I yelled 'Sergeant!' like everybody else when the time came, and then, like the others, I went to be measured up for a uniform, boots and cap.

ABOVE:
Rossco and me on our first day at Scotch College, Melbourne. When we weren't shooting each other, we got along quite well.
SI PRIVATE COLLECTION

RIGHT
Dad was a bloke's bloke. He liked a surf, a beer and a bet, and was a champion with a shotgun - a skill he taught me that came in useful later.
SI PRIVATE COLLECTION

With Mum on graduation day. Mum was just as keen for me to join the Victorian police force as she was later for me to get out of it. SI PRIVATE COLLECTION

The drill sergeant screamed something barely comprehensible about the boots, which I learnt meant Rule 3: Keep boots shiny. This culture of cleanliness was going to be a change for me; I hadn't put much Nugget on anything since my brother and I made $12.50 at our shoeshine stall ten years before. But for four months I was the obsessive keeper of a cheap pair of boots that demanded Nugget daily, with 30 minutes of unrelenting polishing.

The academy life became quite easy; I enjoyed the physical training and was probably the fittest I'd ever been. My running was on par with a few of the fittest recruits and I was quite good in the pool as a result of my surf lifesaving days. But it was my old man's shotgun tutelage that really came in handy when I had to hit targets with pistols. In the end my pistol accuracy won me the Academy Triathlon award, the other two legs of which were swimming and running.

After four months I graduated. My drill sergeant turned out to be a great guy who was doing a tough job. When I was about to leave he told me, 'Life on the street is hard. You'll find out, Illingworth.'

My first placing was in 1988 at the Russell Street police station, the scene of the horrific bombing a couple of years before and the major station in the city. The station looked like a police building in a comic book. On the streets during the day people wore suits and buzzed from place to place, by night the area came alive with nightclubs, drugs, prostitution, sleazy bars and no hopers.

The central Melbourne business district was, and still is, surrounded by overcrowded high-rise Housing Commission apartment blocks built in the 1970s, a legacy from a 1938 decision to house the poorest, least educated and most vulnerable people in the state of Victoria. These ugly monstrosities are made of concrete and vary in height from twelve floors to more than twenty. If these buildings were part of a 1970s experiment into overcrowding, someone should have realised how soul-destroying they are for most of the people who have to live in them.

All Melburnians have seen the towering blocks of low-grade housing from the outside, but very few people see the state of affairs inside these buildings as comprehensively as the police. The worst flats are called 'caves' by some seasoned cops. The lifts in these blocks always smell of urine, cigarette burns and graffiti adorn most walls and the lifts, despite the 'video surveillance' warning signs, which are often burnt and written on as well. They were also laboratories for crime, though nothing like on the scale I was shortly to encounter.

The years leading up to my policing career were believed to be the most bloody and corrupt eras in Australian policing history. New South Wales was in the news for all the wrong reasons and disgraced Detective-Sergeant Roger Rogerson of the NSW Armed Robbery Squad had become a household name all over Australia. Queensland was temporarily the 'moonlight state'. Questions were also being asked about the integrity of the police in Victoria, but the answer was a definite: 'Nothing to see here!' And so our media continued attacking our interstate brothers. I too thought Victoria Police was corruption-free; in fact, as I left the academy I was more concerned that I might be too undisciplined for the Force rather than visa versa.

When it came to owning respectable motor cars I certainly wasn't a snob. I had an old VE Valiant, a gas-guzzling sedan that had a few scrapes and love-taps in the panels. The state of the car's exterior reflected the time lapse it took for my drum brakes to work, during which I could be seen wrestling a steering wheel that chose to turn left every time I braked. It wasn't the sort of car a policeman should be seen driving, although the engine purred and my mechanic Pete said you could rest a pot of beer on it and you wouldn't spill a drop. I haven't quoted him word for word because he would have said no fewer than three 'fucks' in that sentence, which makes it difficult to understand.

'Fuck, mate! That's fuckin' fucked,' Pete once said, describing the Valiant's steering; nevertheless, he always managed to fix it. The Valiant was great because the boot fitted two surfboards and it could handle bush bashing to my favourite surf spots. Its value depended greatly on how much fuel was in it at the time. I used to park it on the street in Collingwood with a smashed window and all the doors open and no one ever stole it. Crooks won't often steal a stolen car without first knowing its history. No one wanted to get caught in a car that had been used in a murder or an armed robbery. My Valiant was given a wide berth on the road where driver courtesy was at a premium. A quick glimpse in the rear-view mirror of a beaten-up Valiant was enough for most drivers to pull aside and let me through. The probability of having insurance for such a car was always considered minimal. I had the same experience when cruising in police squad cars, although I suspect their motives were somewhat different, particularly because the Valiant wasn't fitted with flashing blue lights and a siren.

My first patrol shift was in January 1988. I was rostered to work a marked squad car, one of the early Ford Falcon series. It was the latest model at the time and it had 'POLICE' written on it in bold capital letters. The lettering on the cars changed a while later when someone thought it was best to have 'Police' so it didn't look too aggressive. Of course, some cops, who were waiting patiently for things such as personal issue bulletproof vests and better defensive weaponry, struggled with the idea. At best cops saw it as a lame marketing exercise; at worst they thought the softer image was bowing to minority groups and hardened crooks.

My first shift was with an experienced policewoman, Kate. I'd only had my driver's licence for about twelve months, so thankfully she drove the police car. As we pulled out of the Russell Street garage, I felt a chill up my spine. This was the start of a new and exciting life. And, echoing the perception given by the bold police lettering on the side of the car, within seconds I was perceived as a seasoned cop on the beat.

Of course the ignorant public didn't know I'd only been on patrol for thirty seconds, but I knew the reality of it — I was a young kid on 'P' plates who did four months of training and I knew nothing. Like all young rookies fresh out of the academy I was an impostor, completely reliant upon my superior for direction. But, despite my lack of experience, the fact that I was wearing a police uniform meant that I could stop the flow of the city's traffic in one arm movement — a cop has power.

But, like everyone else at their new job I just wanted to fit in; stopping the flow of Melbourne's traffic was the last thing on my mind. I was more concerned with my new leather belt forcing me to sit uncomfortably upright in the squad car seat. Its stiffness meant that it took me about two minutes of wrestling to force my service revolver into my new holster before I even got into the car. My new status, then, escaped nobody. An old senior constable looked at me wrestling away and said, 'Bloody hell, lad, if you were out on the street you'd have been shot and buried by now.' I knew he was right, but I didn't appreciate a safety tip coming from a man who handled guns all day who had a beer smell similar to my old man's. He did, however, suggest a solution: hit the belt with a hammer, oil it and cut the strap across the bottom of the holster, the one designed to hold the gun in its pouch during fights with crooks. I thought of cutting the gun strap as my beer-smelling friend said, but decided against it. I could never live with myself if someone pulled my gun out of its holster and used it on a colleague.

Although I'd spent much of my time indulging myself in beer and surf, I did know that my career as a policeman had begun at a time when it was Victoria's turn to be awash with dog-eat-dog violence. The garden state was leading the way in breeding violent criminals, some of whom were household names there and elsewhere. Bank robberies and shootings were regular occurrences and the situation was spiralling out of control. In Victoria, high-profile bank and armoured van robberies took the focus of the Armed Robbery Squad, while the other major crime squads busily mopped up after murderers and the relatively new, large-scale drug traffickers. The rest of the evil was pushed around to other squads and local CIBs.

As a rule, Victorians staunchly defend their police officers' ability to control crime, and they sincerely believe them to be the best in the country. In hindsight this appears to be based on rivalry between New South Wales and Victoria rather than anything more substantial. Over a few years members of Victoria Police had been threatened with guns, knives, axes and other weapons and as a result Victoria had an enormously disproportionate rate of police shootings compared to the other Australian states. Victoria has produced more than its fair share of hit men, armed robbers, sleaze merchants and racketeers over the years, most of whom graduated from petty crime. Generation after generation of neglecting truancy, unemployment and poverty ensured that a generation of young men were born to hate. Many of these people were raised in the ring of Housing Commission flats that surrounds the city; others were born into dysfunctional families where parents provided little in the way of discipline. Over time these children became immune to domestic and other violence, where shouting matches and abuse were the norm.

Many of these young men were expected to be yet another generation of underdogs, but for some reason many chose to be different — they wanted more and they didn't care how they got it. Victoria now produces a brand of criminal that appears to have no conscience. They are specialists, and with that comes the money and power many of them craved as adolescents. In Victoria, unlike many of their interstate brothers, they like to carry weapons, and the underworld weapon of choice in Victoria is the gun.

For seasoned cops, the combination of Victoria's underworld carrying guns and having a rookie as a partner makes for dangerous policing. Rookies are liabilities, especially one like me, a kid who couldn't get his gun in the holster without drawing attention to himself, let alone trying to get the bloody thing out. Eventually, I'd forced the gun into the holster and was excited to be going on patrol. But I was nervous: what if something happened? So I listened intently while Kate showed me how to use the police radio and, briefly, what the codes meant. She told me it would be a slow night, and remarked that nothing had happened for ages.

Kate snatched the radio out of its cradle and said, 'Russell Street 299 Code X.' That was the end of my on-the-job training. Seconds later a mint-green Holden Commodore dangerously mounted the curb in front of us. A shower of sparks flew from its undercarriage as it accelerated away. Kate looked at me, turned on the siren and ordered me to turn on the 'Luna Parks'. I fumbled around searching for the switch for the flashing lights, finding the spotlight before getting it right.

'Looks like we've got a bad 65 [drink driver],' Kate said. I agreed, although I didn't have a clue what she was talking about. Even when we took off after the Commodore, the driver didn't pull over, and so my first shift started with a car chase through Melbourne's inner suburbs. It was more of a rat-run through alleys and lanes than anything you might see in a movie about San Francisco, and we screamed through East Melbourne, Fitzroy, North Fitzroy, Carlton and Brunswick in hot pursuit. The crim flattened street signs and jagged back and forth, showering us with sparks and side-swiping the corrugated iron fencing of the narrow laneways. We screamed through red lights and stop signs after him. It was anarchy. My adrenaline was pumping, a mix of excitement, fear and the rush of the unknown, similar to the thrill of surfing really big waves, but lasting longer.

Kate drove superbly, teaching me how to use the police radio at the same time. The driver eventually crashed into a bluestone roundabout and I leapt from the car and sprinted up, ready to arrest my first crook. When I arrived at his car I expected to see a young hooligan covered in tattoos behind the steering wheel. Instead I saw a man, old enough to be a grandfather. He was bleeding from a fresh cut on his head, and he was going nowhere.

That was the first time I heard the distinctive thud, thud, thud of the police helicopter over my head; it arrived just as the pursuit finished. But there were plenty more times I'd hear that noise during my career and it was rarely a sign of good fortune. The police helicopter generally spelt doom for someone caught in the wrong place at the wrong time, sometimes a crook, sometimes a victim, sometimes both.

When I asked the old guy for identification, he proudly announced that he was a member of the Painters' and Dockers' Union, a notorious union with a reputation for crime from theft to murder. Those who controlled it relied on well-known hardened criminals, such as Billy 'The Texan' Longley, for muscle. But this particular crook wasn't hurting anyone, and remained behind the wheel of his ageing Commodore, staring out of a broken windscreen onto a crushed bonnet with steam spewing out of the radiator. He was also drunk, claiming to have had a few cold beers with the ex-secretary of another powerful Melbourne union. 'I didn't know you were after me,' he said. It was an interesting statement.

Another copper who'd joined the chase got out of his car and walked over to us. I stood over the driver after wrestling my handcuffs from their new pouch and managed to handcuff him without any problem.

The copper looked at the handcuffed crook and quipped, 'You fuckin' dog.' He then turned, walked back to his police car and left. I thought that maybe he knew the crook, but it was unlikely — he just hated him anyway. The crook was an idiot, but it seemed pointless to spell it out to him. But how was I to know? It was my first shift. My first shift had taught me one big lesson: I was now a cop, and cops hate criminals. But I didn't hate anyone.

I found that many cops want to have the last word when dealing with crims. It's often a cheap shot, the sort you see on TV delivered by a dirty cop before he takes a final swipe at the unsuspecting and disadvantaged crim. In the real world these cheap shots regularly made the difference between cooperation and resistance from hardened criminals. Hardened crooks know cops are going to lock them up; they just don't like the bullshit that goes with it. I didn't care if I was called a pig while I locked a crook up for something. A crook could have the last word as far as I was concerned, as long as I closed the deal. But some cops wanted both.

3

Caging crims: early days

After just a couple of years on the streets, I found I was catching criminals one after another. Police colleagues never gave anyone a break, so I was considered arsy or told I just tripped over them. Nevertheless, within three years I had arrested a number of major criminals, and had helped lock up one of Victoria's Top Ten most wanted. This crim was the first of three ex-most wanted crims I caught until the system of grading our most wanted was abolished. It was a rare feat.

It wasn't my knowledge of law or any of the other stuff I learnt in the academy that helped me make these arrests. Surfing, football and my old man's communication skills had given me an information network that reached across the state. Unlike most cops, I didn't spend my time drinking coldies with police; I socialised with civilians, from stockbrokers to council workers and knockabout surfers. These people provided me with normality, so I was never engulfed by the whole power trip that some cops suffer from. If this book has a tip for any would-be cop out there, this is it — don't break ties with your non-police friends, you need them. I always found conversations with strangers and civilians more interesting than the chest-beating war stories that spewed from some cops' mouths, so I avoided most police functions, even at an early age.

I learnt many of the skills I needed in the police force from non-policemen, and quite a lot from my father. Dad had been a surfer, a big wave man according to his mates, but his greatest skill was his ability to communicate. He was an outstanding car salesman, and he later became a property developer on the Surf Coast from Ocean Grove to Lorne. I learnt many unassuming traits from Dad and his good mate Teddy, including the subtle and non-confrontational mannerisms they used to sell cars. I copied many of their techniques as a cop, and eventually, was able to sell something much harder to move than cheap, secondhand cars; I sold jail sentences.

Copying Dad's laidback attitude helped me in my role as a policeman. I never lifted a finger to get a confession from a criminal. The way I figured it, bashing someone for a confession meant you weren't smart enough to catch them fair and square. It was an indictment of your own ability as an investigator. I expect plenty of cops don't agree with this point of view.

I completed my training at Russell Street and began work at City West police station in William Street, on the opposite side of the city. The station was on the bottom floor of the new Victoria Police headquarters. On most days, only a few floors up, you'd have found Chief Commissioner Kel Glare seated at his desk. The station formed the foundation of the police headquarters, and with that came trouble. Police headquarters around the world are renowned as places that appeal to strange people, the kind who are irrefutably insane, mostly through drugs and drink. City West was no different. Many people who were 'flying blind and solo into the jungle of bonkers' or 'several cages short of a puppy farm', as one of my colleagues used to say, wandered into the station watchhouse. It was rare not to have a drunk, drugged or emotionally charged person walk into the station during nightshift, wanting to confess to a major crime or claiming to be the victim of one. The station was a magnet for criminals, no hopers and night clubbers drunk or high on mind-altering drugs and complaining of being assaulted by bouncers at one of Melbourne's many seedy nightclubs.

It was a challenging place to work, to say the least, and a workplace where you really did help people. We often gave the old drunks clothes, blankets and food or a ride to hospital for stitches. The Salvation Army provided most necessities when we needed them. We often found drunks passed out on city streets with their arms stuffed into a drainpipe. I couldn't work out why until I pulled a comatose drunk by his legs and saw his arm pop out of a pipe, still firmly clutching an unfinished bottle of cheap liquor. It was an example of the law of the jungle; once street drunks had drunk themselves into near-unconsciousness, they knew the others would be circling like vultures for their unfinished bottle; so they'd stuff it into the 'overnight safe'.

One day, around noon, we heard the police radio: 'Any unit clear to back up South Melbourne in a car chase heading through Spencer Street, Melbourne? Chasing a black Ford Falcon, driver a drug dealer. Any unit clear?' My partner and I sprinted to the car at the front of the station, as the boss yelled at us, 'We're down to one car, don't stack it!' I knew the other two station cars were being repaired after two recent car chases and the pressure was on to save our last car. No one liked foot patrol.

The chase was a beauty. It involved four cars, the crook's evil-looking, undercoat-grey Ford Falcon with mag wheels, and three marked police cars. We weaved through the city streets into the vibrant, often seedy, western suburbs. The crook's mag wheels were screaming and smoke was pouring from his exhaust as he trebled the speed limit of a road normally full of pedestrians while throwing a gun and two bags of white powder out of his driver's-side window and onto the street. We passed the Footscray shopping centre and the drug dealer kept pushing his car, harder and harder. The three police cars worked hard to stay in touch, the flashing lights and blaring sirens masked the squeal and smoke of our white-hot brake pads and our tyres that were straining under the pressure of an urban rally. These weren't cars you would like to buy later, despite the low kilometres on the clock.

Eventually, the crook's misjudgment of a roundabout launched his car into the air, landing it on a small fence. The two police cars either side of ours followed suit but I slammed my foot on the brake and we skidded to a stop just centimetres from the crook's back bumper.

We didn't sit around admiring the mayhem. I climbed over the boot and roof of the crook's car and extracted him through his open window.

Taking my cuffs out of my softened leather pouch I cranked them on his tattooed wrists, nice and tight. I also secured him with my knee between his shoulderblades.

When I had finished I looked around and noticed a crowd had formed around us. Many were older people, but they all looked as if they were tired of crime, a legacy of living in the western suburbs of Melbourne where hardworking dockers and migrants are now inundated with illegal drugs and violence. An old Greek man stood there sipping from a foam cup, witnessing yet another violent arrest in his neighbourhood. His face was expressionless, despite the havoc of smashed police cars, a Falcon resting up on a fence and a faulty police siren that wouldn't turn off.

My partner called the crash details into VKC from the scene, ordered a divisional van for the crook, three tow trucks for the cars and some council workers for the fence, and proudly added: 'the City West sedan is *undamaged.*' Back at the station the coppers clapped and roared with approval, and no doubt the boss smiled with relief — we still had a car left. I took the handcuffed crook from his Ford Falcon to another one. Unfortunately, our Ford didn't have bucket seats, fuzzy dice and tinted windows like his did. Our seats were metal and the windows were caged; it was a divvy van and he was going to jail.

Of course we all thought we were making a difference by locking up these hardened crooks, but I dare say the old Greek man knew that this arrest, like all the others he'd seen, would make little difference to the local culture. As the scene was cleared of crashed police cars, smashed fences and the crook's written-off Falcon, the old man vanished. The only evidence left of him was an empty foam cup lying on its side in the gutter, waiting for a gust of wind to take it somewhere else.

There were plenty of other heart-pumping car chases and arrests, and before too long I managed to charge many of the west and north Melbourne crooks with a range of crimes. For me police work was the ultimate hunt, mind versus mind. Catching drug dealers and armed robbers was a thrill. I loved it, it was like a drug.

I was stationed at City West from December 1988 until January 1991. During this time an ex-Armed Robbery Squad detective arrived at the station. Like the other Crime Squad detectives, Sergeant Steele (not his real name) came with a reputation of being ruthless and switched on to criminal networks.

I was only twenty-two years old and, like many other ambitious young cops, I was impressed with the aura that surrounded any detective, let alone one from the Armed Robbery Squad. The 'Robbers' were always considered to be brutal compared to some of the soft, paper-shuffling detectives. At the time, the Armed Robbery Squad had been plagued with far more than their fair share of corruption investigations, so the officer in charge of our station set down the rules for our new sergeant in no uncertain fashion. The boss had done it with all of us, but Sergeant Steele was said to have been given a double dose.

Steele immediately took a liking to me. He'd asked another sergeant who the crook catchers were and, in particular, which constables wanted to get into the CIB. He was given my name and told that I'd caught numerous 'good crooks' and was 'one of the lads'. At the time I was expecting an Internal Affairs inquiry into my conduct, because a crook I'd arrested had threatened to say I'd assaulted him, among other things. (I had belted him a number of times, and opened him up, but only after he had swung a couple.) As it turned out the crim never bothered to make a complaint, but that didn't matter because the old Armed Robbery Squad was a place where complaints often indicated how hard you worked. Of all the corruption allegations made against the Robbers, I can recall none that led to convictions by the Internal Investigations Department (IID), and this at a time when a number of criminals had been shot dead by police.

Melbourne's reputation for violent armed robbery and police shootings had grown rapidly since the early 1970s, when professional bank robbers armed with cut-down guns and wearing masks and balaclavas had preyed on small suburban banks. These men picked banks with minimal security and no more than a handful of staff, then set about maximising their victims' terror in an effort to ensure that they were given all the available bank loot and not just the 'piss-off' or 'show' money held in the teller's drawer.

By the late 1980s Victoria's banks and building societies were still being hit by gangs of organised armed robbers but they'd been joined by amateur smack-fuelled criminals looking for a quick buck to buy some more of their favourite 'white lady'. I don't know which group I'd prefer to be robbed by — a greedy and extremely violent yet professional armed robber or an unprofessional, out-of-control druggie who's likely to point a loaded gun at you and pull the trigger by mistake.

Anyway, in 1987 it was reported that an incredible 500 armed robberies had been reported to police. One man who had served almost six years for a series of armed robberies told a reporter from the *Australian* newspaper, 'Armed robbery became a dangerous profession: people were getting killed. Towards the late 1980s there was definitely awareness that if you were committing armed robberies you were at risk of getting shot by police.'

A string of police shootings was said to have scared many criminals away from the once lucrative criminal skill of bank robbery. I don't subscribe to this view. The claim that police shooting criminals was the sole reason armed robbery statistics dropped was ludicrous suggestion, an idea based on the opinions of a handful of paranoid crooks and a few rogue ex-cops and their mates, not on any research or specific facts.

The profession that involved sticking a gun into the face of a low-paid bank teller came to an end for a range of reasons, none of which involved cops and allegations of itchy trigger fingers. They include the use of security devices, suburban bank closures, pop-up screens, video surveillance, dye bombs, time delay safes, increased credit card use and the introduction of automatic teller machines. Add all that to a new low-risk yet lucrative criminal trade called drug trafficking and of course the armed robbery statistics fell rapidly; professional crooks aren't stupid.

But every police shooting is scrutinised, and some of the detectives were charged with the murder of a criminal named Graeme Jensen in Narre Warren, 40 kilometres from Melbourne. It was alleged that Jensen had been shot and then set up with a firearm, but the case was so weak that the charges were withdrawn against all detectives except one, who was duly acquitted. During a coronial hearing the prosecution alleged that a gun had been planted on Jensen after his death, a claim rejected by the state coroner Hal Hallenstein. Hallenstein said it was 'hard to envisage anything like those events', despite the professional criminal lying dead in his car with a firearm that was not cocked, not loaded and with the magazine upside down with two bullets on the floor. Nevertheless, he was an armed robber and known to carry firearms.

The detectives charged with offences relating to the death of Graeme Jensen included Goran Black and Brian Reece (fictitious names). These names meant nothing to me until Sergeant Steele arrived at City West, followed shortly by another ex-Armed Robbery Squad detective, Senior Constable Reece. At the time media pressure was building and while many in the force believed that the violent nature of armed robbery was the reason for the high number of complaints directed at the Armed Robbery Squad, the Force command changed the squad's name to the Armed Offender Squad. This wasn't the last time a squad suspected of getting a bit whiffy was cleansed via a name change. As I'll explain later, the Drug Squad was one of the next to undergo a literary cleansing.

Ironically, the Armed Robbery Squad's name change signalled an apparently permanent fall in the number of armed bank robberies. But this didn't mean a reduction in the number of criminals: they simply moved into the heroin trade, where potential lucre far outweighed the increasing risks in getting money from bank hold-ups. Especially enthusiastic about heroin, I suspect, were a few of the paranoid crooks worried that Victorian detectives suffered from very itchy trigger fingers. But the drug market brought another culture change: it fractured the criminal code of silence. Crooks turned on each other and informed on their rivals. They also began to use the police to eradicate competition and to intensify their fight for more drug territory.

Within the Force, IID investigators were widely regarded as inept, unwilling to take the hard ball, or both. It was obvious that many went there to accelerate their way to the next rank, because few would admit they went to IID to lock up their colleagues. Nevertheless, a number of meticulous investigators tried hard to stem the tide of corruption, despite having their investigations leaked into general policing, which rendered them useless. The sort of person who leaks information at Internal Affairs has the spine of a jellyfish. They're so weak they want to have a foot in both camps, taking promotion into IID but still wanting to be mates with blokes in the general policing area so they can transfer back later. Such investigators are weak-gutted and useless. But who better to receive a difficult or embarrassing complaint file than someone you know will write it off?

I later found the difficulties faced by internal investigators are wide-ranging and varied, but one of the greatest comes when investigators have been compromised before coming into IID. These investigators are toothless tigers because, inevitably, the person they're investigating finds their skeleton in the closet and puts in a friendly reminder. IID investigators need to avoid coppers calling in favours. Internal investigators must be able to divorce themselves from ties to their old mates until they return to their departments.

Easier said than done.

4
In the giggle

Sergeant Steele was a drab, quiet individual: he couldn't have had a better disguise for his real disposition. He started by asking me to drive him around our police boundary, and to the whorehouses and gambling joints. I was eager to impress him with my street knowledge and took him to a brothel in West Melbourne. It looked dark inside and gave me the creeps. I stood around the corner without going inside, but I could still hear Sergeant Steele talking to a woman who had come out to see him.

Steele asked who was running the place and was told that they ran the place themselves. 'Not any more!' Steele told her. 'We'll be fuckin' back.' He walked towards me and we got back into the marked police car. I didn't realise he might have just taken the first step towards standing over the brothel owner, although I certainly felt something wasn't quite right.

We drove a short distance to the corner of Arden and Victoria streets in North Melbourne. This was the area of some of Melbourne's gambling hot spots, where a regular clientele made use of the many cafes and warehouses that posted regular card games and illegal gaming. Melbourne was a conservative gaming state at the time, without a legal casino or poker machines, so the illegal gaming venues prospered. Most taxi drivers would know where to take a punter who wanted to enjoy some illegal gaming. Despite the venues being nomadic, they weren't too secretive. This low-risk crime prospers because the illegal sex and gambling industries are victimless (without identifiable victims apart from the community) and no half-smart illegal gambler, gaming organiser, prostitute or sex client would be stupid enough to report a corrupt cop who had stolen their money, whether illegally earned or not.

What these individuals fear more than losing a few hundred bucks are publicity and attention. It's the relative secrecy and covertness of these trades that enables these people to prosper. A crooked policeman also knows he'd be very unlucky indeed to be convicted on the evidence of a hooker, pimp or illegal gambler, so these types of earns for dodgy cops were money for jam. Even today, the so-called victimless crimes are the sources of greatest temptation, the hot spots for corrupt coppers to make and justify a good earn. Of course, the community is never considered to be a victim by the corrupt, so it's a win–win.

Even though the big illegal gaming venues allegedly had some friendly cops on side they would still move locations constantly. Warehouses were hired on a per night basis. Many police knew what was going on, but little was ever done about illegal gaming by anyone but the Gaming Squad; there were bigger fish to fry. But corruption and gaming go hand in hand. It's now well known internationally that licensing and regulation of the industry create opportunity for the corrupt, and the more red tape involved in getting an authority or a licence, the more valuable the industry becomes for crims and bent cops. Risk management is required by government to curtail the potential for corruption before laws are made, because it's too late afterwards.

Corruption prospers in bureaucratic delays, bungling and anywhere humans are relied on to judge, authorise, test or inspect another's destiny. Even in Australia it isn't unusual for a poorly paid public official to inspect a multimillionaire's application for an abalone licence or multimillion-dollar residential building site. Unfortunately, many councils and governments fail to assess the risk of corruption. It can so easily escalate from 'It was just a lunch. What's the problem?', to 'It was just a weekend away he gave me. The wife and kids needed a break. So what?', and finally, perhaps, 'It was just a few extra dollars he gave me. So what? We don't get paid enough. Everyone does it.'

Sergeant Steele and I drove past one of the cafes and spied an illegal game taking place at the rear. I said to Steele, 'Game on! Money on the table and all!' I stopped the car and we walked up to the front door. I went up to the table and told the men to leave the money and cards where they were; I was keen to impress my sergeant. One of the small Italian men took his money from the table and I told him to put it back; it was now evidence, or so I thought.

Meanwhile, I looked around and saw Steele walk behind the counter of the shop. I thought his actions were strange so I watched him from the back of the cafe. I heard the ring of the cash register opening and the snapping of the money clips followed by the sound of notes being stuffed into his pocket.

I'd turned back towards the table. *Shit! What the fuck do I do now?* I asked myself. *What the fuck did I just see and hear?*

The owner of the cafe took it all in his stride. 'Do you want a coffee, sergeant?' He then turned to me: 'What about you, sir? Would you like a coffee or something to eat?'

'I'm right,' I said as I looked at the floor. At twenty-two years of age, that was the first time I'd ever been called 'sir'; it made me feel like scum.

The sergeant moved over to the card table and I heard the same stuffing sound I'd heard previously at the cash register. Steele's actions were very unassuming and matter-of-fact, but his pocket wasn't cooperating as he stuffed in the cash. I looked around and started heading for the door. My mind was racing. *What about cameras? It'll look like I'm in on it. Steele never even asked me! He assumed I'd be happy to go along with this stuff!* I've no doubt this is one of the ways young people are corrupted. They are effectively forced into it, as Steele had just forced me.

We got back into the marked police car and drove off. I remained cool and waited for him to offer me half. *What am I going to say then?* I thought. I asked what I should write on the running sheet. He told me and we drove away. Somewhat surprisingly, he never offered a cut of the gaming money. Thank God! Not only was he a thief, but he was greedy as well.

Now that I'd apparently passed the corruption test, although my agreement to Steele's cash collection was passive, I was considered 'in the giggle' (often known in New South Wales and Queensland as 'in the joke' or 'laugh'). This meant you were considered to be part of the corrupt brotherhood. I don't know how other police made it into this exclusive club, but I didn't have any choice.

It was fairly obvious to me that once one joined the giggle there was no exit clause. In essence, there's no going back. *No one would believe a constable over a sergeant*, I thought. The cafe owner was hardly going to complain and bring attention to himself and his dodgy business. So, despite not being happy about what had happened, I was sure that being in the giggle would help me get on in the job and, in particular, to become a detective. I wanted to test my skill and wit against the worst criminals, those who commit the heinous crimes that catch public attention. Until now I had never considered that anyone would join the police force because of the opportunities it gave for corruption.

Until now I'd always been a team player with plenty of mates. I hadn't lagged in Sergeant Steele for snipping the money and had remained steadfastly loyal, despite his ethical indiscretion. Anyway, I thought about the short cuts to promotion, the career fast track that came with mates secretly looking after each other. I was happy to reap the benefits of being in the giggle, wasn't I?

Well, no, not really. I knew this wasn't right. I tried to justify to myself that I wouldn't be cheating anyone out of a detective job because I'd already proved myself; I was only getting what I legitimately deserved. But even though I hadn't taken the cafe gambler's money I had an overriding and constant sense of guilt. My conscience wouldn't allow me to consider myself as not involved, nor could I justify what I saw as 'everyone does it' — an old favourite we all use time and time again. I'd seen it, I'd heard it, and my bank account was collecting a fortnightly cheque from society to stop it from happening. I hated myself and the uniform I was wearing for the situation it had put me in. I felt I'd lost something — my soul.

Temporarily, though, I justified my failure to report Sergeant Steele by convincing myself I hadn't done anything wrong. I didn't get any of the money and the victim was running illegal gambling anyway. Oh yeah, there were benefits for me if I shut up as well, but that was just a bonus side issue.

In a very short time, I felt rudderless. I'd broken the oath every police officer takes, the oath well described by Mr Justice Cummins during the trial of two murdered police officers in 2003: 'As a member of the Police Force of Victoria to well and truly serve the community without favour or affection, malice or ill-will, to see and cause the peace to be kept and observed, to prevent to the best of his power all offences against the peace, and to discharge to the best of his skill and knowledge all the duties legally imposed upon him, faithfully and according to law.'

While my head was still spinning, the sergeant put me on nightshift to work with him. What made nightshift different from any other shift was that some sergeants often hand-selected some of their crew members to ensure that they were surrounded by people they could trust. The giggle's definition of someone you can trust means, of course, someone you can trust *not* to tell the truth, someone who will fabricate things, or cover up any wrongdoing by you or another colleague. This can be reversed for those who were honest. I can only surmise why I was selected for this particular nightshift, but I reckon the cafe incident helped the situation along.

I later found that the difficulty of getting honest police to come forward against corrupt police was their fear of being targeted for special attention, singled out for constant harassment for breaking minor rules, put on nightmare rosters, given extensive supervision. It's so easy to do this. No police officer can claim that he or she has always followed the strict Victoria Police code of ethics and conduct to the letter. Any cop who claimed such extraordinary and impossible cleanliness would be either joking or lying. There are such complicated networks of policy, regulation and legislation. Seasoned cops called the manuals '150 years of fuckups' because every time someone fucked up a new rule would be made.

Ironically, the purpose of such rules is to actually curb and control unsavoury behaviour, not to dissuade potential internal witnesses from reporting corruption. Unfortunately, the policy writers never realised that the only people who try to abide by fresh new rules are the good people; the bad guys are already breaking the old ones.

The unworkability of today's laws is exemplified in the usual police stop. Say a police officer stops a vehicle after seeing that the driver is an aggressive drunk who was escorted from a local hotel. He calmly talks the violent assailant into the back of a divisional van, ducking violent outbursts and ignoring verbal abuse. He completes all the paperwork — arrest sheets, charges, property book, jail documentation, running sheet, leap reports (if the drunk is charged with anything apart from drunkenness) — and puts the drunk into custody. This process routinely takes an hour at most, yet the results of such a routine incident weave uncontrollably through unworkable legislation.

If this story is later played out in a court, it will probably take at least two fully qualified lawyers the best part of half a day just to agree on the legality of the police officer's initial assessment of the offender 'alleged' to have been 'drunk'. Even the best and cleanest police in this state can easily fear that they have unwittingly done something wrong or have innocently failed to do something that is required of them by law. This fear ensures loyalty, no matter what, a fact seized upon by the corrupt.

Meticulous record keeping is an innocent policing skill you learn very early in your career, but, like many skills, it can be used by the corrupt, whose best form of defence is usually attack. The only comprehensive notes most corrupt police keep relate to innocent, hard-working members of the Force or their own corrupt colleagues. They carefully log minor breaches, rule breaking and any criminal activities (that they themselves are not involved in, of course). It is the corrupt coppers way of arse-covering. Corrupt police use the innocent mistakes made by others to blackmail and bully potential witnesses whom they fear are considering lagging on them or, in the case of one of their own accomplices, rolling over on them.

I didn't believe I had that problem because I hadn't done anything wrong, nor anything that could have been perceived as wrong. I'd passed the test and was considered one of the lads. Apart from my nagging conscience I didn't have a care in the world; police life was great. I soon discovered how naive I was.

Before we went on nightshift that first time, Sergeant Steele read a brief of evidence I'd written, a sizeable brief about Raymond Edward Baxter, once considered a career criminal. Baxter was one of the old-school crooks, a knockabout crim who sounded as if he had a mouth full of gravel when he spoke. He was small but tough and was very well connected in criminal circles. When I came across him he was living with the previous partner of a violent and unpredictable armed robber named Peter McEvoy, a name synonymous with hatred for police.

Baxter came to my attention on 18 May 1989 at 3.15am. He was sitting on an old-style council bench connected to a table in full view of four blocks of towering Housing Commission flats in North Melbourne, quietly smoking dope. He had a few back-up bags of cannabis with him. I had driven the police car, its headlights off, onto the grassy area near the flats and caught Baxter red-handed. In trying to outsmart crooks, I tried to think laterally so I often drove the police car along city arcades at night, down one-way streets the wrong way, with the headlights off. I rarely took the police car out of second gear. Few other coppers had the patience to drive so slowly, but you don't see, hear and smell the street if you're travelling at more than a few kilometres an hour.

At the time the Commission flats in North Melbourne were the roughest in Melbourne. The blocks were almost on top of each other, and overcrowded in the extreme; not surprisingly street crime in the area was high, drugs were rife and violence was a nightly occurrence. Nobody bothered to report a crime since nobody believed the police would solve it. This was an area that believed in self-regulation, often regulated by the lowest common denominator, not the highest.

As soon as I turned on the headlights, Baxter dropped the packet of drugs he was holding and made for the stairs to his flat. While the policewoman who was my partner radioed for backup I leapt from the car, ran after him and caught him at the stairs. I grappled with Baxter, and our voices echoed through the flats as I tried to handcuff him. Punches were exchanged. The fight went for so long that it was almost in slow motion by the time backup arrived. The other crooks from the high-rise flats began to whistle loudly to each other, something they did whenever the police came on site.

Baxter put up a good fight. My police shirt was ripped and bloodied, and a couple of other police officers were damaged, but I managed to get him handcuffed and into the divisional van under a hail of abuse. 'You fuckin' rats! Pigs! Let him go, you cunts!' More than one bottle was thrown to the street. We were not surprised that the 3.15am abuse from the flats was directed at us, not Baxter. During the day it probably would have been a different story. Those flats catered for two extremes: hard-working battlers during the day, thugs and drugs at night.

Back at the station Baxter was put into an interview room. He wouldn't say much apart from announcing that he intended to complain to the ombudsman about my treatment of him. He said he was doing it through the ombudsman rather than through police investigative channels because — as he later said in Melbourne Magistrates' Court — 'Police can't investigate police. It's a waste of time.' I ignored his comment at the time, but later in my career I found that Baxter was quite right.

Baxter grabbed the chance to make a phone call to his lawyer, Andrew Fraser. Fraser was one of the big criminal lawyers in Melbourne, one of a handful trusted by Melbourne's most notorious gangsters when they needed legal advice. He was arrogant, impeccably dressed and had a high profile. His clients included some of Australia's most prominent gangsters and fraudsters, including failed business tycoon Alan Bond, gangsters Jason Moran, Peter and Dennis Allen, Victor Pierce and Anthony Farrell. Compared to these men, Baxter was a nobody. Interestingly, in 2001, Fraser was jailed for cocaine trafficking.

A few minutes later Fraser was at the station. I remember being surprised at his speed so I asked him whether he had been around the corner or waiting out the front for a call. He ignored me, of course: a cheeky constable didn't merit a reply. Baxter selectively answered the interview questions and alleged I'd assaulted him during the fight under the flats and stolen his money. He had obviously taken part in many more police interviews than I had, and even though I had a sizeable ego at the time, I was fairly sure he won the verbal exchange on a technical knockout. I was happy, though; I'd won the fight under the flats and got to the bags of marijuana before it was set upon by druggies looking for some free mull.

Baxter was on bail at the time Sergeant Steele read the Baxter brief of evidence with interest. He told me that he had something on Baxter and wanted to 'see what he knows'. I asked him what it was about, but he wouldn't say.

There was station gossip that Baxter had some connection to a crook called Gary Abdullah and a heavy crew of armed robbers from Kensington. Abdullah had been shot dead in a North Carlton flat by a detective from my station. He was shot in self-defence. Abdullah allegedly held an imitation firearm and threatened the police detective, who then shot him with his own gun. This was one of many fatal police shootings during this time. Even so, I couldn't understand what the big deal was with Baxter; all the crooks in the area knew each other, and as far I as knew Baxter wasn't one of the three wise monkeys.

Shortly after I started nightshift with Sergeant Steele I had arrested Baxter. Steele drove to the Armed Robbery Squad, where we arrived under the cover of darkness; it was five-thirty in the morning. He collected a very heavy sports bag that had a baseball bat protruding from one end. The bag's weight made me think it contained guns; I couldn't imagine anything else that could be so small yet so heavy. I later saw the bag hidden in our police station, so I took a quick look in it. It did contain guns — a sawn-off shotgun and an imitation pistol. I also saw a hessian bag with 'Reserve Bank of Australia' stamped on it and a set of car number plates. I didn't delve further — I'd seen enough.

I was a tough lad who liked to swear and talk blokey shit while having too many beers too many times a week. I liked crunching through packs of players during hard-fought footy games and booting the pill through the goals. I liked surfing in really crazy places and jumping off 15-metre cliffs to get in there. I was used to shotguns and seeing Dad whack a bird or net a fish. I took people on their merits and never cared about a knockabout mate's tough stickers (tattoos) who 'arkst' instead of 'asked'. Steele must have added these things together and pigeonholed me as someone dodgy. I wasn't. I was my own man — and I was straight.

Steele started talking to me about helping him and others kidnap Baxter. He said some mates would help out, that he had stolen a car for the job and wanted me to get a boiler suit and balaclava. When I asked who else was helping out, he said only that I would find out soon enough. Steele wanted to take Baxter for a ride, he said, and he mentioned a quarry. I tried to explain that I couldn't help because Baxter and his girlfriend would know who I was. Steele assured me that with boiler suits and balaclavas on we would all look the same. If I was really worried, he said, I could always just be the driver.

When I asked what he was going to do with Baxter, Steele told me: 'I'll see what he knows, and then . . . boom!' At the same time he levelled two fingers like a shotgun. His meaning was pretty clear.

I felt sick when I realised that Steele wasn't bluffing about shooting Baxter. That bag of guns and goodies had been just sitting on top of a locker in a shared office of the Armed Robbery Squad. I figured that Steele was either very careless about leaving such incriminating implements around the office or that others were also in the giggle.

I had to make a choice, right then: join the corrupt brotherhood and accept the rewards, or salvage what was left of my soul and wear the consequences.

I guess there was a third choice. I could have walked away from the police service altogether, but that felt like repeating what I had done when I saw Steele operating that day at the cafe. Later in my career, an old man in Tiananmen Square, Beijing, told me something that will stay with me forever: 'Some people get on the bus, some run alongside it. Very few stand in front of it.' I think most people are happy to run alongside the bus, as I had done in the early days with Sergeant Steele. But running alongside the bus allows the corrupt a free ride. You do their work, you cover for them, you accept them and you live in a state of limbo at best. You might talk about them behind their backs, but whatever rank you have achieved, you are weak.

I could either get on the bus or stand in front of it. But I knew there was only one choice: to take this head on. I had to stand up and be counted.

The thought was not a happy one. It has always baffled me that those who do evil seem to have a monopoly on reward and recognition, while doing the right thing almost always means taking the hard road. And it is a very hard road.

What made the choice a little easier was knowing I didn't have it in me to do what Steele wanted me to do. I knew I wouldn't get any prizes for my choice, yet I thought good would prevail over evil in the end. I believed that what goes around comes around, and that if I kept my head down and tail up, I'd be OK. While the Police Internal Affairs unit was not perfect, I thought I could rely on it to see that justice prevailed, that it would look after me and minimise the consequences of being a police witness (a whistleblower). As I said, I was naive.

I spoke to a cop I knew to be honest and who was an experienced detective and I told him everything. He had connections, one of whom was a legendary boxer. But I wasn't after contacts — I wanted advice. I knew what he was going to say before he said it. 'Simon, I agree with you — you'll have to tell the toeys'. Internal Affairs are commonly referred to as the 'toe-cutters'.

In hindsight, I wish I'd asked for a few boxing lessons from his mate instead.

5

The rat trap

I finished nightshift that morning and went to bed. I tried to put my conscience to sleep, hoping that I'd wake up with some sort of special answer to the shit I was in. Then, the telephone rang. I was hardly asleep so I answered it. The call was short. 'Simon, we know everything about it. Come into IID now.' The rest of the call was a blur as I was still half asleep. I began getting dressed almost automatically, feeling a strange sense of relief and nervous expectation, a similar feeling, I dare say, to someone on death row when they're told it's time.

I'd been on nightshift for a while, and this was the first sun I'd seen for days as I walked out of my house into blinding sunlight. *What a joke!* I thought. *Here I am, a supposedly upstanding cop, leaning through my uninsured, bomb of a car's broken quarter vent window trying to open the fucking door to drive somewhere to become one of the most hated whistleblowers in the country. What the fuck have I got myself into?* I asked myself as I grabbed my $5 petrol station sunglasses out of the glovebox and drove to IID.

A sign that my eyes were still red and bloodshot from the glare was the fact that I was wearing my sunglasses as I walked into IID. I was very weary, but I knew I was doing the right thing. I felt uneasy and slightly sick in the stomach because I knew from that point on, my life was going to change. This was the day I became a rat or, more formally, a whistleblower.

I don't like the term 'whistleblower'. It conjures up the image of a petty, weak bastard, or a snitch. It's often used in the media to describe a disgruntled employee making a mountain out of a molehill. However, I do accept that my actions were those of a whistleblower and I cannot think of a better term, so it will have to do. I still prefer it to some of the other names my colleagues gave me.

That day in July 1989, while I was meant to be sleeping, I gave a verbal, recorded statement to Internal Affairs. Nobody else knew. In the late afternoon I was asked whether I wanted to continue my nightshift with my bent sergeant while the investigation continued and, if so, whether I would wear a listening device to record our conversations. I refused the device, feeling that my inexperience in using such things would make it too risky. I was smart enough to know that if there was an information leak at IID and Steele heard I was a rat, he could orchestrate a false conversation with me all the while, knowing I was wearing a secret listening device. What most civilians fail to understand is how cunning bent cops can be, especially if they are under a cloud of allegations. There was also the chance that Steele could suspect something and then search me for the listening device.

I decided to go back to work that night so as not to create suspicion before IID had executed any search warrants and made an arrest. I made this decision because I wasn't rostered to work any further shifts alone with Steele, or so I'd thought.

I arrived at work looking tired; I hadn't slept for over thirty hours due to the time spent at IID. I acted as if nothing had happened during the day, apart from sleeping poorly. Then I discovered that, for some reason, Steele had changed the typed roster. I would now have to work with Steele tonight: I would be alone and out in the car with him.

That made things far more difficult for me. Suspicion and tension grew second by second. My mind ticked over frantically: I had to work with the same man I'd accused of conspiring to kidnap someone, a man with guns and balaclavas and a man I had accused of perverting the course of justice. These were some of the most serious corruption allegations that the Victoria Police had faced at the time. If my allegations were proved, Steele would be sent to jail for a long time. Why had Steele changed the roster? He still had a 'Freddie' (police badge), but that didn't mean he should know anything about my secret meeting with IID. But did he?

I had to act normally, as if nothing had happened during the day. I reluctantly collected the equipment for the shift and we both got into the car. Both of us were armed with loaded .38 calibre service revolvers. This fact was difficult for me to ignore, and didn't help my exterior remain normal. It's sometimes said that, 'If you can fake sincerity you've got it made.' Well, in that case I had it made right up until we were alone, when I sensed something was up with Steele. He wasn't a big one for social chitchat, but he wasn't talking — not at all.

My mind was racing. I asked myself: *Does he know? Or am I being paranoid? He's acting differently. Is it a coincidence that he wanted to work with me tonight?* I said nothing. I just sat in the car. My gut feeling was that Steele had been tipped off. Could someone at IID have put me in danger? If so, what now? What was Steele going to do? It was dark, we were on our own and we were both armed.

Finally, Steele said, without any particular expression in his voice: 'I've been having a chat to my mate "Five".'

He didn't need to say another word. Five was working at IID and I had been talking to him. I trusted Five, but it mattered little to me at the time. Someone at IID had knowingly put my life in danger. I'd been sold out in less time than it took for the sun to go down. Steele had apparently been given the heads up just hours after I'd completed my top secret/highly confidential statement. I was sure Five hadn't been involved in passing on the information; Steele had just used his name to intimidate me or perhaps to provoke comment. He didn't know the detail but he knew I'd been there.

I just nodded to Steele in defeat and looked at the floor as we drove around in silence for a while. I slowly unsnapped my holster, freeing my revolver slightly — the leather was much softer than when I first got it at Russell Street — preparing myself if I needed to draw it quickly. I realised that I could be heading the way of Ray Baxter, so I prepared to shoot my sergeant if I had to defend myself.

Steele drove me around the night streets and then dropped me back at the police station. Not another word was said. As it turned out I don't believe Steele knew exactly why I'd been to IID. He had obviously heard of my daylight movements via the giggle's grapevine in Internal Affairs because no one else knew what I had done, not even my own family.

Steele changed the roster, and then initiated the conversation as to why I'd been seeing his so-called mate at the toe-cutters, no doubt expecting me to respond in kind. But I was caught unawares with no cover story. My silence told him of my new species: rat.

The IID investigators pounced. The head of the team was Detective Inspector Leigh Delmenico, a slightly built man, impeccably dressed, and whose only noticeable habit was to cough before speaking. His gentle demeanour was an excellent cover for his inner courage. I was lucky to have Delmenico to investigate the case. He was a fine investigator and a man of honour. Unfortunately, not all the people at IID had the same integrity.

I still cannot understand the mentality of some police officers who choose to be responsible for the investigation of crime and corruption by police, yet who are unwilling to make the hard decisions or take on the brotherhood. Worse still, I have regularly found people within these departments willing to sell out corruption investigations. The rumour mill works very well among police, especially the corrupt propaganda specialists.

Delmenico found the cache of guns, weapons and disguises, still in the sports bag where Steele had left them. Steele had hidden them in the station. This in itself gives you an idea of the nonchalance of these people. But even if Steele knew he was being investigated for corruption relating to the sports bag he couldn't have got rid of it; far too risky. Bent cops are always aware of walls having eyes; video footage of the sports bag with its owner is evidence with a capital 'E'. During the IID search a bag of cannabis was found in a locker used for paperwork, but it couldn't be linked to any person in particular. It didn't belong to a crook; none were ever in that area. That dope probably originated from a police raid or a drug search and never quite made it to the property store. It was probably snipped by someone with a drug problem or big debts, or to plant on someone.

Internal Affairs spoke to a number of other young police, and they found that Steele had put other cops in a similar situation to me. Two other constables came forward with information and made statements; others, I suspect, didn't. Another who had been selected for Steele's compulsory mentoring was Steve Brown, a skinny, good-looking, country lad who had the misfortune of being very handy at locking up crooks. Constable Brown was one of the few police who stood by me after I became known as a rat. He's a gutsy bloke and a good friend. Our friendship began with a common bond in the corruption involving Sergeant Steele, but we worked together on a few occasions and managed to rack up some horrendous incidents.

I've always told Steve he was cursed, because every time I worked with him something major happened. The first involved Sergeant Steele, which was quite enough, but it didn't stop there.

The second time we worked together we were on nightshift crawling the divisional van down Franklin Street. It was 19 January 1990 at 12.55am when we smelt smoke. We soon saw where it was coming from: it was billowing out of an abandoned terrace house near the Victoria Market. We stopped the van and called the fire brigade. While we waited for them, we sat on the bonnet of the car and lit up cigarettes. Both of us had decided that we couldn't get through the Victorian solid wood door, security door and the secured windows, so we had no option but to relax, watch the disused building burn and wait.

Then, for no apparent reason, Steve and I simultaneously looked up at the second storey window and saw a young boy peering out. He looked down towards us and then collapsed to the floor. Steve and I looked at each other, threw the smokes away and bolted to the locked front doors in a panicked state. We knew we had limited time to break down the door to save the street kid.

Remember the solid door that we had assessed as impossible to force entry without equipment? A couple of minutes later, we'd managed to yank the security door away and had started to elbow, punch and kick the main door. Then it started to crack. Life's like that, isn't it? As a football coach once told me, 'Winning or losing anything often comes down to one thing; how much you want to win.'

The result of this battle to gain entry and save the street kid's life depended upon how quickly the fire took hold, how much smoke there was and whether we could break in in time or, in fact, at all. But the door had started to crack and the frame was splitting. We ran onto the street and charged at the door to force it open. I planted my shoulder into the middle of it at full pace and the door buckled, swung open and spat out the deadlock into a hot, smoke-filled hallway.

The boy's life was the only thing that mattered to us. Steve and I felt our way along the hot cement plaster wall to the stairs. There was no banister and no electricity, which meant no lighting, except from the carpet, which was alight under our feet. I felt Steve behind me and grabbed him so he could follow me upstairs. Of course, after a couple of pots of beer Steve's account of this is that I dragged him into the burning house backwards, but I know Steve was just as committed to put his life in danger as I was. Country lads always love a good yarn.

We worked our way up to the second floor: the smoke made breathing almost impossible. I ran into the bedroom, where I found the young street kid. We heard a cough, and then spied another boy on the floor a few feet away. I handed the first kid to Steve and I took the second. Both kids were groggy but we managed to drag them downstairs onto the street. The fire brigade arrived soon after, followed by an ambulance. The boys weren't the only ones getting treatment for smoke inhalation.

The television and newspaper reporters didn't take long to get to the scene and the resulting footage was shown on all the major channels. Unfortunately, that footage of one of our proudest moments was later used by a television station on the day Steve and I were giving evidence in Sergeant Steele's corruption case. Giving evidence against Steele was stressful and clearly not something either of us enjoyed. But the television story showed us smiling and being jovial. It neglected to mention that the footage had been taken from the successful conclusion of a fire rescue and not from the day we gave evidence against a corrupt colleague. People in the media say that perception is reality. It was very damaging when that news story went to air with the jovial footage. It gave the public and the police the impression that I was a whistleblower who clearly enjoyed the limelight.

Steve and I were given bravery awards from the Royal Humane Society of Australasia for our rescue. Predictably, this went unremarked by any police in the brotherhood; they were still happy seeing me as a weak-gutted bastard. I was one of the first called to the stage in front of a few hundred people to collect my award from His Excellency the Governor of Victoria. As I stood on the stage, I thought he looked a little tense for a man who performed these official public roles on a daily basis. I also noticed he had a shocking nervous twitch in his right arm. I soon realised I had forgotten to salute him and that he was giving me a not too subtle hint.

Nevertheless, we got over it with a smile and a quick photograph, and I took off as soon as etiquette would allow. Steve got his award immediately after me and I watched as he made it two non-saluters in a row. I was reliably informed afterwards that every other uniformed recipient down to the boy scouts had saluted on the day except for Steve and me.

On my way out of Government House, I noticed sandwiches that looked to be of very high quality. I couldn't help myself, so I snatched a couple of travellers on my way out. My early lunch caught the attention of one of the Gov's butlers, who gave me a nod and a wink.

Steve had become involved with Steele because of Anthony Coffey, a regular around the North Melbourne Housing Commission near where I'd arrested Baxter. I knew Coffey quite well. He hated coppers, like most punters in the area, and would take a verbal swipe at any cop who spoke to him. In police jargon, he had an attitude problem.

On this particular night, some time before I blew the lid on Steele, Brown had been with him as they moved around the North Melbourne Commission flats. Steele arrested Coffey, planted a gun on him and dragged him back to the station where he 'confessed' to carrying the gun he'd never seen before. Coffey was a tough kid but not the carrier of firearms. As soon as I saw Coffey's name in the attendance register for possession of a firearm I knew something was suspicious. Steele had forced the confession from Coffey through violence. Unbelievably, all this happened underneath police headquarters, literally a matter of floors from the Chief Commissioner's office. That still leaves me scratching my head.

I don't understand the mindset of a rogue cop. Fabricating a charge against a punter be it Anthony Coffey or anyone else, just defies logic. These briefs of evidence, entailing entirely fabricated evidence and leaving the defendant with little or no chance of defending the charge successfully, are referred to as bricks. What does a brick achieve? A deeper hatred of police? A propensity for more serious crime? Increased distrust? Police assaulted? I can't think of anything good that comes out of such a low act, no matter who the criminal is. Ironically, Anthony Coffey, like Baxter, became another unlikely ally. Despite being a young punter Coffey found something that a few of my colleagues couldn't when he too stood up against corruption: guts. He took to the stand and gave evidence too. I have no doubt Coffey's life changed from that day on, hopefully for the better.

As soon as I had carried out my decision to tell the IID about Steele, I was ostracised by many of the people I had thought were my friends; only a handful stuck by me. I was no longer welcome at police functions, where I became the focus of staring matches and finger pointing or where I found myself ignored to the point of being unable to get a drink. Inexplicably, my work ratings also went down, despite my workload being extremely high. I didn't complain, just worked harder despite the white-anting that went on under the surface.

Once a caller rang the police station and asked to speak to me regarding a car accident. A new constable, who probably wondered what he had got himself into, took the call and passed on the message: 'I just took a call for you, Simon. Apparently, you are going to be shot dead.' Around the same time another police officer, a woman who was a staunch supporter of mine at the station, received a pair of animal testicles in the internal mail.

I met Ray Baxter, Steele's would-be kidnap victim, twice after I'd broken ranks and became a rat. By prosecuting him for minor drug offences, I had probably saved his life. I saw him for the first time in the Melbourne Magistrates' Court in Russell Street and started talking to him about the foiled kidnap attempt. It became obvious very quickly that this was the first time Baxter had heard of such a thing. He said one word: 'What?'

Baxter's lawyer, Andrew Fraser, took one look at his distressed client and ordered me to explain what I'd said. But I'd said enough, and we both looked at Baxter. He said, 'Simon stopped me from being kidnapped by a bent cop.' Even Fraser was gobsmacked.

Baxter pleaded guilty, avoiding a contested hearing between us. I left the court and headed back to the station.

The next time I saw Ray Baxter he was playing pool in a knockabout pub in the inner suburbs. There were a few hard-core crims about; some had just been released from jail, and the others were probably positioned somewhere else on the conveyor belt of hard knocks. They were men full of hate, who loved getting pissed, tattoos and smoking heavy cigarettes. Baxter fitted in well.

I walked into the hotel wearing the clothes they hate most — a police uniform. The place stopped, as I'd come to expect in this type of pub. I saw Baxter but didn't acknowledge him — this could have put him in a potentially dangerous situation with his peers. No one would like a cop sympathiser in this particular pub. Baxter would have had more reason to hate cops than anyone else in that pub, except for one cop: me. I feared these men's notoriously short fuses wouldn't allow Baxter enough time to explain why he spoke with me. Nevertheless, I walked past Baxter and asked if he was winning his pool game. Baxter replied in the affirmative and paused for a long while before saying, 'Thanks.' I nodded and gave him a smile.

'One day you and I will play a game of pool,' I said.

Baxter replied, 'Yeah, one day.'

When I walked into that smoky pub my career was in tatters, and I had to handle constant threats and fear. I walked out the same way. But I also walked out with the respect of a criminal, and, most important of all, with my own self-respect.

Steele's preliminary hearing was held in the Melbourne Magistrates' Court, Russell Street. When the day came everyone in the office was too busy to drive me to court, so from William Street I walked the two kilometres across the city. When I arrived I stood in the upstairs foyer next to the courtroom. I was to be called as the first witness, immediately after the standard legal argument.

I stood on my own outside the courtroom in front of a group of detectives who glared at me. I could tell some were detectives from the Armed Robbery Squad because they had big bushy moustaches, black suits, white short sleeved shirts and thin black ties with the motif of crossed pistols and the initials ARS. I wondered why they bothered wearing plain clothes; they might as well have been in a uniform. But soon I realised I wasn't on my own. The second witness was there: Anthony Coffey, the young petty criminal who had been fitted-up with a gun.

As I waited to be called into court, Steele's ex-Armed Robbery Squad mate, Senior Constable Rod Reece, walked up to me. At the time Reece was suspended, facing charges arising from claims brought by a woman that she had been assaulted, shot at and offered $400 for sex by four off-duty policemen at a barbecue in St Kilda on 10 April 1989. But now Reece glared into my face and lifted his left hand slowly to his temple. He mimicked a pistol with his fingers, pointed it at his head and said: 'Boom, boom, boom.' He then pushed past me into another court.

I felt a sense of disbelief, then real anger, a deep anger I'd never felt before, as well as helplessness. Turning to Coffey I said, 'That's what you get for being honest.' Coffey nodded hopelessly and we both looked at the ground. Coffey and many others who live in Housing Commission flats among grinding poverty, with little hope of getting out, probably knew the feeling of helplessness quite well. But for me it was a new feeling — I'd lived a privileged life, despite Dad's rough camping trips, and this was the first time I saw life from the position of the downtrodden minority. I didn't like it and knew I had to act.

I didn't know whether Coffey had witnessed what Reece had done, but as I stood there my blood felt as if it were boiling. I didn't wait to be called into the courtroom, just pushed open the door and told the prosecutor and anyone else who happened to be listening exactly what I thought of Reece's death threat, the judicial system and the culture of the Victoria Police. Luckily, the magistrate had left the bench for a short adjournment or I would have pushed the boundaries of contempt myself.

The case against the highly popular Sergeant Steele was adjourned. Meanwhile IID investigators came rushing into the courthouse to check on the welfare of Victoria's most unpopular policeman — me.

Reece's blatant threat meant another statement to Internal Affairs and so I was acutely aware that the whole whistleblower process had started all over again. I already figured I was tagged as a rat, perhaps now I'd be King Rat or at least one with a gold tooth. Reece had threatened to kill me, and once again IID laid a charge for which I was the only eyewitness.

A day later Reece was acquitted in the Melbourne Magistrates' Court on the charges he was facing. The magistrate made a less than subtle reference to the way the investigation had been handled by Internal Affairs when she said: 'The case has been riddled with mystery and uncertainty, and it leaves me with a number of suspicious . . . I was concerned some witnesses were ignored or at least not pursued as energetically as one would have hoped.' She continued that 'Photographic identifications of Reece and [name deleted] were clearly not conducted in the proper manner.' I heard the news, but it didn't fill me with any great hope that IID was on the ball.

Reece walked from court a free man, only to be charged with contempt of court following his death threat the day before. It went direct to the Supreme Court for hearing, and Victoria Police hired John Winneke QC to prosecute the case.

Winneke was one of the best barristers in Melbourne at the time and later served as an Appeal Court judge. He also appeared for Lindy Chamberlain, but, most important of all for me, he played in the AFL 1961 premiership team. This was one of the hardest eras in the history of Australian Rules football, so I knew he could help me tough this out.

It was May 1990 when I walked to yet another court hearing, this time in the Supreme Court. I wondered what was coming next. A sergeant took the stroll with me; he was a good man who asked if I wanted some company.

We arrived early. My sergeant patted me on the back as I opened the courtroom door and walked in. The large courthouse was packed with loud detectives, many of whom had the familiar big bushy moustaches, black suits, white short-sleeved shirts and squad ties. They weren't there to support me.

The people in the court were standing, thereby making it impossible for me to see where I was expected to go. As I took my first steps into the courthouse the noise abruptly stopped. It was obvious that many conversations had stopped mid sentence. The rat had arrived.

I walked halfway down the room under everyone's watchful gaze, wondering whether there were any seats left. I hadn't expected to see a packed court. In the silence, all I could hear were my own tentative footsteps. I stopped, eager to see the ex-Hawthorn Football Club strongman, Jack Winneke QC. I was now considered some sort of goody two shoes, although my old squeaking R.M. Williams boots told the tale of very different bloke. I stopped and tried to look for Jack, avoiding row upon row of beady glaring eyes. *Fucking hell, this is worse than last time.*

Then Jack's face peered out from the front row. 'Down here, Simon.' *Good on you, Jack.* There was no chance of me being eyeballed in the front row, where all I had to do was look towards the judge. Winneke was unfazed, calm and focused, which helped me greatly and gave me confidence to stand up once again.

The court rose at the knock of the judge: 'All stand,' demanded the tipstaff. 'The matter of Rod Reece.' The judge, in his white horsehair wig and black gown, sat down. Soon afterwards Winneke, who was at least 1.9 metres tall, stood up and called me to the witness stand.

Here goes nothin'. My squeaky shoes made a noisy comeback. I walked to the witness box and began giving my evidence; Winneke was painfully slow and methodical. Then it was time for cross-examination. Again the defence examination of my evidence was slow and I was asked to show the court how the threat had been made. Instinctively, I imitated a gun with the fingers of my right hand and began moving my right hand up to my temple. But I stopped midway. 'Sorry, your Honour,' I said to the judge, 'he used this hand,' and I substituted my left hand for my right and said, 'Boom.'

It was said that I'd imagined the events at the Magistrates' Court and that I was deluded. But the judge quickly dismissed that idea, saying: 'It is clear that the case in which Constable Illingworth was a witness has divided the police force. Although he was only doing his duty, some policemen believed he betrayed the accused sergeant. Constable Illingworth was caught in the crosscurrents of factional strife and morality standards in the police force.'

Reece was fined $3000, convicted and sentenced to three months' jail. Fortunately for Reece his sentence was suspended so he avoided incarceration, but Reece was now formally branded a crook. I too was branded, but I had to wait for my punishment.

My experiences with Detective Reece and Sergeant Steele were never far from my mind. On one particular occasion, they were thrust back in my face. It was 1 March 1992 and I was working ringside security at the Carlton football ground, the scene of one of the biggest boxing matches Melbourne had ever held. Forty thousand boxing fans were barracking for Jeff Fenech to avenge a drawn bout with reigning champion Azumah Nelson. The winner would claim the WBC super featherweight title.

I could hear the super featherweights trading blows behind me as I crouched and watched the mobsters, dodgy lawyers and other colourful identities cheering them on from ringside. No draw this time: Nelson punched Fenech's lights out. The result was obvious, as was the illegal gambling cash being passed between crooks and local identities to settle bets. There were many more winners and losers outside the ring than in it.

As the crowd dispersed and I strolled around the oval herding the people out of the stadium two men in bomber jackets walked into me. They were Rod Reece, freshly convicted and with a jail sentence hanging over his head, and a mate. Barging into me didn't appear to be a mistake. A few minutes later the two of them staged a fistfight only metres away from me. I just walked past them, much to the disgust of a number of bystanders who, understandably, expected more from their local police. Reece and his mate stopped fighting immediately it was clear I wasn't going to be lured in. I risked being bashed, the outcome of which would probably be hospitalisation, followed by more intimidation and another round with a legal process for which I was quickly losing respect.

6

Organised and disorganised crime

Until that point I had tried to keep my head down in a doomed attempt to resurrect my career. But as one of my colleagues used to say, 'You can't turn shit into strawberry jam.' Trouble jumped out in front of me whenever I got into a patrol car. It followed me like a curse.

One evening my partner and I arrived outside the King Street nightclubs. Some of these seedy clubs were very close to a busy overpass. Rain never penetrated under there so it reeked of urine, stale beer and the occasional patch of vomit. This was — and remains — a notorious location, known for its drugs, drunkenness and high-profile crooks; if violence was what you were after, it rarely let you down. We crawled along in the divisional van down King Street towards the glow of the nightclubs; through our open windows we could hear the *doof doof doof* of the music a block away.

Suddenly, cars began darting viciously around the road. We sped up and saw the obstacle: a young man was crazily wielding a baseball bat at passing motorists, while late nightclubbers urged him on and screamed at him. We skidded to a halt and jumped out with batons raised. Our repeated requests to drop the baseball bat fell on deaf ears, so we tackled him with our batons. Strike, strike, strike. The speed and velocity of my hits could have felled a medium-sized tree. My partner wasn't exactly a small guy either. Quickly, the batsman was cut down, the bat now safely out of hand. I yelled instructions. 'Put your fuckin' hands behind ya back!' I kept a knee on him; he complied and I cuffed him. I was happy to get this bloke squared away before he did anything really bad or, indeed, before anything really bad happened to him.

Midnight baseballers in King Street risk getting shot; it's that simple. This was a gangster hot spot, where you either 'carried' (a gun) and were prepared to use it or you went unarmed. There was no shortage of guns. So, apart from the obvious amusement value, a fuckwit with a baseball bat was very low on the food chain and therefore ripe for a disgruntled crook's venom. Most fair dinkum crooks wouldn't bat an eyelid at putting off such a bloke if he came at them. Then, they'd happily stroll down to the Homicide Squad office and claim self-defence. But the wallet of this midnight baseballer fell open on the roadway as I was cuffing him, revealing a familiar metallic star. Our sore and sorry man was another cop. I couldn't believe it, but I told my partner I would do the charges; there was no point in dragging someone else into the shit. My name was already mud.

In my free time I simply tried to blend in like any other young lad. I played football and enjoyed surfing with my mates. Very few of my friends knew what was happening to me inside the Force, and I avoided telling them. I was embarrassed because many of them had told me I was an idiot to join up in the first place and I figured they wouldn't understand the situation anyway. But I had to come clean when one of my mates was threatened with violence by a few pissed Victorian detectives. He was in Bali at the time. His offence, according to the drunken slobs, was knowing me.

The long tentacles of the bent cops stretched all the way to my footy games with my mates. Opposition players and club officials would yell 'Whistleblower' and 'Lagger' while I was playing. I didn't care much about the players saying it; they could be dealt with when the opportunity arose, but some of the officials looked old enough to be my father. I was often involved in many verbal stoushes, wrestles and a bit of push and shove before the umpire stepped in. My normal response to sledging would be to settle down and set about kicking a few goals.

But very occasionally the frustration would become too much and on a couple of occasions I unloaded huge biffs on opposition players.

One day my younger sister Binny came to watch me play. She knew what I'd been through in the Force and when she heard the tirade of abuse I was getting from the opposition coach, who was yelling 'Whistleblower' and 'Lagger' from the comfort of the grandstand, she could sense I'd had enough. Binny was probably the only person not surprised at seeing me run from full forward to get into this bloke, but when I jumped the boundary fence and pushed through the crowd even she looked on in disbelief. I began yelling at the coach and headed over to punch him, but he quickly apologised and sanity prevailed, so I ran through the crowd and back onto the field. Things went rather quiet at the oval after that. No one said a word to me about it — no players, no umpires, no officials, nobody. It was as if it hadn't happened. That was a strange moment in my life because I'd naively thought that only a handful of people knew about my whistleblower experiences, but the silence around the ground confirmed my worst fear: they all knew.

My youthful innocence was gone. I was a young man who'd experienced the wrongs of a corrupt world well before my time. I'd grown up very quickly and it was isolating me from my peers. In the years to come I'd lift my trouser leg, take my revolver from my ankle holster and drop it in the team valuables bag before getting changed into my football gear. By then everyone knew I had a gun for protection. The lads didn't flinch, they just shook their heads.

A different group of my mates kept an eye on weather maps rather than footballs. They knew the surfing conditions all around the country. On a few occasions we drove to Queensland to tackle the big cyclone swells. We all loved getting away, nobody more than I. When Queensland trips weren't on the agenda we surfed our regular big wave spots that were far less inviting than the warm water of Queensland, including Easter Reef at Port Campbell and the appropriately named Massacre Reef at Peterborough. Both places are on the southwest coast of Victoria where surging waves hit underwater reefs and create waves that aren't easily measured. There were days down on that rugged shipwreck coast where the waves were every bit of 6 metres high.

Anyone who tells you they aren't scared of surfing 20-foot waves is a liar or mentally ill — we were all scared, but we pushed each other to the point of stupidity. That coastline combined huge waves, razor-sharp reefs, cold water and long distances from medical assistance, so when we paddled out we knew that drowning was always a distinct possibility. Even so, we tested our courage by pushing ourselves down some gigantic mountains of water in search of Australia's biggest wave.

It was ironic that after such adventures I would return to work only to be branded gutless by police who didn't even know me. I knew I couldn't fight everyone and it would be juvenile to try, so I ignored the backstabbers, misinformation and shit spreaders, bent cops and gossipers and just did my job as best I could under the circumstances. I worked harder than most other cops I knew, often arriving for work two hours early, and I set about catching as many crooks as I could.

What I wanted was to join the Criminal Investigation Branch and become a detective. A detective senior sergeant offered to be a referee for me. He knew the implications of being associated with a whistleblower, let alone writing one a job reference, but he did, saying that I had 'the most potential of any member [of the police force] coming to my notice'. This was a big statement considering the station had an estimated one hundred police within it and he'd been in the Force for thirty years. But his reference didn't help me; I wasn't even getting interviews for detective jobs. I decided to move branches, hoping life would be different. It wasn't. I was slammed into a clothing locker by a colleague who said he was a mate of Sergeant Steele. I gave him the usual response, 'Go fuck yourself', rather than be lured into a fight.

Work was a constant battle but I managed to save some money and I bought a small Victorian cottage in Collingwood. The house was a wreck but I scrimped and saved to repair it. I lived among broken floorboards and a second bedroom with a dirt floor but I didn't care. I did one room at a time and slowly transformed it into a very attractive little house.

In the meantime, I kept applying to become a detective, again and again. I still couldn't even get an interview, despite an excellent resume. I desperately wanted a detective's job and I also needed the extra money. My previous reference had become outdated so another detective was asked to provide me with one. He refused. The only thing worse than a poor job reference is no reference at all. This detective and I had an altercation that involved some swearing and raised voices. I told him I knew he couldn't give me a reference because he knew it would have to be a good one, but he also knew Sergeant Steele. I received the report two hours later.

Interestingly, he gave me 8 out of 10 for every field with the exception of the teamwork category which was dropped to 7 out of 10. Teamwork was always my stumbling block, at least according to some who expected loyalty no matter what. Years later Professor Sawyer of Melbourne University described Australia as a mateocracy in a speech I heard in Melbourne about whistleblowers. Our mateocracy makes an Australian whistleblower's lot far more dangerous. But bent cops swiping loot don't like loyalty to be a lottery — they demand staunchness to the bitter end. The evils of breaking the code are unspoken but everyone suspects that they will be quick and harsh.

The inner-city suburb of Carlton is renowned for its Italian culture. But part of that culture — as, indeed, for other cultures — was the existence of organised crime. Hidden within that culture was a group of gangsters known as the Carlton Crew. Its members include Alphonse Gangitano a well-known celebrity crim who basked in the glory of being a suave thug. There are many others whose names and *modus operandi* I know well but I won't give details here for legal reasons, not yet anyway. I can name Gangitano because he's dead; I hardly need to lead you by the nose as to how you think he might have died — he was shot in the head. But, like all people of his ilk, his evil lives on long after his death. His victims can't forget the not-so suave things he did.

Many crooks appear to be legitimate businessmen, some of these men came from well-known Italian families and some were just hired thugs. But there was a definite group, and they never talked about each other or about what they did. They followed *omerta*, the code of silence. This was a tried and trusted characteristic of the real Mafia and these men followed a similar code outside Italy.

After working in the city for a few years, I decided to move to the Carlton police station. This wasn't a promotion, but a sideways step.

I thought it would do me good to move somewhere else and try to make a clean go of things away from the stigma of City West and Sergeant Steele. I wanted to keep my arrests ticking over and wanted to chalk up a few big crims.

When I got to Carlton I noticed most other cops knew very little about the Carlton Crew at uniform level, but I wanted to know them so I could catch them, so I made it my business to know. I spoke to as many coffee shop and restaurant owners as I could and I built a genuine rapport with them. Some were very guarded in speaking about the local Mafia, some weren't. It was clear that none of the owners liked them. In Sicily they were just part of business. But what about in Carlton? Was silence part of doing business here? I couldn't ask; that was far too insulting and direct.

In the community rumours were rife about a courageous Italian businessman who fought the Carlton Mafia by meeting fire with fire. His defiance came in the form of blasting the facade of a mobster's house with a shotgun. He wasn't going to pay.

Stories like this one fascinated me — it was a new world, an underworld. I soon realised how tunnel-visioned most police were in their outlook on crime. Their main focus was street crime that involved petty crooks, pimps, prostitutes and minor thieves, but it was all superficial, a pimple on the back of a really ugly monster.

It didn't take me long to realise that the best crooks weren't driving stolen cars; they owned the latest European models. So I began targeting specific types of cars and people I believed were members of the secret society. It didn't take me long to strike gold in the heart of Little Italy.

It was 1992 and everything was buzzing as normal in Carlton as I intercepted yet another new sports car as part of my new routine. The driver wasn't doing anything wrong; he was cruising slowly and simply drove a car that fitted my new strategy. It was time for a licence check to break the ice. But it soon became apparent that this interception was different. Shopkeepers and waiters stopped to observe and whispered in Italian to each other.

The moment we intercepted the car, the driver was on his mobile telephone making a call. I wasn't sure who he was calling until after we'd arrested him and were met at the police station by his lawyer and barrister team. He had called his lawyer before my partner and I had even got out of our police car.

We searched the car and found a large quantity of cash and some handwritten notes. The notes were very interesting indeed, involving some well-known colourful identities and, perhaps more importantly, some not so well known. For those named it would be their worst nightmare to know such a document was in possession of police. It appeared to be intelligence in its purest form. But someone back at the station didn't put too much weight on it being of any value, because they took the evidence away. It was eventually located, torn up and scrunched into balls, an interesting way to treat another policeman's evidence.

The Carlton identity was seated opposite me in the interview room as the evidence made its way back to me in its altered form. I tried to hide my anger but it was clear I was upset. He slid his hands through his slick black hair and laughed as he rocked forward and stood up to show himself out. Considering the state of the evidence, he obviously thought the case had collapsed and that the interview was over. The matter never went to court, which at least meant I didn't have to produce scrunched-up balls of paper as evidence.

From that day on I was treated differently by some of the local businessmen. It hadn't been my intention to arrest the man where we did, it just happened that way, but it was clear that many of the locals approved. It was a monumental win for Victoria Police, despite the foolish actions of one of our own. I still don't know why the evidence was tampered with; one can only surmise.

One of the most meaningless tasks I did while I was at Carlton was to issue a penalty notice for about $25 to a person whom I'd alleged was riding a bicycle without a helmet. The date was 20 February 1992. You may well ask why I have mentioned that bit of trivial information, but this was to be no ordinary on-the-spot fine; it resulted in a great deal of embarrassment and made the newspapers. Why? Because I sped through the process of typing up the most minor brief of evidence I'd ever done and made a fatal mistake. I wrote down the name of the person I believed was my partner on the day and got it wrong.

The brief of evidence was checked by a supervisor and the error wasn't picked up, so no one, with the exception of the defendant, knew things were amiss at the first hearing that occurred seven months later. He knew very well that my partner had been a Caucasian female, not a black male police officer and, understandably, appealed his conviction from the Magistrates' Court.

When I received notification that the bike helmet guy had appealed his conviction, I couldn't understand why he'd fight such a trivial matter so hard. Something was fishy, so I double checked the old running sheet. After a while I found the answer, and realised my mistake. No wonder the policeman whom I thought was with me on the day said he couldn't remember anything. I voluntarily contacted Internal Affairs and explained my error. I explained the situation and, as they say, I threw myself on the wire. I also apologised to the bike helmet guy.

On 20 October 1993 the matter went before the County Court and we lost: no surprise there. But when I opened the newspaper the next day I saw an article titled 'Perjury claimed in helmet case'. Life wasn't meant to be easy. I wrote a letter to the editor of the newspaper in response to the article, explaining the difference between perjury and an honest mistake. I explained how the mistake happened and what does — and does not — constitute perjury. I also subtly let it be known how peeved I was with the way the article had been written. It was great that the publisher printed my response. I felt the matter had been settled and I put it down to one of my life's more embarrassing moments.

But, as I've explained, anything that causes embarrassment to honest cops is ammunition for the corrupt ones. This is the type of thing they never forget.

And sure enough, the $25 bike helmet case did raise its ugly head again fifteen years later as part of a smear campaign by a very desperate person who sent copies of the article to two journalists. Thankfully, these people saw through it, and the campaign never got off the ground. Another campaign began when a politician received a copy of the bike helmet article from an anonymous source. When I was told about this I didn't try to locate the source until I was shown some of the other documents the politician received. They were top secret police documents that should never have been released.

The only valid reason for confidential police documents to be in the hands of anyone except their author or some other appropriate person is if a defendant or defence lawyer requests their release in preparing the defence. I doubt a judge or magistrate hearing a disclosure argument would be told that a document was intended to form part of a smear campaign or to be passed around by criminals. People who receive files under disclosure provisions are morally obliged to honour the integrity and confidentiality of the documents. But that doesn't seem to be enough. There needs to be a greater deterrent for people who use the discovery provisions to embarrass an innocent third party or to provide them to a rival crook.

Information intercepted by police phone taps and served on the defence often contains subtle threats between crooks about other crooks. A dodgy lawyer needs only to hand the transcript to the wrong person and it's like gunpowder for an already turbulent underworld. Indiscriminate and corrupt releases of confidential information and documents can be a very deadly game.

Less than two years later I moved from Carlton to the Collingwood police station as a senior constable. This wasn't a real promotion, but I'd done my time. Collingwood was an arena of hardened blue-collar workers, druggies, drug dealers, Asians and yuppies.

The station was run by a well-respected senior sergeant who was a gentleman and a man of underestimated talent. The small crew of sergeants, senior constables and constables of Collingwood knew the patch well. It was no mistake that in six months we had seized amounts of illicit drugs in our 5-square-kilometre patch that rivalled the hauls made by the Drug Squad, responsible for the whole of Victoria.

One or two years' experience at Collingwood was worth four or five years elsewhere. It wasn't the reported crimes, such as burglaries and thefts, that kept you busy, it was the other crimes that Collingwood had in abundance: drug trafficking, stolen goods, illegal gaming, bribery, blackmail, standover merchants and unreported assaults. More serious crime, too. The boss often said, 'If it's criminal, it normally happens in Collingwood or thereabouts.' He knew what he was talking about. On 9 August 1987 a rogue ex-army officer named Julian Knight had run riot with an automatic weapon in Hoddle Street, Clifton Hill. He had mercilessly shot and murdered seven civilians and wounded another nineteen in what was known as the Hoddle Street massacre. The dead and wounded civilians' only offence had been to be wandering around Clifton Hill trying to catch a train or to drive up Hoddle Street through to nearby Northcote. Thankfully, such outrageous crimes are still unusual for Australia, although nobody in the Melbourne police was in disbelief where it happened. More a case of, 'That'd be right — in Collingwood's patch.'

Ten years before, on 10 January 1977, another hideous crime had occurred in Collingwood — the infamous Easey Street murders. This ghastly crime involved the slaying of two young women who were stabbed to death; one was believed to have been raped. The savage maniac had stabbed the women a total of eighty-four times and left a sixteen-month-old baby in the house to perish. The murderer or murderers have never been caught.

But my boss's comments weren't about either of those crimes; he was talking about the vibe of the place. Collingwood was a place of heavy crooks and big stakes — there was never a time you could take your eyes off a suspect's hands. Some could break out of handcuffs quicker than I could get them off with a key. It was a breeding ground for crime families, where kids were born into a cycle of bad luck, violence, drugs and false dreams. Many of the criminals had connections to the docks and they were often used to stand over any person with unpaid credit in the crime trade.

In such an environment it was always more dangerous to be owed money than to owe it to someone. This was because the crooks who couldn't pay their criminal debts often chose to clean the slate permanently rather than be stood over by someone debt collecting on another criminal's behalf.

Collingwood was a place where perception and reality were the same. Small-time crooks and off-duty sex workers often walked into Collingwood pubs where they were very quickly assessed as such and left alone; as long as they kept to themselves they were OK. Pretenders, would-be Mafia types or wankers who prey on small-time crooks and off-duty sex workers were not treated with the same respect. The cone of silence in Collingwood was far better than the one on the American sitcom *Get Smart*; very few people spoke out in Collingwood. It was amazing how many people would have their backs turned or were in the toilet at the crucial moment.

Collingwood was largely self-regulated. Pubs did not often have the need for security because the locals regulated who drank where and when. It was a place where you could drive the divisional van around the streets for an eight-hour shift and continually see people getting up off the street with bloodied noses, swollen or cut faces and bruised elbows after they'd 'tripped over'. It never ceased to amaze me how many people would trip over backwards out of Collingwood pubs, yet suffer facial injuries consistent with forceful punches to the front of the head.

It wasn't all doom and gloom in Collingwood, though; there were plenty of characters. A great local identity was (the late) Harry Rizzetti. Harry and his crew of hard-working men made up the last generation of workers at the Cox and Rizzetti iron foundry.

The lads worked over white-hot coke furnaces in soaring temperatures to melt down some of the old city pipes to make iron lacework, outdoor seats, real Victorian-era fireplaces, real fence spears and fire grates. In winter, Harry's lads would come out of the foundry for a cigarette, their faces sweaty, their arms ash-black, their tattoos barely decipherable through the soot. Harry and his family had kept the family tradition going until the very last moment. This kind of ironwork is all made overseas now, but George from Steptoe's (another Collingwood icon) says, 'No one makes 'em as good as Harry made 'em.'

At Christmas, Harry and the lads always made a generous contribution to the Collingwood police charity raffle. Harry also insisted on purchasing a couple of handfuls of raffle tickets. Every year it was held Harry won most of the prizes — it was karma, we'd say. He actually put some of his prizes back into the draw one year but won them all back again minutes later. These blokes were the true hard men of Collingwood, bar none. It was the end of an era when the foundry closed.

After the bike helmet saga, I was never one for traffic offences so I rarely handed out fines. But I couldn't ignore a 1-tonne utility driving along Victoria Parade, Collingwood, with what appeared to be 1.5 tonnes on it. The back of the ute was almost touching the ground.

As it pulled into the curb the driver got out and approached me. He smiled cheekily and enquired, 'Is there a problem, officer?' I looked at his rear number plate almost touching the road. We both laughed. I told him the Road Traffic Authority was on its way to weigh the ute. The driver quipped, 'She's over, but not by that much. I'll put five bucks on it.'

'Done,' I said.

I was very confident of a win but I had decided that I wouldn't take his money, figuring he would have a fine to pay as well. The RTA arrived and the utility tipped the scales at 1.2 tonnes, it was just over.

I opened my wallet and handed the driver a fiver. I was careful not to be a sore loser, so I also gave him a warning. We all laughed as he drove off with my cold hard cash. I said to my partner, 'What chance has he got when he gets to the pub and tells his mates that story: "This cop pulled me over, handed me five bucks and drove off . . . Fair dinkum!"'

I would have thought that after seven years the threats and abuse would have dried up, but no. While I was at Collingwood I received another threat, this time from a cop who had asked to speak to the roster sergeant. I identified myself to the caller, who stopped mid conversation and asked my name again. I confirmed who I was and he asked me if I recognised his voice. I said, 'No', although I did.

The caller then called me a 'fucking give-up c—' and hung up. I didn't tell anyone about it, I just shrugged my shoulders. Seriously though, what was I going to do? Go to court again as a whistleblower? I was tired of being a victim but I used my knowledge to my advantage for a few years. It's more important to know who your enemies are than it is to know your friends, but this advantage was limited because this bastard had also been a bystander at Steele's case when I was threatened with being shot in the head. He knew it and so did I.

A few years later Chief Commissioner Neil Comrie created an award, the Police Service Medal, for ethical service. It was awarded to me — and another recipient on the same day was my abusive caller. By then he knew I was aware of his identity. Unfortunately, I had to sit and watch him proudly collect his Police Service Medal before I received mine. I watched as he walked off the podium and raised his middle finger at me. *Typical of his outstanding ethical service.* A few moments later I walked up to the podium, received my medal from the Assistant Commissioner and successfully restrained myself from throwing it until after I left the presentation hall. I didn't want the fucking thing after that prick got it; it was a medal of shame. How could more than 90 per cent of the Force deserve a medal anyway? I thought awards were meant to mean something.

7
Hooray for Collingwood

The Collingwood station was always a hive of activity whenever a search warrant was taken. A handful of the more seasoned officers were often put together as part of the raiding party. Each individual possessed particular skills: some were good in the meticulous art of searching, a skill that requires patience, others had the ability to defuse tension or violence, some cared for children and some were just good at kicking in a door, clearing rooms and handcuffing scumbags. There are very few ex-Collingwood coppers who don't have a solid repertoire of war stories.

I risked my life while working at Collingwood, as did many other cops over the years. One of these occasions was during a house raid. The house itself was an unremarkable, small, Victorian terrace house situated in a quiet street in the suburb of Clifton Hill. We already knew it was frequented by a number of criminals involved in organised crime because our most recent raid had netted all their handguns. We knew the guns were safely locked in the police safe and out of harm's way, and this next raid was conducted with the expectation of finding drugs. Expecting one thing and not the other can be a fatal mistake.

It was early and the sun was just coming up as I moved to the side lane of the premises with the others. One after another we scaled the side fence as quietly as possible.

Then we came to the sobering realisation that the house had altered since the last raid just a few weeks before. On that occasion our entry point had been a flimsy wooden door but now it was all glass. We knew we were in trouble because we only had a 12-pound key with us. Sledgehammers aren't particularly helpful entry tools for anything made of glass — unless, of course, you like losing fingers. The old adage 'Time spent on reconnaissance is never wasted' was going through my head. The silence was deafening.

Then I saw one of the more gutsy things I'd seen in my time in the Force. Using his body as a battering ram, our sergeant threw himself through the glass window, then lay on the broken glass and screamed, 'Go, go go!' I ran at full pace over him and I assumed my original role of clearing each room.

I moved quickly through the house but missed seeing a discreetly positioned bathroom. Not only did I miss seeing the bathroom, but I also missed seeing a criminal arming himself with a shotgun. Thankfully, one of my offsiders dealt with him as I ran into the master bedroom where I saw a middle-aged woman and a young girl lying on the bed under a blanket.

I pointed my pistol at them and yelled, 'Police, put your hands where I can see them.' They didn't respond. The young girl was screaming in terror. Again I made my request, again nothing. I felt terrible and considered lowering my gun, but decided against it — I still hadn't seen her hands. I pulled the blanket away. The woman had a loaded automatic weapon next to her left hand. I seized it and, shortly after, when I checked the breech of the weapon I found it was fully loaded.

The woman said she hadn't been sure if we were real police so she hadn't known whether to shoot me or not. She was soon to be a star witness in an organised crime trial so she feared an ambush. I found it ludicrous at the time that someone would sleep with a loaded gun nearby. But if I had seen what was in store for me later I would have thought differently.

Collingwood challenges the people who live there. It isn't easy for people from different cultures to live in such close proximity to each other. Every high-rise flat has the same layout, all blocks of flats suffer from graffiti, syringes, grime, dodgy people and night workers coming in and going out at all hours. It's hard for the tenants, many of whom have been born into spiralling poverty. This builds resentment of the wealthy and of some employers, but most of all they distrust authority. The loathing and distrust of police is passed down from generation to generation and many of these young people believe they have no choice in life. If they want to be someone, they often turn their hand to crime.

I was still at Collingwood in 1994. It was a Friday the thirteenth when my old colleague Steve Brown arrived at the police station. I greeted him as I normally did: 'Sniveller? What the fuck do you want?' Steve's nickname was a tribute to his constant moaning about being ill and his non-stop complaining about (his version of) having influenza. Sniveller greeted me with his usual, 'G'day, Arsehole!', his nickname for me.

He then announced that he was now, apparently, fatally allergic to eating cheese. This caused me to put on a look of concern and pretend to reach for the police hotline to call an ambulance, as I pointed out that he had gobbled up a hot pizza served with cheese while we were out drinking a few hours before. Sniveller quickly said, 'I'm allergic to cheese, except on pizza!'

Every time Steve and I had worked together we had found trouble — as in the house fire near Victoria Market. We were clearly not a good combination for a quiet shift. But our insistence that we were bad karma didn't penetrate our sergeant's head when he decided Steve and I should work together on Friday the thirteenth, despite our pleas. Steve then offered to take one of the trainees from the academy out with us as well. The recruit jumped at the chance of joining us rather than answering the telephones at the station and he was ready to go on patrol in a couple of minutes.

Once we were in the car, Steve warned the recruit of our pending trouble, explaining in graphic detail that every time he and I worked together the shift would somehow instantaneously turn to shit. He reeled off the scandals one by one, the car chases, fires, fights and shootings we had been in. The young recruit just laughed it off (obviously not a believer in karma). Steve hadn't quite finished his repertoire of grim stories when we heard these words over the police radio: 'Any unit clear in Wellington Street Collingwood for a man gone berserk? Two women down, one possibly deceased. Any unit clear?' I looked at Steve; we shook our heads in disbelief and swore at each other.

Steve took the job and I drove 500 metres to Wellington Street. En route Steve gave the recruit a well thought out lesson in the finer points of critical incident policing: 'Do what you are fucking told!' The recruit nodded nervously.

I skidded the car sideways into Hoddle Street and saw a number of pedestrians pointing up the road. Then we saw a woman, severely beaten and crushed under a car. An ambulance was already on the way and Steve turned to our recruit and yelled, 'Get out!' The recruit jumped from the car and ran over to help the woman and begin first aid. Steve and I continued up the road in the police car as a crowd of pedestrians were screaming, 'He's up here, quickly, quickly!' and pointing. I pulled up outside a petrol station where the crowd had gathered and Steve and I got out.

We headed towards the automatic doors doing the usual macho cop walk, the one that announces that the police are here to save the day. Our strut didn't last long. The doors opened and out hurtled a madman covered in blood, speaking in tongues and running straight at us.

I was normally one to talk things down and avoid violence, but this time the crook just came out swinging and I didn't even get a chance to begin. Steve and I avoided most of his punches and scratching before we instinctively returned fire with a barrage of well-placed fists. The fight continued. The buttons popped from our police shirts, which soon became smeared with blood. Our bare chests were exposed by the time I hit the crook very hard between the eyes and his head rocked backwards. A fine spray of blood flew into the air and over my fist and arm; the crook jerked backwards, lost balance and headed for the concrete. A sickening 'crack' temporarily stopped the commotion around us, but incredibly, a couple of seconds later the crook was fired up again.

Steve and I tried to pin him to the ground but he tried putting his bloody fingers into our mouths and began snorting and spitting blood. A bystander snatched the keys from my pocket and opened the police car. He grabbed a heavy metal torch and handed it to me. 'Hit him with this!' he urged. I couldn't use it; one blow with that would have killed him. The wrestle continued until our assailant tired, only a shade faster than we did. He was completely overpowered and Steve got him cuffed. A divisional van arrived at the scene and I pushed the crook in the back. Steve and I took a bit of time to compose ourselves while the television cameras and reporters began arriving at the scene.

Steve and I thought it was all over, but we didn't know what was to follow. On our way back to the station we were radioed with an urgent message — the crook was dead. We were told that we had bashed him to death and he was being transported to the emergency department at St Vincent's hospital while the ambulance officers tried to revive him. His victims were already there and they too were hanging onto life by a thread.

To say that we had mixed emotions at this stage was an understatement. I slowed the car down and we drove slowly back to the office. The TV cameras were still a short distance away, blissfully ignorant of the fact that the offender was now being transported to emergency clinically dead. We all knew that one sniff of a headline like 'Cops bash suspect to death' would have television reporters crawling all over us. Our timing wasn't the greatest, either. We knew we had acted in self-defence, but police behaviour, especially towards members of the public, was under scrutiny: we'd be crucified if there was even a hint that we had beaten someone to death.

Luckily for us, the hospital brought the crook back to life. The women also survived, thanks to the quick work of our new police recruit. He was commended for his work, which I have no doubt included a notation about his strict adherence to Steve's critical incident briefing in the car. He had a war story to take back to the academy like none before him.

Later that night we saw news footage on the main channels. The service station attendant vividly described the fight blow by blow and told everyone how tough it all was. This was the third time in three years that Steve and I had hit Australia's national news bulletins, an interesting fact, especially considering Steve and I had only worked with each other five times. (A shooting and a car chase were the incidents that didn't make the news.)

While Steve managed to find some peace for the rest of his career, I didn't. For me, these national news bulletins were just the beginning.

On Thursday, 1 September 1994, I was working nightshift with my sergeant, Blake Hartwell. We were both in uniform, rostered on the divisional van together. I always enjoyed working with Blake, who was widely regarded as a very good operator. In police terms this meant someone who coped well in difficult situations and had the runs on the board as far as catching crims went. Blake had worked with the National Crime Authority and, like me, he had locked up one of the top ten most wanted criminals.

The weather plays havoc in policing; the hotter it is the more drunks, fights and domestic arguments there are. But this night was cool and we expected a quiet shift as we drove out of the station. I was looking forward to more of Blake's war stories from his detective days. I couldn't get enough of them. Despite racking up many big arrests myself, I was still considered a rat and disloyal and so still couldn't get into the CIB, so I loved hearing Blake talk about it. Blake trained me in such things as the use of surveillance and undercover operations. I lived on his every word. I craved Blake's knowledge and I loved suggesting lateral ideas to catch crooks. If I was ever accepted as a detective I wanted to be the best I could be.

As the night wore on and the exciting stories and my questions wore off, we found ourselves cruising slowly along Victoria Street in Richmond. This was the closest thing to Vietnam that Melbourne had. Small shops lined the street. Out front were tables and racks covered with unusual vegetables. The street was very crowded during the day, buzzing with Asian people darting in and out of the shops. But this was very late at night and the only thing that provided evidence of the day's activities was the litter drifting around in the summer wind. Deliveries were stacking up at the front doors. Blake and I were almost falling asleep. At 3.08am, this thriving street was dead.

Blake raised his weary head and told me to pull the next car over; we were both about to nod off. 'No worries, I'm feeling a bit tired too,' I mumbled. We knew that the best cure for tiredness was to get some fresh air, and we were overdue to talk to someone else anyway.

A lone car pulled out and past us — it was like any other car. Blake pointed at it. 'That'll do.' I accelerated and turned on the blue flashing lights. This routine happened time and time again, shift after shift, day after day, but this was different. The car didn't stop. This sometimes happens when people don't look in their rear-vision mirror. But in this case, not only was this car not pulling over, but it had also sped up.

Blake and I were now awake and the siren went on. 'Collingwood 300 in pursuit,' Blake shouted over the radio to D24. Our screaming siren didn't slow the car down either. Blake and I watched as it crashed through a red light and almost bottomed out through the uneven intersection. The driver hadn't even touched the brakes through a red light. 'Shit! Hold on, Blake,' I said. I held onto the steering wheel of the divisional van as it launched over the intersection. The lights had turned to green, which kept us close to the fleeing car.

Then the car took a sharp right hand turn at considerable speed. We watched as the passenger side hubcaps peeled off the car as it turned. At the same time the unflappable Blake was screaming something about 'speed' and 'divisional van braking systems not being built for …' something. I couldn't quite hear him properly.

We were halfway around the same corner when the divisional van started skidding sideways at about 75 km/h. I still couldn't quite hear what Blake was yelling at me. Nevertheless, sliding sideways and watching helplessly out the front windscreen at the passing footpath, I realised that these divisional vans weren't made for this sort of stuff and so I aborted the chase — or, more to the point, the divvy van aborted it for us.

As our van screeched to a halt I saw the crims had crashed a few metres from the corner. Blake and I unbuckled ourselves and I ran towards the crashed car as Blake pumped out directions and a situation report to D24 on the radio. As I ran towards him, I saw the driver get out; he just stood at the driver's door and looked at me menacingly. He was cornered. His skinhead passenger on the other side began sprinting down the side street into the darkness. The driver squatted next to his car. I figured he wasn't running so I left him where he was and focused on the fleeing skinhead. As I made up ground I saw a black pistol-like object in the skinhead's hands. About 50 metres down the street I was one pace behind him and jumped on his back, driving him head first into the bitumen with every bit of my 100 kilograms. It was a heavy rugby-style tackle that was all shoulder-driven into the kidneys.

That was when I got a better look at the weapon that had been in his right hand. The tackle had dislodged the gun as we had hit the ground, and it was skidding down the road. I pulled out my cuffs and cranked them on tightly; this big bastard wasn't going anywhere. After a few moments I flipped him onto his back and that was when I realised that this gun-carrying skinhead was female.

Blake was running towards me from the police car. I asked him if he saw the other one. Blake said, 'What other one?' He hadn't seen the driver who had squatted next to the crashed car; he assumed there was only one offender, so he ran to back me up.

I picked up the weapon off the road and I took a look at it. It was an American Taser gun. These weapons don't shoot bullets; they shoot a few thousand volts. They immediately disable people by electric shock. Most people recover from being shot with a Taser, but there have been deadly consequences for people with weak hearts.

I ran back to the crashed car as Blake radioed for further assistance. That was when I saw it. A pistol lay on the front seat where my skinheaded crook had been. A sawn-off .303 rifle was standing beside the driver's door, loaded, cocked and ready to fire. The rifle must have been in his hand as he stared at me menacingly.

Blake coordinated the manhunt via the police radio; his experience in this type of situation had the driver scooped up by a roving patrol within minutes. The arresting patrol was from a nearby police station. The Richmond area was not unfamiliar with violence and armed offenders; it was much the same as Collingwood. They arrested the driver at gunpoint.

Once both crims were in custody the CIB swooped in and took charge of the case. The crashed car had been stolen after the owner had been ambushed by a man and a woman brandishing a gun. But that was just the start. The crooks were also wanted for a robbery at a Blackburn beauty salon where the shopkeeper had been held at gunpoint and handcuffed.

I strolled around the perimeter of the scene with a fresh roll of chequered crime scene tape; I'd done it many times before. The adrenaline drained from my body and I began noticing my knees and elbows were stinging from cuts and abrasions after the rugby tackle. It was 3.30am and cold, but I was still sweating. I turned away and lit a cigarette and waited for the detectives to come in. We had done our job.

As I smoked I saw a few police cars with young rookies driving slowly past. They were like me when I first started, major crime drawing them in, just for a look. This arrest was big news: anything to do with car chases and crooks caught with guns always is. It was all part of the inspiration of being a young cop — I had been no different when I joined. But the thrill and excitement were wearing thin; I'd had far more than my fair share of it.

I stood there for a minute and looked over at the stolen car, smashed up, leaking oil and green fluid. I looked over to where the crook had stood at the open driver's door; the gun was still resting there, ready to fire. Blake and I had been lucky. A muffled alarm wailed in the background: a hubcap had smashed a shop window and set it off.

We had originally pulled the car over in the first place because we were getting drowsy. Ironically, when I got to bed twelve hours later I couldn't sleep.

8

The courage of a coward

I always seemed to know how to talk to crooks and to violent men and women; I rarely had to use my fists. Nevertheless, I had seen and taken part in plenty of fights over the years — most of them playing country football for Port Campbell or in the police, fire brigade and navy football competitions. Years ago, when there was a fight in a pub or a club, people rarely king hit someone who was not expecting it, so most fights began with a verbal altercation and progressed from there. The coward's punch is still not common, but dirty fighting has crept into our way of life and street culture. I wonder if this is due to the influx of kickboxing and the anything goes style of fighting so popular on pay TV or pub television? The criminal code of conduct and culture has changed over the years. People were rarely shot in front of children or in open and public places — now it happens quite often.

My life took a turn for the worse while I was stationed at Collingwood. In 1994 I arranged to meet two girls and three of my work colleagues at a nightclub bar in Carlton after work. The bar was chosen by one of the lads. I had never been there before and I was somewhat concerned when I was told it was called the Hellfire Club. I told my colleagues I didn't know what the girls, whom I didn't know very well and who were from the country, would think about the name. The lads just laughed. 'Do you want a drink or not?'

When I arrived at the Hellfire Club I immediately saw the women at the bar. I am not normally great with small talk until I get to know someone, but I thought they were quite nice and, like me, not really suited to the Hellfire Club, but we stayed there because no other pubs were open. I offered to buy the first round of drinks.

It was a really strange place — somewhat of an underground club, plenty of strangers in the night and people you wouldn't want to take home to meet mamma.

Once I had purchased the drinks I glanced around briefly to see if I could find my workmates, who should have already arrived. I couldn't see the lads, which meant I had to continue struggling to make small talk until they arrived to save me.

I was about to take the first sip of my Crown lager and continue chatting when . . . *bang!* My head rocked back from the force of a vicious hit to my mouth and chin. I couldn't see anything, my vision left me completely and I felt my teeth puncture my bottom lip. My mouth filled with blood as I slumped to the floor. In a state of shock, I put my head up and looked around trying to get my bearings. I thought I had had a stroke or a heart attack, but quickly realised that I had been king hit by a coward, a strong fighter judging by the force of the hit, but a weak-gutted coward nonetheless.

The two women were screaming in horror. I covered my face with my hands, sensing from the commotion around me that my attacker was still around. He was. And because I wasn't finished off he started laying in the boots. I kept my hands over my face and tucked my elbows into my chest as my attacker kicked me in the ribs and stomach. It was damaging and painful but I knew I was better off covering my face than the rest of my body. I stayed as still as I could, I was confused and concussed. The concussion and sharp pains in my chest and stomach continued but the beating had stopped. My life was flashing before me — my family, friends and schoolmates flicked through. *He is assessing the damage.* I was right.

Don't be a weak bastard, you have what it takes, a whistleblower has what it takes. Get up. I knew I couldn't fight, not after being king hit. My vision was blurred but I was determined to stand up and show this guy I had the mettle. I also wanted to see who my attacker was. I made my way up to one knee and then to my feet, blood trickling out of my mouth. I got my bearings and looked towards the exit, and then I saw his back as he forced his way out of the club towards the street. I didn't know who he was until he made one big mistake. He looked back. I knew him, not by name, but definitely by sight: he was a cop. He was standing in the dark behind the front entrance of the club as I'd walked in. I'd been ambushed. He looked at me as I stood up, wobbly but defiant. Then he came back at me, no doubt angry that I'd seen him but wanting me to stay down.

I knew his return wasn't a good sign. As I waited for another punching spree to begin, I promised myself to remember his face. And I knew why I was being bashed: I was a whistleblower and I was being taught a brutal lesson from a brutal police force.

He hit me in the mouth again and I hit the floor once more. Not one bystander moved. I think he kicked me some more, but I was really concussed by then. Again my pride surged through me, pushing me to stand up and show my attacker he couldn't break me. I got up again but this time I lost balance, my legs collapsed and I fell, head first, to the floor.

My attacker fled. The clubbers jumped aside as he ran out of the club as my colleagues had arrived on the scene. They'd seen the last blows of the coward bashing someone, realised it was me and took off in pursuit. The lads caught him down a side street and arrested him. He was handed to the local patrol car. I was helped from the floor and taken to nearby St Vincent's hospital where I was put under observation.

I suffered severe concussion and took a week off. The shock had left me with diarrhoea and I didn't eat for days. I lost weight and spent most of my time pondering. I wasn't interrupted by visits or telephone calls from Internal Affairs, the police hierarchy or the Police Association, though. My mates from Collingwood station were good — bloody great police station, that one, from the top down.

I started to think about resigning, but every time I talked about this with people outside the police they always made the same statement: 'You can't quit, that'll mean they [the corrupt cops] win.'

These people spoke about my predicament as if it were some sort of game. I guess everyone's the same; we're all great at suggesting the hard road for someone else to take. I knew very well it wasn't a game, and I knew how much courage it took to go back to work after my flogging, but I did it; I went back.

I stayed with the Victoria Police, not because I wanted that elusive win everyone talked about, but because I had to break some new ground for people in my situation in the future. I did believe I would be OK in the end.

That was a big mistake, thinking my fight against corruption had a finish line. I naively believed that one day good would defeat evil. I never expected so many people would choose to be indifferent to corruption, turn a blind eye or passively agree with it; in essence choosing neither good nor evil. I soon realised there's no finish line in life.

When I went back to work, I was put straight into working the Collingwood divisional van at my request. Soon afterwards my partner and I received a radio message to check a suspicious male driving north along Wellington Street. This type of job was common in the Collingwood area and often amounted to nothing but an empty street.

But we found him. He was a clean-cut young man wearing casual clothes. Seated in the driver's side of a dirty green Ford Fairlane with a briefcase next to him, he was stopped in a service station. When he saw us drive the divisional van up behind him, he got out and came to greet us. I sensed something was wrong. He was very nervous, his eyes had pinhole-sized pupils and he was sweating profusely. I immediately suspected he was a druggie and demanded as a matter of routine that he empty his pockets. He didn't. Instead he flashed his police badge, mumbling from the side of his mouth, 'I'm in the job.'

This druggie was an officer with the Federal Police. I looked to the sky, swallowed and wondered: *What do I do now? Let him go? Just drive away?* But I had made up my mind what I would do about bent cops a long time before, and repeated three of the most repugnant words one cop could say to another: 'Empty your pockets.' Those three words said many things, possibly the harshest being, 'I think you're a crook.' I didn't want to find anything, but I had to do my job. Sure enough, he had a few illegal drugs on him in tablet form.

We took our Federal Police colleague back to the police station and began an interview, then raided his residence in the northern suburbs.

The first thing we saw when we walked in was a cannabis plant. I was now a highly experienced street cop, and the occupant's lack of criminal discipline in hiding this incriminating plant indicated that any other contraband might not be hidden either. It wasn't long before we found large bags of white powder, more drugs than I had ever seen in my life.

Although this bloke was a Fed, our big find made the taste in our mouths — the one you get when you lock up a colleague for a serious criminal offence — a little more palatable. No one liked the bitterness of dragging a fellow cop through the court process and finishing his career for nothing but a couple of 'eckies' and a mull plant, but I had no problem taking this bloke out of the system. He was a crook. I guess when you're a drug dealer and a cop, one tends to take some things for granted. He obviously hadn't expected a police raid.

I enjoyed Collingwood and continued to work hard, racking up more commendations and awards than anyone of my age and experience I knew. I received a bravery award from the governor of Victoria, a chief commissioners' commendation for outstanding professionalism and a further two commendations for persistence, judgment and restraint.

My boss at Collingwood rewarded a few of us for our hard work by selecting us for counterfeit duties at Melbourne's Grand Prix Formula 1 race meeting. This entailed checking the stall and street sellers for counterfeit goods being sold without licence or against trademarks, not particularly stimulating work, but enjoyable because of the hype of the race.

Early on the first day of the race we spoke to a thirty-something nobody who was apparently selling unauthorised caps or T-shirts (I can't remember which). Ron was pleasant, seemed harmless enough and was cooperative. We parted on good terms and, although I had joked with him, he expected to get a bluey (summons) in the mail for his alleged misdemeanour which, I have to say, never overly impresses anyone. Ron took it in his stride.

The next time I saw Ron was on national television on 28 June 1997. He was standing on Bondi beach with police around him, reportedly threatening them with a knife. Ron was mentally disturbed at the time and, tragically, the police shot him dead. The two police officers involved were later found to be cocaine users. In March 1998 the New South Wales state coroner concluded the inquest into Ron Levi's death with the finding that the two police officers had a case to answer. The New South Wales Director of Public Prosecutions declined to proceed. It's a mad world.

Despite my commendations and awards, five years of detective applications had passed and I hadn't been granted a job interview as a detective. This was the brotherhood striking back, silently, in a cold war. No matter how hard I worked I knew that I was never going to get a position without appealing to the Police Appeals Tribunal. So I did.

I'd applied for an inner suburban CIB job and didn't even get an interview, but after a day in the Tribunal the chairman reversed the decision of the police convenor and gave me the detective's position. The candidate who had been selected over me did deserve to get a detective's job, he was a good operator, but I'd hung on for a long time, writing resumé after resumé and, unfortunately for him, I'd randomly picked that job as the one I decided to fight for. It was a big turnaround considering I'd been marked 'unsuitable' and wasn't even granted an interview.

In the beginning everyone was cautious of me at my new CIB, and no doubt the jungle drums had been beating long before I arrived. I was cautious of them too, fearing I was in for some special attention, particularly when I noticed that my name on the whiteboard had been circled in red. Thankfully, it was just paranoia. Morale in the office turned out to be great. The unit was working so well we rarely had a moment where we weren't locking up crooks for some of Melbourne's major crimes or having a laugh, or both.

One of our biggest jobs was arresting seven armed robbers who had been firing shots and doing home invasions and drug rip-offs. The office teamwork also resulted in some other notable cases being solved, including large frauds, arsons and rapes. But sometimes it's not the major crimes that bring out the characters.

One character was an old-school break-and-enter crook who I'll call Lucky Phil. He was an active burglar who chose the rosiest spots around our area to swipe expensive goodies and any loot he could lay his grubby little hands on. His *modus operandi* was known to me well before his name. He often burgled heavily alarmed houses while people were home, and often at night. He had an eye for the finer things in life (owned by others) and he knew what was valuable and where to sell it. Lucky Phil was causing us a few headaches; every detective who was responsible for overnight crime spent most of the following morning tracking Lucky Phil's night time shift. His identity was discovered when I received a phone call from a man who found his classic marble statute in a city secondhand shop. Lucky Phil had kindly left his name with the shopkeeper.

I charged him with a number of similar burglaries, deciding to give him bail rather than making him ask for it in court. But before we let him go I had an idea. In the office I had a silver ball on a stand, an adult novelty toy designed to help a person make decisions. Once the ball was pressed, a robotic voice would give one of eight random answers, including, 'Good one, dickhead!' and, 'No way, you loser!' We found that the odds were heavily stacked towards a negative response. Considering the scales of justice often went against us, we thought that it might be interesting if we used it now.

I asked Lucky Phil if he would ask the ball to confirm my decision to give him bail rather than risk going to court. Being a gambling man he said he would be delighted; he hated judges and they hated him. But now we witnessed the greatest run of luck I have ever seen. When Lucky Phil rubbed the top of the silver ball and asked, 'Can I have bail?', the reply was, 'Of course, arsehole!' We didn't need to tell Phil twice; he was off. We were pretty sure he would be back: some people just cannot help themselves. Lucky Phil's driving record ensured that he needed to be arrested and bailed every time he was caught in his car. Every time the bail issue came up, Lucky Phil insisted on taking his chances with the ball. It never let him down. He began to rack up arrests for minor offences, and his luck continued. We couldn't believe it.

But one day Phil came under the watchful eye of one of the lads while driving disqualified for the second time in less than twenty-four hours. It must have been his twentieth disqualified driving charge. The lads broke the bad news: Phil was going to court and this time there would be no bail. He agreed, but insisted on pressing the ball for luck anyway. We agreed and spent the next twenty minutes rigging the ball to provide a negative response before putting it in front of Phil in his interview room.

I smirked as I put the ball in front of Lucky Phil. He gave me a long look, and patted the ball. 'Will I get bail?' he asked defiantly.

'Sounds good, idiot!'

Lucky Phil smiled widely. He was taken to the local court in front of the magistrate affectionately known by lawyers as the Whispering Assassin. Phil represented himself and, not knowing the magistrate, he thought his whispering voice meant he was soft, maybe a bit of a nancy boy. So, thinking he had a soft judge, and still feeling lucky, he took the opportunity of cleaning the slate, and pleaded guilty to all his offences, expecting a suspended sentence.

The magistrate summed up the charges in a barely audible voice and finished by sending Phil to jail for six months. Unlucky bastard.

During my time in the CIB, I met and married Tracy. She was a very pretty girl with a quick wit, one of the best corporate personal assistants in Melbourne.

We were engaged on 8 November 1998 and married at Scotch College chapel twelve months later. Tracy and I sold my cottage in Collingwood, which I had almost finished renovating, and bought a large double-fronted Victorian house nearby. We transformed it into a masterpiece with colourful gardens and a beautiful interior that blended old with new.

One of our new neighbours was extremely popular with people of all ages and at all hours of the day and night. His friends were always very busy and could only stay a minute or two. Our neighbour was very generous to his busy friends, often giving them a bag of green vegetable matter to take away with them. Unfortunately, this was not the kind of vegetable matter you cover with nanna's salad dressing, so it didn't surprise me when he got a visit from some of my very busy work colleagues early one morning. A few weeks later I noticed some beautiful red and mauve poppies growing in our back garden. I liked the look of them so much that I collected the seed from the pods once they finished flowering and dried them out to grow some more next season.

The stress of the police force began to take its toll. Almost daily I was intimidated or stared at by groups of detectives who knew someone I'd locked up for corruption or who just hated 'that cunt' because it was the cool brotherhood thing to do. I say 'groups' because rarely, if ever, did they find the courage to try and intimidate me on their own.

Nevertheless it began to wear down my tough facade and I took the stress home.

I began drinking regularly, working excessively hard on the house and isolating myself from Tracy. It was not unusual for me to renovate the house from 6am and not finish until well into the evening, when I would set about drinking enough to sleep. Doing the physical work of renovating stopped me thinking about the week's subtle abuse by workmates. When I wasn't working on the house or at work, I would be at the pub. My local had the best and coldest beer in Australia and the tastiest and cheapest pub meals. It was a pub that many people called home. I was often greeted with a laugh and a wisecrack as soon as I walked inside the door, and I loved the friendly atmosphere, joking with the other punters while shooting pool or throwing darts.

It was at that pub that I met a few of the local lads from good old Collingwood town. Knockabout tough men, battlers who lived hard and played hard, most worked for a living yet lived on the poverty line. They had seen their share of dodgy police in their time, but, thankfully, because I was straight, they accepted me as a mate despite my being a copper.

I stayed in the CIB for a few years before I decided to try for the Homicide Squad. I figured that I would be partially vindicated if I were to be part of that elite squad. Only 2 per cent ever make it into the Homicide Squad, so when I applied I was thrilled just to get an interview.

The convenor of the interview was a legendary detective senior sergeant. He was an honest, strong and well-respected homicide detective and leader. Like me, he had had a past battle with some alleged corruption, and had quit the force because of it but had been persuaded to return. He was, and still is, the most experienced and dogged homicide detective I know. His main problem is that he takes on too much work, a flaw he readily admits to. He has his enemies, like every decent courageous person does.

I had a reference from a seasoned detective senior sergeant that described me as 'the most successful, most active and most diligent detective currently at this office, in fact he is equal to any detective I've had working under my supervision'. With a referee like that and a fair convenor of the selection process, I became a homicide investigator on my first try.

9

Homicide Squad

In December 1997 I started at the Squad. I was putting my belongings into my desk two hours after walking in the door when my new detective senior sergeant walked over. 'Welcome to the Hommies, mate,' he said. 'Oh, and by the way, you'd better get down to the morgue. The car accident hit-and-run at Brighton on the weekend had a bullet in his head.' I had just broken the squad record for getting my first murder investigation.

It was going to be a hard case; tracking a murderer's car down is always an unforgiving slog that involves plenty of red herrings. My colleague, another young detective who had done his apprenticeship under the legendary senior sergeant, showed me the ropes and we set about catching my first killer.

It was a bizarre crime. The victim had been out to a party, became uncharacteristically drunk and began wandering along Station Road in Brighton, causing a bit of strife with passing motorists. A southern suburb of Melbourne, Brighton is a sleepy area with a few commercial enterprises scattered among the houses. Its quiet nature was probably why this particular case received so much media attention.

The victim reached a major intersection and was canvassing cars for a hitch. As the light changed to green, he selected his would-be murderers' car at random from the line waiting to turn. He innocently asked for a ride back to the party he had come from, but not only did the driver fail to grant his request, when the victim grabbed the roof of the car he also sped off with the victim holding on for his life. It was the last time anyone saw this bright young man alive.

I was able to decipher from the traffic collision experts that the victim fell from a vehicle travelling at high speed down a street. That part seemed obvious, but identifying the perpetrator was not. I surmised that the victim was holding onto the roof of the car with both hands, which would have rendered him completely harmless. Meanwhile, the passenger in the car slowly raised himself out of his seat, pulled out his trusty .32 Browning pistol and fired one shot out of the sunroof before calmly firing the weapon at point-blank range into the victim's head. This caused the victim's instantaneous death and made him slide from the moving car onto the road.

Owing to the victim's injuries and the lack of eyewitnesses to the shooting, the death was treated as a hit-and-run. The case became mine when the pathologists at the Coroner's Court found a bullet in the victim's head during the autopsy. The newspaper article headlines were 'Dragged to Death' and 'Find my son's killer'. A devastated family and friends put themselves in front of the media to plead for witnesses to come forward. These tragedies never involve just one person — scores of people are scarred by these types of events.

I used the intense media coverage to flush out multiple witnesses. A number of people came forward, all of whom had viewed the same event from many different angles; they all described how the victim was holding onto the roof of the car as if rollerblading beside it, but most struggled to provide an accurate description of the murderer's car. We were left with many varied accounts, a jumble of different makes, models and colours — no two witnesses' accounts were the same.

This search needed to be based on gut feeling so I knew I had to pick the description given by the most convincing witness. This was hard. Everybody had desperately tried to remember the make and model of the car and provided a description; no one said they couldn't remember. Every one of them wanted to help bring the killer to justice, but all eyes had been instinctively drawn to the victim holding on for grim death.

For the most convincing witness, I chose an Irishman, who had been sitting at the traffic lights, because he said: 'Simon, don't worry about what all the other witnesses are saying, forget it, and just listen to me. I am 100 per cent sure it is a champagne-coloured GD model Mazda MX6. My mate used to have one.'

Was that insignificant point enough for him to divert his attention from the horror that was unfolding before him and correctly identify the car? I had to trust his judgment, so I began the long search of champagne-coloured Mazda MX6s. There were hundreds of them and I knew I was back to instinct should I come across the murderer. I was looking for a needle in a haystack, although in the back of my mind was the possibility I might be looking in the wrong haystack.

With the assistance of the Victims Unit I built a good relationship with the victim's family and friends. We caught up with a regular phone call or a coffee and I provided them with an update; they were good people — all of them. I found it hard to say to them that I mightn't be able to solve their son's murder case for them, but I knew it was a very realistic outcome.

Then, a young Turkish man appeared in two of the investigative traps I set up. We had a suspect. My new colleague, Mick, and I laughed anxiously when our hard-working and underpaid analyst announced that this man, Mehmet Ince, was not only the proud owner of a champagne-coloured Mazda MX6, but was also known to carry weapons.

Mick and I sat among a mountain of paperwork that identified every Mazda MX 6 in the state. If our hunch was wrong we were in for an awful lot of work. Mick and I carefully planned every move we made, and no one was contacted until we assessed the risks involved. When you're tracking a killer you must tread very softly; a misplaced telephone call to the wrong person could alert your suspect. Melbourne has a reasonably large Turkish population, but we figured it was small enough for most Turkish immigrants to know each other. We needed to work slowly, gathering piece by piece of evidence.

Ince had every reason to be cocky — he knew more than anyone that it was a random act, the end result so ghastly it was thought to be a hit-and-run car accident. He had the right to think he could walk among us all keeping his secret.

A week later we had positively identified Ince as our killer: he carried a gun, owned a car like our Irishman's mate and had connections to the area. Mick and I are good lateral thinkers and we thought up some wily evidence-gathering techniques (none of which I intend to explain in this book). By the end of the week we also had another witness. This one had a close-up view of the bastard doing the job — he had been driving the car. Loyalty runs thin for criminals who kill for the sake of killing.

Mick and I successfully arrested and convicted Ince for murder. It is one of the very few murders in this country that was solved solely through eyewitness descriptions of a murderer's motor car, with no other identifying clues.

Before long, we were once more required — as an old homicide detective put it — to turn chicken shit into chicken salad. This time it was a soul-destroying crime for everyone in the police brotherhood. Two of our own officers were killed in the line of duty. One lay dead on a roadside with his weapon still holstered. Sickened by these murders, I agreed to join the investigation team.

As soon as I did, my Turkish murder investigation came back into the limelight. Mehmet Ince's forty-five-year-old mother, Nurdane Enges, decided she wanted to get involved in the internal workings of her son's case. She attempted to convince my star witness to alter his account of the murder. I accommodated Engez's wish for involvement in the matter. I arrested, interviewed and charged her with perverting the course of justice in September 1998. She was later convicted in the Supreme Court. But this was extra work I didn't need at a time when I was trying to help unmask two cop killers.

Perhaps the smartest Melbourne crook during the 1980s and 1990s was the most evil of them all. His name was Bandali Debs. Most of the time he flew well under the radar while his well-known criminal competitors took the limelight by robbing high-profile businesses, such as banks and building societies, taking potshots at innocent people and police officers who were arresting them. These crims, most of whom wound up dead or in jail, almost had celebrity status in Victoria. Of course, once they got out of prison many were quick to tool up again with a gun and balaclava and charge into another bank for a quick cash withdrawal.

Debs moved through this era relatively unscathed. His success as a crook was best displayed by his lack of arrests, testament to his keenness to avoid capture at all costs and to his good fortune. Arrogant, pig-headed and violent, like most other armed robbers, Debs was not your average crim. He was much harder to catch. He looked after his kids, his parents and his wife, and lived a very normal, middle-income existence in one of Melbourne's newest satellite suburbs.

Ego, excitement and an insatiable appetite for fast money makes many criminals target banks and armoured vans instead of the softer targets, which are easier but almost as lucrative. Debs was a soft target man. The only reason I expect he even made it onto the Armed Robbery Squad radar was because of his penchant for unnecessary and brutal violence toward defenceless and terrified soft robbery victims. This type of violence doesn't rest well with detectives, even in Victoria.

A string of violent armed robberies had culminated in the murders of those two policemen on 16 August 1998. On that fateful night scores of plainclothes police were on stakeout duties in and around the quiet bayside suburb of Moorabbin. Senior Constable Rod Miller and Sergeant Gary Silk were sitting in an unmarked car, doing surveillance on the Silky Emperor restaurant on the offchance the armed robbers would strike again. They weren't alone. In fact, there were a number of police in similar cars, in similar carparks, waiting patiently around similar Chinese restaurants until they closed that night. Most cops get used to the mind-numbing boredom of static surveillance. It's a skill to sit quietly, often cramped up and in darkness, while assessing the activity of those around you.

The decision to intercept or arrest someone is made in a split second. Miller and Silk were both seasoned officers. They drove out from the darkness in the carpark and routinely intercepted a motor car that pulled into the kerb about 50 metres from the restaurant. During the day this road was a hive of busy mechanics and commercial people, but at that hour of night it was ghostly quiet.

The occupants of the vehicle opened fire on the policemen. Senior Constable Miller courageously returned fire before running to the main road to seek assistance for his soon-to-be fatal injuries. The fact that Miller shot back at these vicious killers in self-defence and defence of his sergeant caused a chain reaction that allowed me and a handful of other detectives to identify the killer's vehicle, even though both policemen had been killed. The exchange of gunfire from Miller probably led to Debs and his accomplice Jason Roberts panicking; such people are rarely courageous.

Bandali Debs began spraying bullets from his .357 revolver as the brave policeman managed to shoot back, despite being fatally wounded. During this exchange Debs fired at least one bullet into his own car and the hatchback window broke. As the two killers made good their escape, some of the glass dropped out and spilled onto the roadway. With one police officer lying dead and the other mortally wounded, the police arriving at the scene were far more concerned with fleeing murderers and urgent medical assistance than anything else. As the gun smoke cleared the ambos came and went with our dying mate: it didn't look good.

In the hour that followed, Rod Miller also died, leaving the culprits, Jason Roberts and Bandali Debs, as the only people in the world who knew precisely what happened in Cochranes Road, Moorabbin, that night. The rest of us were left with thousands of unanswered questions, and so began the collection of evidence to answer them. These scenes are always the same; they crawl with police, all trying to help. No one wants to seal a crime scene off with chequered crime scene tape with a colleague inside because no one wants to admit to themselves that he has passed on. But professionalism and the strict adherence to the rules of crime investigation must prevail and the crime scene tape comes out, a shattering event.

Once the crooks had gone, and as the minutes turned to hours, a refined search began. Spent bullet casings, bullet projectiles, footprints, fingerprints and eyewitnesses took precedence over the insignificant sprinkling of glass cubes amongst the roadside gravel. The nondescript glass lay patiently waiting for collection. But surrounding the glass cubes was a ghastly scene. It was one of Victoria's saddest days.

I was drawn in to the investigation, known as Task Force Lorimer, as part of the car crew; it was our job to think of ways of tracking down the murderer's car. This became a difficult juggling act for me; not only was I working on this case, but I was also working on Supreme and

County Court trials. A murderer on remand, a number of armed robbers and a case-tamperer were already on my plate and I was up to my ears in paperwork, bail hearings, committal hearings and trials. These cases dragged on because of excessive court delays. Still, I rolled out and adapted the same ideas I had used to identify Mehmet Ince and his Mazda MX6. It was relatively simple to tailor the ideas to suit this specific crime scene, but this killer's car was Australia's most popular and this made the traps infinitely more difficult.

We had no idea who had committed the brutal slayings. Hundreds of suspects were nominated by caring members of the public, and the numbers multiplied after a composite Facefit was put in all the daily papers. I set up traps similar to those in my previous murder investigation, confident that I was on the right track. But the stakes were high. There were thousands of cars to filter through and this time even I was doubtful, some others even more so.

I decided to visit my old Criminal Investigation Branch, one of the few workplaces where I felt comfortable, so I stopped for a quick coffee with my old CIB boss, Tim. We talked quietly as I sipped from a foam cup of cheap coffee and dragged on one of Tim's horrible-tasting, high-tar cigarettes. Then my mobile phone rang. It was the Lorimer office. Someone had set off one of my traps and I was told I'd better take a look. I knew the trap had gone off near the house of a prime suspect, where the analytical experts estimated the crooks might live. I knew this was a significant event, but it was unfolding on the other side of town, and I need to get there. I was unarmed and needed backup.

'Tim, I need you to come out to the eastern suburbs for Lorimer,' I told him. 'Grab a gun — you're coming with me!' My coffee cup headed east, as Tim and I ran west towards the gun safe and the car. The cup slapped against the old jail door and coffee splashed and stained the concrete.

Tim snatched a handful of bullets and a gun from the safe and ran out behind me. I was revving the car out front, and, as we sped off, I plonked the portable blue light on the roof. The siren came on, but hidden sirens never work like the ones on marked police cars, and we were going too fast for it to warn anyone anyway.

A few minutes later we screamed through a roadwork area and were abused by the stop/slow road worker. Fresh gravel and tar had just been laid and stones flicked up everywhere. With his head down, Tim mumbled something about 'Fucking bullets' as he tried to feed five rounds into his revolver.

I stopped a few doors away from our destination, an auto wrecker. Tim handed me the gun, the only one we had. 'You take it,' he said. 'Your eyesight is better than mine.' Tim was the type of bloke who would make sure everyone had a weapon before he filled his own holster, but he also knew he was getting too old for gunfights. He gave me a dozen spare bullets he had managed to scrounge from his old brown jacket. Some of them looked like the bullets we had been issued fifteen years ago, which made me wonder how long Tim had owned that jacket. But I didn't care what the bullets looked like; I grabbed all the ammo I could get. We both knew if the shit hit the fan we were in trouble.

We approached the wrecking yard with caution; shells of smashed-up cars were stacked on large industrial racks. It was a graveyard of caved-in car wrecks. A shopfront to the yard opened onto the street and as we approached I opened the door as quietly as possible, my hand covering the loaded gun in my trouser pocket. My eyes scanned the shop for customers: nothing.

Then, one of the auto wreckers identified us and gave us a nod. 'They've gone,' he said. 'You just missed them, but we got the rego for ya.' I'd spoken to him before.

'Well done, mate,' I said. Cops become used to dead-ends and false alarms. I was pissed off that we had missed the bloke by a few seconds. After all, he was only a suspect because he tripped one of my stupid eccentric traps that I was working on, and now he was somebody else we had to track down. I was worried that my eccentric ideas were adding additional work to the taskforce rather than reducing it. I took down the car registration details: Debs, 22 Blacktown Drive East.

A young man had purchased a rear window for a Hyundai hatchback. So what? Many others had done the same thing. But I had a feeling about this one, perhaps because of the timing and proximity to the crime. Tim and I decided to follow up the car there and then.

Tim assured me he had nothing but a pile of paperwork to return to, so he was happy to stay on the trail.

We headed further east. A few minutes later we were cruising into Blacktown Drive East in our unmarked car. We spotted the vehicle seen at the wrecking yard coming towards us. 'That's it!' I said. Tim didn't respond. We kept our heads facing the front so as not to draw attention to ourselves, but as the car drove towards us it began to slow down. A woman was driving and a young man was in the passenger seat. Their car slowed to a crawl as we passed by each other. A young man with dark bushy eyebrows glared in our direction and sat up in his seat. This was the first time we had laid eyes on Jason Roberts.

'Did you see that?' Tim asked.

'He picked us in one. I'd better tell the taskforce what happened. Let's go,' I said.

I dropped Tim back at the CIB and drove to the taskforce, where things were buzzing as specific suspects were being chosen for extra attention. I explained what had happened. As I spoke I realised that a young dark-haired teenager who had bought a rear windscreen and glared at Tim and me didn't really rate a mention compared to some of the high-powered crooks being bandied around the office. He was just another one to add to the collection. I was churning inside. I wanted this car to take precedence over some of the other suspects and cars but it was very hard to explain why.

The people responsible for Victoria's most ghastly crime in a decade had shown us a clean set of heels. If finding the car in my first murder case had been like looking for a needle in a haystack, this one looked like a drop in the ocean. It couldn't have been worse. We were all well aware we could be walking into a cop killer's lair on any given day; most of us had perfected the poker face as we went from suspect to suspect, inspecting, quizzing, assessing and hoping.

After the strange drive-by Tim and I had witnessed I managed to persuade a colleague to leave his mountain of work and come with me to check out the Debs' car. It was difficult to justify any extra attention for this car because no one had reported any suspicions about it. Call it a gut feeling. We weren't looking for a car among hundreds; this time it was a Hyundai Excel, Australia's biggest-selling small car. Aussies had bought hundreds of thousands of them.

It was 27 August 1998, eleven days after our colleagues had been brutally murdered. My partner and I got into our unmarked car and headed east on what was a mild day. I walked up the concrete driveway in which was standing yet another one of Australia's most common cars. It was a standard brick house, in a normal suburb with normal everyday people. This was the Debs residence. When I stopped in the street I saw a clean-cut young man meticulously cleaning a dark blue Hyundai Excel's sports wheels with a small rag. He was cleaning it like a car fanatic would, with over-the-top thoroughness. I hadn't washed my car for three months (and, in fact, I'd never washed the Valiant) so the precision of his cleaning was something I took notice of. Perhaps if I'd cared more about my own cars it wouldn't have struck me as so extraordinary.

My partner and I walked to the top of the driveway and talked to the teenagers. As we spoke, Jason Roberts wiped off what he thought were the last traces of his filthy crime in front of us. Roberts remained cool, calm and collected; not too friendly, not too unfriendly. His girlfriend, Nicole Debs, who turned out to be the owner of the Excel, wasn't cool at all. I showed no surprise when she confidently reeled off a set of responses to my questions. But I knew that she had replaced her car windscreen, and that she was lying when she said she hadn't. But did one lie amount to suspicion? I smelt a rat with the Debs's blue Hyundai, registration OJI 862, and, if I was right, I hoped the rat hadn't smelt me.

After the initial meeting with Roberts, we drove away. My colleague and I talked about what had just happened, and we decided to go back. This worried me for a range of reasons, but I knew we couldn't afford to dabble with krill when we were hunting whale.

So we went back, this time without the poker faces. I played the bad cop. But again, when I engaged Nicole in conversation about the replacement windscreen in her car, she continued to lie, despite being told the game was up and that I knew she had replaced it. I didn't like this situation. We had shown our hand, yet she refused to show us hers. Why didn't she say how her rear window broke? It was no big deal; we would check out her alibi and move on to the next car. But she stuck with her lie.

Finally, she changed her story and admitted to replacing the screen. Apparently her father, who she said was a tiler, had broken it at work. This was hardly something worth covering up, I thought. Roberts stood beside my colleague and remained cool as I asked to have a look inside the house. I walked upstairs into the master bedroom and began searching in the usual places guns are hidden. Nicole's mother, Mrs Debs, stood downstairs, waiting.

I was alone when an adjoining bathroom door creaked open and lit the bedroom, temporarily blinding me. Was someone else up here? 'Hello?' No answer. A chill went up my spine. *I shouldn't have come up here alone*, I thought — after all, we were hunting cop killers. I should have been smarter than that. Suddenly, Mrs Debs walked in startling me for the second time in less than a minute. She stopped, pleasantly raised both eyebrows and looked at me. It was time to go, and we walked back downstairs.

My partner and I left, none the wiser. Roberts stood and watched us drive away. Nicole had given us directions for finding the head of the household, her father Bandali Debs, who was supposed to be tiling at a building site a few kilometres away. The directions led nowhere; he, too, would have to wait. When we got back to the office, where detectives and analysts were poring over reams of paperwork, I tried to write the report on the Debs's car. This was difficult: I had to accept the fact that gut feeling and lies aren't evidence.

A few days later I caught up with Bandali Debs at his worksite. With two other experienced detectives present, Debs pointed to where he said he broke the window of the Hyundai; I searched but there weren't any shattered glass cubes to collect from the ground. But, he said, he had broken it weeks ago. He was gruff and seemed forthright: nothing stood out that led me to believe he was a killer.

Meanwhile, the taskforce was flexing its muscles elsewhere. Well-known criminals were being arrested and interviewed for the killings, and each arrest required thorough investigation and planning. The newspapers followed every move.

The car trail began with the review of the Hyundai motor car manufacturing plant and motor registration records. That narrowed the field considerably but still left us with 25 755 vehicles. Further analysis reduced that number to approximately 19 000, then to 9000, and then to 2808 (by methods that are best not divulged, for obvious reasons).

The final stage was the physical checking of each individual car in Victoria, interstate and overseas, all 2808 of them. The operation was a logistical nightmare, with hundreds of detectives and cars drawn from all over the state to help with the search. Before they embarked on the intricate process of inspecting the cars allocated to them each detective had been shown an instructional video I'd made.

The media whipped themselves into a frenzy over the massive investigative process about to be launched. As a result I walked to the first (strategically positioned) Hyundai for checking. It was parked at the rear of the Crime Squad headquarters where I had my photo taken for the newspapers and television stations. It also meant the detectives checking the other cars could go about their business without interruption. My traps were being set off all over the place and thousands of cars still required checking, so I came up with another way of checking through the remainder of the vehicles very quickly. My idea was a lateral extension of an investigative method used during an English manhunt for a child rapist and murderer and was based on human DNA and the taking of voluntary blood samples. My idea involved cars, not people. My superiors liked the idea but thought it was too risky. It was frustrating to be a policeman with a lateral mind; most detectives I knew above sergeant rank were too conservative. Nevertheless, I am confident my version will soon be the new way of hunting cars, and one that will actually save the Force money.

Older, more experienced detectives prefer to have overwhelming amounts of evidence before committing themselves. This is because detectives often have the belittling experience of clever lawyers minimising or even erasing evidence. Sometimes a jury never even gets to hear it. Seasoned detectives prefer their evidence the way a five-year-old likes a birthday cake — with plenty of extras on top. They like to be confident they've got enough facts added to the brief of evidence so that it can withstand a few slashes and scrapes as it goes through the judicial process.

The Debs's car was annoying me. I couldn't see how to make investigating it seem more urgent. But nor did I want to cry wolf. It was one of many dodgy situations uncovered and it had to wait its turn.

I sticky taped a 5-cent coin to my desk, my token bet that it was the Debs's car. I knew the odds were against me and most of the other suspects had form like Phar Lap. But despite Bandali Debs's and Jason Roberts's apparent lack of form as criminals, I knew that no one else since Nicole had lied about getting a replacement screen. I suspected the car was involved in the murders. *Maybe they lent it to the killers*, I thought.

To my delight my 5-cent Debs file was taken up by one of the investigation crews. But as soon as the investigation started in earnest, an examination of the glass particles located at the scene saw the file temporarily put to bed. I was shattered, but accepted the forensic experts' opinion — it wasn't the Debs's car. My confidence in my ability to read human behaviour plummeted.

Having lost total confidence in my ideas and my ability to judge people, I found myself wandering aimlessly, checking yet another rusty Hyundai wreck in yet another graveyard for smashed cars. By this stage the caryard red dust had turned to mud and it was raining, my suit and shoes hadn't been cleaned for weeks — I didn't bother with it any more. I was still coming to terms with the fact that the Debs's car wasn't the one. Tension was high in the taskforce and we all had different ways of venting frustration. It was hard for us all, but we'd be in greater trouble if we stopped arguing over suspects.

A new bloke arrived at the taskforce; I'll call him Reg. He began reading the car files and asked me what I thought. 'I thought it was the Debs car but the lab reckons the glass didn't match. I'm fucked if I know now,' I said.

Reg's fresh set of eyes looked over the file. 'How many pieces of glass did they check from the crime scene sample?' Reg asked.

'I don't know,' I said. Moments later, Reg was on the phone. I heard him say, 'Check all the glass — you never know.'

I always showed interest in the technical side of the investigative process but there was nothing technical in my response when Reg told me the Debs car was alive again: 'You fuckin' beauty!'

The investigation was far from over when I left the taskforce, an exhausted wreck. I had achieved what I had set out to do — find the car I believed was responsible. I'm proud that one of my lateral ideas identified Jason Roberts and Bandali Debs as persons worthy of suspicion. But I take no credit for identifying them as the killers or building the evidence against them; this was done by a handful of detectives and many analysts. These men and women managed to last the distance — I wanted to continue but after having a hand in checking over 2000 cars, I was tired.

There wasn't one person in that taskforce who didn't make numerous personal sacrifices to locate and convict Bendali Debs and Jason Roberts, but in the end, Justice Cummins's words were some of the sweetest I'd heard: 'Mr Debs, for the murder of Sergeant Silk I sentence you to life imprisonment. For the murder of Senior Constable Miller I sentence you to life imprisonment. No minimum term of imprisonment before eligibility for parole is set. You are sentenced to be imprisoned for the remainder of your life. Life means life . . .

'For the murder of Sergeant Silk, I sentence you, Mr Roberts, to life imprisonment. For the murder of Senior Constable Miller, I sentence you to life imprisonment. I direct that you serve, upon the sentences I have imposed upon you, a minimum term of imprisonment of thirty-five years before eligibility for parole.'

The Russell Street bombing on 27 March 1986. Less than two years later, my first police placing was at this station. NEWSPIX/TREVOR PINDER

This article appeared after we rescued those kids from the burning house early in 1990. COURTESY NEWS LTD.

Page 22—The Sun, Saturday, January 20, 1990

Fire heroes save youths

By MICHAEL EPIS

TWO policemen risked their lives to rescue two squatters from a fire in an abandoned house in central Melbourne yesterday.

Constables Simon Illingworth and Greg Stewart were on patrol in Queen St when they saw smoke coming from Franklin St.

Knowing a local house was being used by squatters, the two police investigated.

"We got there and heard voices so we called for backup," Constable Illingworth said.

But before help arrived, the pair spotted a youth behind a window on the second-storey of the house.

"He seemed very disoriented and couldn't answer our calls," Constable Stewart said.

"The front door of the house was locked and tin sheeting in the windows was scorching hot."

The police could hear the sirens of an approaching fire truck, but took on the rescue themselves.

They fought their way through flames and thick smoke and found two teenage boys in an upstairs bedroom.

The youths were distressed by the smoke.

"I grabbed one of them and gave him to Greg," Constable Illingworth said.

"Then I found another one of the boys, and we then carried them both downstairs."

Once outside, the boys were treated by ambulance officers while firemen put out the blaze.

"One of the kids came over, thanked me, and shook my hand," Constable Stewart said, but in the confusion the youths left.

● Constables Simon Illingworth (left) and Greg Stewart ... rescued two teenagers from a fire.

Jason Roberts (far left) and Bandali Debs: the cold-blooded cop killers.
NEWSPIX/TREVOR PINDER

Receiving a commendation from Chief Commissioner Christine Nixon.
SI PRIVATE COLLECTION

10

Professional practices

Murders had once fascinated me, but I'd seen my fair share of killing over the years and had tired of it. The stench of dead bodies and the look of hundreds of wiggling maggots in a corpse would turn most people's guts, but I'd become hardened to that. I didn't like being desensitised to gore the way some cops do. I couldn't help sharing the anguish of the victims' families; that made the job hard. In that respect I wish I could have been less human. I'd made it as a detective, but bent cops still labelled me a rat, despite my work on the police murder investigations and other major crime. Even while I worked on the murder of our police colleagues, bent cops would stare through me. That baffled me. What the fuck did they want me to do — erase history or turn back time? I just wanted to mix with real people again so I decided on a change.

After the Homicide Squad I successfully applied for a transfer to Broadmeadows police station. Broadmeadows was an easy place to get promotion into because it was a tough area to work. I became a sergeant. I had to go wherever they desperately needed someone. A person considered a rat couldn't really choose where to go, despite his operational experience.

Broadmeadows was a challenge. It had a large migrant population and many of the residents had seen the worst the world had to offer. To them, Australia was a land of hope and opportunity. But Broady's mix of migrants came with a downside; people of different cultures had clashed overseas and many of them had been the victims of abuse.

Migrants often find they have to compromise the strict values they have grown up with when they arrive on Australian soil. Sometimes this is a challenge for even the most moderate person. But the uniformed police around Broady worked hard, and it never ceased to amaze me how the region operated with such diverse groups living in such close proximity to each other. That is the beauty of this country — it is still a land of opportunity and a safe haven for many. I found that many settled Australians constantly strive for more and more: a better house, better car, favourable work and pay conditions and bigger handouts from the government. I often think of these immigrants when the going gets tough; we often take our freedom for granted.

Broadmeadows was a hard place to work: while I was there I managed to rack up no fewer than four sieges. It was a change from Homicide but definitely not a holiday. Shortly after I started there the boss told me that Broady had more baseball bats per capita than anywhere else he'd worked. He was right, the number of baseball bats far outnumbered the baseballers residing in the area; I don't remember ever seeing such a sporting club. Perhaps a few of the locals carried the sporting equipment on the offchance such a club would open.

It was literally a baptism of fire for me at Broadmeadows. First came the pyromaniac who constantly set fire to anything flammable on fire danger days. Then I was threatened by a would-be baseballer swinging his favoured apparatus, shortly after by a bloke firing lead shot at his neighbours, a handful of domestic assaults, violence and a fight or two. Then there was the bloke who barricaded himself in his house after loading his microwave oven with aerosol cans. I became proficient at talking to people on roofs. What is it about madmen and rooftops?

Taking charge of the Broadmeadows cells was meant to be the respite a sergeant got when not working on the streets. But my run of bad luck continued and I was forced to spray the prisoners with pepper spray more than once in response to things ranging from attempted escapes, picking the locks, lighting fires in the cells and having crooks punching each other. That was Broady. All go. During one nasty altercation we had to forcibly enter the cells and use two cans of pepper spray to control a violent prisoner. We hadn't taken into account the swirling motion of the air-conditioner and we were soon dodging a noxious, burning haze. Everyone was in pain; both prisoners and cops were crying uncontrollably and suffering a sharp burning sensation around the eyes, nose and throat. This became a combination of pain and laughter as one of the bosses ran into the cells to see that everything was OK. We tried to tell him to stay back, but too late.

While I was at Broady, the Force commanders brought in physical health experts. Everyone was given blood pressure tests and asked to ride an exercise bike. Our fitness was then graded using a special formula. On the day of my test I was in charge of the cells, which contained fourteen of Melbourne's finest. It was a jailer's usual shift — sorting out violent arguments between prisoners about important things such as the temperature of their hot lunch or the volume on the TV.

I walked upstairs, had my blood pressure tested and was put on an exercise bike. I rode for a kilometre or two, before being retested. The tester told me something was wrong: after the bike ride my blood pressure had gone down, not up. I gave the examiner a few details about the job I was doing and invited him down to the watch house to see for himself. He thanked me but declined. He did, however, give me my final results: I was clinically obese.

This was ridiculous because I was playing football regularly and, although I was carrying a few extra pounds, I'd always been solid but hadn't ever been considered obese. I was a draughthorse, I told him, not a racehorse, and not everybody is built like a hyena. I told him he'd given me the wrong test, and assured him that if we had a few hours to kill I'd still be riding the bike. My examiner laughed as I lifted my enormous fat gut down off the bike and waddled my way back to the pressure of the Broady cells. The constables laughed at my assessment and spent the rest of the shift calling me 'Barge' instead of 'Sarge'. A large strawberry cream cake appeared on my desk in case I got hungry. Cops have a special way of making the unbearable bearable — and more often than not, it's humour that saves the day.

I received a commendation for leadership while I was at Broadmeadows, a place I really enjoyed. What it lacked in tranquillity it gave back in knowing you were helping people in genuine hardship. A handful of the uniform cops had spent years there, a credit to them and their capacity to work under stress. It was a very well-run operation from the top down. It had to be.

While at Broadmeadows I saw a detective sergeant's position advertised in the *Police Gazette* for the Ethical Standards Department (ESD), a department that rooted out bent cops. ESD was widely known among cops as 'the filth' or the 'toe-cutters'. With my history as a rat, I knew it was probably the only detective sergeant's job I had a good chance of getting. And without putting too fine a point on it, I needed the extra money because I'd had to take a pay cut to get promoted. I applied for and got the job. Now I was formally a corruption investigator and informally 'a rat from the filth'.

I started at ESD looking forward to being treated as an equal, not as a whistleblower.

Neil O'Sullivan, the boss, was a tough customer who stepped aside for no one. He was known as Donga, from an old Paul Hogan comedy skit in which a barrel-chested detective bounced crooks off walls with his gut. Donga was feared. He targeted anyone in the Force with a split personality. Any mix of cop and criminal was fair game for O'Sullivan and his men. His delightful wife once said to me, 'If I stuffed up, Neil would lock me up, honest, Simon. He wouldn't bat an eyelid. That's just the way he is.'

Donga and I formed a lasting friendship. Despite his tough, old-school exterior I found him to be a very proactive and lateral thinker. O'Sullivan and his team knew that proactive methods of investigation were the new way of policing, but more importantly, that they were the only methods likely to be successful in catching corrupt cops. He had already begun seizing cops' official diaries. After all, Al Capone had been caught for tax evasion; there were lots of ways of catching corrupt cops too.

When I arrived I was given an old school 'welcome to the unit' speech, which consisted of O'Sullivan laying down the law in a not too subtle way. His no-nonsense approach was a breath of fresh air. Some of the other leaders I had seen in Victoria Police spoke cryptically and unsuccessfully tried to fake sincerity — a trait best left to undercover operatives. I guess it is horses for courses, but I always felt comfortable knowing where I stood with O'Sullivan, something that I valued greatly.

Soon after my arrival, O'Sullivan encouraged me to apply for the Sir Vincent Fairfax Fellowship, a prestigious Australian scholarship that selects up to fourteen potential leaders from a diverse range of occupations and puts them through an intensive ethics and leadership program. The Fellowship also sponsors candidates to travel and study around the world. But I felt uncomfortable applying, sure I would be buried by all the prestigious people who applied. They'd have walls covered in academic qualifications and could talk the talk. But O'Sullivan wouldn't hear of it.

I started to read the application form. Question 1 was: 'Do you know of anyone who has been adversely affected by sticking to their principles?' The second question was: 'What experience do you have in making ethical decisions?'

I wrote my story down. *Cop that!* I thought they wouldn't believe it anyway. When I'd finished, I handed the form to the boss. *That's got you off my back.* I returned to work.

A short time later I was informed I had an interview, and decided I should just be myself and tell it like it was. A while later I found out I had been selected. Finally, my experiences and decisions were valued. Wow! I never thought of being considered ethical. I was too much of a bloke. When I told the boss about it he smiled and nodded, like he wasn't surprised.

Being selected was wonderful, until I found out that the others chosen included people such as doctors, political advisers, chief executives and radio producers — even the manager of the Bionic Ear Institute.

It was during the ethics program that I realised that being a policeman was not a guarantee you knew the world better than anyone else. Being a cop, in fact, guaranteed tunnel vision. Cops process, label and judge people; they operate on gut instinct. A person who looks like a druggie is treated like one, someone who looks like a crook is treated like one. If you're wrong, it doesn't matter because at least you're still alive. As they say, 'Better to be tried by twelve than carried by six.' Police believe that it is better to have a self-defence case in court than to risk prematurely winding up in a morgue. But part of the job of being a cop is judging others, and how do you do that without prejudice? Police assess and judge others all the time. Things like tattoos, clothing types and intravenous track marks signal danger. They tell police to be cautious. Eye movement, fidgeting or a lack of eye contact can arouse curiosity in an experienced detective.

The ethics and leadership program took me to places where I saw the effects of unchecked corruption. In some places corruption had systematically moved through whole communities, cities and countries. It was like an octopus, sucking the life out of freedom, free speech and a fair go. Some countries, such as Indonesia, Malaysia and Mexico, were gripped so strongly by corrupt systems that bribes were expected to be paid to public officials simply to retain a place in a public waiting list. I travelled through countries where every person I spoke to admitted that every one in their police force was corrupt to some extent. I saw the effects of crime left unchecked, with no independent crime commission to keep tabs on things.

In many of the places what really astounded me was seeing impoverished people displaying genuine happiness. It made me realise that we often wrongly connect wealth with happiness. Mind you, there were plenty of people desperately unhappy because they didn't know where their next meal was coming from. I learnt that people need a certain amount of money to be happy, but the rest depends on attitude. I studied ethics, international anti-corruption and terrorism and culture and visited Aboriginal settlements in far north Queensland. I met people suffering from incurable diseases. Ironically, some of them were legitimately happier than some of the fully fit, wealthy Australians I've met. Why? Because of their attitude to life.

A Tibetan monk put this situation into perspective: 'Don't say, I wish I was, say, I'm glad I'm not.' Whether we like it or not, we have all been handed a baton by our predecessors: we have a choice, we can run, walk, stand still or hand it back. For us to achieve, it is not good enough to be a copy or a clone of our predecessors. We must be better than that. It's time to run!

Before my arrival at the Ethical Standards Department my unit had already created some waves. On 10 May 2000, the St Kilda police complex was searched by ESD. It was in all the papers and on all the news bulletins when Detective Superintendent Neil O'Sullivan and his detectives located a cache of illegal substances in the ceiling cavity of the building. The unit expected to find out who had hidden the drugs and guns there, and why.

I wasn't unfamiliar with St Kilda, having locked up a former colleague who knew many of the people who worked there. I didn't really want to go back and investigate, but I was told to, so I did.

The last time I had gone into St Kilda CIB the first person I saw looked at me as if I were a maggot on a clean black suit. I was familiar with the look; it was the same one he'd given me after I'd locked up one of his bent mates. I wanted to leave immediately, but had to wait for my colleague to finish what he was doing. Then the detective walked behind a partition and I heard him sliding the load and unload mechanism of a pump-action shotgun, an unmistakable sound even without the experience of camping with my old man. Not pleasant, but I'd had to put up with worse.

On 29 July 2001 the Victoria Police or, more specifically, the Victoria Police Drug Squad, was put under the microscope by the media. Detective Sergeant Blue of the Drug Squad, on sick leave at the time, was caught up in buying 10 kilograms of hashish from a person connected to slain gangster Jason Moran, and 15 000 ecstasy tablets linked to Mokbel, a well-known Victorian crime boss whose cases are still before the courts. The search of a hotel room rented by one of Blue's criminal associates revealed a cache of 12 500 tablets, plus another 40 000 and $10 000 in cash. The associate pleaded guilty to trafficking a commercial quantity of ecstasy, and was jailed for eight years with a minimum of five years, fined $18 000 and ordered to forfeit $10 000 and two mobile phones.

Another related criminal pleaded guilty to trafficking a commercial quantity of ecstasy and cultivating cannabis, and was sentenced to seven and a half years' jail, with a four and a half year minimum. Eventually, Blue himself pleaded guilty to trafficking in a commercial quantity of ecstasy, two counts of conspiring to traffic in cocaine and one count each of trafficking in cocaine, cannabis resin and ecstasy and possessing ecstasy. He had joined the force at the age of twenty-two and had received four commendations.

Blue was not the only policeman heavily involved in organised crime at this level, but he was one who suffered the consequences. A handful of strong-willed men worked relentlessly on that investigation.

The newspapers reported that the corruption investigation netted 52 500 tablets worth up to $4.4 million, but that would make the tablets about $83 each, an excessively high estimate, even as a per tablet street price. Needless to say, these people weren't at street level. The higher up the drug chain you are, the cheaper the price: like buying or selling anything else wholesale or in bulk. My guess is that the tablets at this level of trafficking would be worth about $18 to $25 each, so the value (to the players involved) would be about a quarter of what was reported; somewhere between AUD$1 million and AUD$1.375 million. Either way, it's still huge coinage.

As the dominoes started to fall the Feds jumped in on the action. Blue's arrest triggered a number of worldwide ecstasy arrests. One day after Victoria Police ESD arrested one of their detectives, Spanish police struck. Using information supplied from Australia they seized 252 000 ecstasy tablets. The people arrested in Spain included the world's biggest ecstasy trafficker and eleven Israelis whose role was to send the drugs around the world, including to the world's most livable city, Melbourne.

While one arm of the Victoria Police was tediously counting 50 000 plus ecstasy tablets, the Victoria Police Assistant Commissioner (for Crime) was reported as saying he still had confidence in the Drug Squad, whose detectives had been selected 'because of their high integrity . . . they continue to demonstrate strong ethical character'. I suspect that a few of my colleagues counting eckie tablets would have viewed the situation with a little more scepticism, especially after they passed the 49 999 mark.

My role in this operation was to take part in the raid on a house near the Flemington racetrack. The detective inspector who led the charge, an astute detective whom I'll call Tails, was renowned for having a cool head under pressure. Because of my physical strength and size, Tails handed me the metal window reamer, a heavy, sword-like instrument used for extracting glass from windows. George, another detective who was also powerfully built, was chosen for door duties and handed the key, a 20-kilogram sledgehammer.

Six solidly built men crept up to the house. An innocent civilian, noticing that we all wore tabards with 'POLICE' emblazoned across them, slowed down for a closer look. We didn't need any extra attention from someone driving slowly past a house we were going to smash into, so I looked towards him menacingly, held my metal sword high and mouthed two words that meant 'please leave'. Understandably, he decided he'd seen enough and accelerated away.

We took position and Tails gave George the nod. George lifted the huge sledgehammer over his shoulder without making a sound. A small bird tweeted as the hammer reached its pinnacle, then George let out a roar as he launched the sledgy at the door lock. *Crunch!* Wood splinters spat out and the bricks shook. That was the signal. I lifted the reamer and waited for Tails to give me the nod. *Bang, bang, bang.* The door failed to give in to the sledgehammer. *Bang, bang, bang*... Ten hits and the door was still holding. Tails turned and I got the nod. This time I swung the reamer into action with full force. *Smash!* The cheap glass broke into razor-sharp, jagged edges.

George kept hitting the fortified door, but he was starting to loosen bricks. 'Stop, George!' The entire entrance wall had started to rock. 'Simon's got us an in.' I continued to swing the reamer and smashed out the sharp points. Time was of the essence here, and we needed a safe entry — now!

I expect that a crook would be up and at 'em after hearing one or two sledgehammer hits on their front door — let alone ten — or the window being smashed with a reamer. But no one came.

I'd cleared an entry through the main window, but the combination of George's sledgehammer and my reamer became too much for the house facade: as we watched six windows cracked and broke in sympathy.

The rest of the detectives went inside and cleared the house, just as you see it done in the American cop shows. 'Police, don't move. Police, don't move.' A long silent pause, then, Tails looked at me as we cleared the rooms of the house. I knew that look well — I think all my bosses had been taught that look at the officer training school. It said two things: 'Thanks for that, Simon' (sarcasm) and, 'The paperwork you have caused me for caving in the front of this house will finish my career.'

The look intensified when we realised no one was home. This was not a mistake on our behalf but part of the risk that investigators have to take in simultaneous arrests and searches. It didn't help Tails though; it meant he had to get another officer to inspect the damage. That was like rubbing salt into an open wound. 'Aaah, come and see the damage my detectives have done.'

While we were standing around the occupant arrived at what was left of his premises. He must have thought a semitrailer had side swiped it: the entire row of windows had caved in and the front door and brickwork were either loose or badly damaged — or both. George's dozen or so love taps with the sledgehammer ensured that the house required a bricklayer, not just a locksmith. But much to Tails's relief, the damage bill was no longer ours. We searched the place and I found the occupant's pistol. This alleviated the damage bill.

As I picked up the pistol, the crook said, 'It's loaded.' I appreciated crooks with the decency to tell you when guns were loaded or if there was a syringe at hand. I located something else near the pistol, something metal, long and quite heavy. 'Oh yeah, don't muck around with that either,' he said.

'Why?' I enquired.

'It's a grenade.'

That sounded like a good reason not to muck around. Tails called in the army explosives expert. The crook said he had brought the grenade to Australia from Israel, explaining that he had it in his backpack while travelling in a commercial aeroplane. I hope this wasn't true.

Within hours the newspapers told the sorry tale, further evidence that elements of the Victoria Police were bad. A new generation of competitive young reporters took the bull by the horns and they weren't going to let go. Twenty or so journalists were breaking major corruption stories on current affairs programs, while others provided the impetus for the headlines. It was a new era. Many journalists took a back seat. It's difficult to write stories about people who have been sources for you over the years. I understood that; some didn't. Longevity in journalism is a delicate balancing act because, like cops, few journalists like the smell of a burning bridge.

I'd waited for a long time to see news articles digging deep into Victoria's corruption. Many journalists had scratched the surface over the years, but these arrests put corruption squarely in the headlines. Finally, reporters printed the words I had desperately wanted to see more for more than a decade — 'Independent Anti-Corruption Commission'.

11

Ethical standards

On 16 March 2001 Christine Nixon became the first woman to command an Australian police force. Instantly, she became popular with the rank and file police after she relaxed some of the dress rules and supplied the first of hundreds of extra police recruits. Some of the wise old cops suggested that casual dress encourages a casual attitude. Time will tell, but the lax dress codes were popular with the majority of the younger cops. The additional recruits were part payment of a pre-election promise made by the Labor government led by state premier, Steve Bracks.

The most recent corruption operation was largely unchartered territory for the ESD, so all eyes were on Chief Commissioner Nixon, who had been in office only three months. What was she going to do about it? Many police and media saw this challenge as Nixon's first major hurdle and rumours about her apparently minimal organised crime experience began to circulate. Which way would she go? More of the same? A reshuffle? A cleansing name change?

ESD had already undergone a name change, having previously been known as the Internal Investigations Department (IID). Whatever the name, these departments are, and will always be, known around the world as Internal Affairs, or IA for short. The structure of ESD had been well thought out years before, but it had degenerated through a lack of resources and manpower and was a skeleton of what it should have been. ESD had been created to cope with all the crime and misconduct a corrupt police officer could think of, but no one would have guessed that a Victorian Drug Squad detective would be only a step or two from members of an Israeli drug cartel. These were people involved in international organised crime. Was Blue on his own in this? The question was answered shortly afterwards by a small crew of detectives. Blue was quite possibly one of many. But how many? At the time of writing, we still don't know the answer to that question, but more than a handful have been under suspicion.

The media spotlight was fixed firmly on the police hierarchy, so it was time to deal with the problem. What could be better, then, than a cleansing name change to keep the media at bay? The decision was made to rename the Drug Squad and so the Major Drug Investigation Unit was created. A few people took the opportunity to move voluntarily into different areas. At this point the Police Association stepped in, saying no detective should be moved without consent, that such a move would arouse unfair and completely unjust suspicion of a former Drug Squad member's character — and they were right. You can't punish good employees because there are bad ones. The revelations kept coming, flagging an obvious need for immediate change. The stress of working within high-risk areas required the Force to create a system in which employees straining under work pressures could voluntarily request to move into a less stressful role.

Anyone working in high-stress areas shouldn't have to wait to transfer. Over the years, detectives knew that applying for lateral movement within the Force's antiquated promotional system took months, if not years for some, and once that was achieved the court cases followed them around like a curse. Court delays and holdups aren't only unjust to defendants, but they also add extra weight to a detective's lot. The only speedy way to move within the Force meant taking a job that very few others wanted. These were often high-stress roles in places like Broadmeadows or Footscray, which defeated the purpose.

Corruption reporters forced an immediate rethink, and the media were informed of the creation of a new anti-corruption strikeforce called Task Force Ceja. That fixed it, didn't it?

*　*　*

Blue's arrest occurred at an unforgettable time in Victorian criminal history. A long-standing, simmering feud between criminals went haywire. Gangsters began shooting each other in what most believe to be an egotistical fight over drug territory. Apparently, it was a good old-fashioned dash for cash as the territorial boundaries became blurred. The old-school criminal code of conduct was thrown out the window, to become a situation of kill or be killed. For the first time in living memory Victoria's criminal networks were unsettled, not by the police, but by the crooks themselves. At least two major criminal networks and other peripheral criminals took the opportunity to eliminate one another. It was unstoppable rogue violence. As time went on, rapidly escalating violence had deadly consequences.

There was one interesting fact, though: the all-important crime statistics showed crime was down. In August 2004, the chief commissioner seized upon this in a media interview.

> The latest data show that overall crime is down 12 per cent, burglaries 39 per cent and stolen motor vehicles an incredible 44 per cent. There is a lot that Victoria Police is doing right. Our strategies to combat speed and road trauma have been enormously successful. Last year, Victoria recorded its lowest road toll since records began. Driver culture is changing, and more people are alive as a result. Victorians feel safer in their homes than [they do in] any other state or territory in Australia. The most recent COAG report on government services showed without doubt that Victoria Police initiatives were successfully targeting crime and were tailored to meet the needs of all members of the community.
>
> The report showed Victoria had the lowest rate of recorded crime per 100 000 population for crime against the person and the lowest crime rate of all jurisdictions for murder, assault and unlawful entry.

I have no doubt the statistics made everyone feel much safer.

I wasn't on my own when it came to scepticism. *Age* reporters Gary Hughes and Fergus Shiel weren't convinced either. Six months later they reproduced an internal police email that gave credibility to the story that the crime stats had been fiddled somehow.

Nevertheless, during this apparent downturn in crime, some of the tough, unshakable mobsters looked decidedly flustered. It was a time when underworld chaos reigned supreme, no matter what the statistical bean counters said. Why was the underworld unsettled? More importantly, what happened to agitate the territory that caused this urban warfare?

It would be naive to believe that this boiling pot of crime had nothing to do with some of the corruption being unearthed. Untangling corruption almost always leads to the disclosure of secrets and the erosion of underground loyalty. To save their own skins corrupt police and criminals often turn on each other after they've been arrested. Underworld secrets and once confidential information and intelligence begin to circulate during these times. Some of it is true, some of it is untrue.

In times of gangland warfare mobsters assess the links in their criminal chain. Weak links are a liability. Gangsters don't want to take the risk of an associate rolling over (lagging), so they release dirt to a person they know will take action. There's no honour among thieves — mobsters often hope that any potential lagger or other weak link might just drop off the planet. As dirt is spread in the underworld and an issue comes to the surface, it often reopens old wounds, a vengeful situation that creates a heightened sense of anxiety: death is often the result.

But underworld upheaval and killing were far from my mind early in 2001. My new career in Internal Affairs began when my boss threw me an official yet handwritten document. It involved a notorious CIB, and one of the police working from that office was a well-known police detective with a reputation. I'll call him Mr Pink.

Mr Pink had been stationed at the Armed Robbery Squad, the squad involved in the shooting of convicted armed robber Graeme Jensen on 11 October 1988. The detectives present alleged that Jensen brandished a weapon (while also driving his car), forcing some of the police to shoot at him in self-defence. Jensen died of a gunshot injury and his car speared into a pole.

Less than twenty-four hours later, two young uniformed police officers were gunned down in an ambush, allegedly in a payback for the police shooting of Jensen.

One of Pink's Armed Robbery Squad partners was Detective Reece, the same man who had mimicked threatening to shoot me in the head at the Melbourne Magistrates' Court moments before I was due to give evidence against my corrupt former partner Sergeant Steele. Reece was involved in the fatal interception of Jensen with Detective Blue. Another cop found to be corrupt, Blue was later found to be a drug trafficker, no less. Blue was part of the team keeping Jensen under surveillance prior to the fatal interception. Eight armed detectives waited in position from about 7.30am but none could act until surveillance confirmed Jensen's identity. That was the job of Blue's crew.

I knew the Jensen connection between detectives Blue and Reece, as did most members of the public. The arrest had figured prominently in the news. I'd never had anything to do with Pink, but I had been told that he was quite tall, solidly built and had an icy stare. I later found this description to be reliable.

The day I was thrown the handwritten documents and handed a foam cup of cheap instant coffee by Neil O'Sullivan was the day that, if I had my time again, I would like to change. It marked the beginning of the end for me in several respects: it turned out to be the day my marriage, my job and my life began to slide uncontrollably into an almost lethal journey of crime and corruption allegations.

An hour after getting the documents my suspicions rose and, like all corruption detectives, I began to salivate at what I'd found. There were suspicious underworld connections and networks. I walked into O'Sullivan's office and told him that something didn't seem to add up. He told me to run with it but to be careful about making enquiries. 'Don't trust any of your previous contacts,' he told me. 'It's different when you're investigating corruption. You have to identify the contacts you can trust when you're investigating anything to do with police. Assume nothing.'

My investigation took many strange twists and turns. I spoke to drug importers and traffickers, colourful racing identities, gangsters, thugs, bank managers, informers and an assortment of criminals and their lawyers. I went to racetracks, jockey yards, country jails, city jails, remand centres, sheriffs' offices, courts, country towns, farmhouses, doghouses and my fair share of slums and pubs. The documents created an investigation that spread far and wide in many directions.

This investigation was going to take time, but as we found, time had run out. Our unit was disbanded in a reshuffle of the Ethical Standards Department, a perplexing decision to many, because the Professional Practices Unit under O'Sullivan had delivered results time and time again in routing out corruption and was, arguably, the most successful unit in Victoria Police Internal Affairs history. Superintendent Neil O'Sullivan was a tough cop who had spent many years at the sharp end of humanity. He was a proud man who had helped many people over the years, particularly within the Indigenous community. Yet my boss and mentor had his unit dissolved from under him. The hierarchy had decided that resources would be better placed in a new taskforce.

That was the end of the Professional Practices Division, the proactive division of the Force was replaced by the other reactive investigative body I mentioned previously, Task Force Ceja. This change was seen by many as a knee-jerk reaction to the scandal caused by the arrest and later incarceration of Detective Sergeant Blue.

On O'Sullivan's last day I walked him out to the dingy, poorly lit carpark at the back of the Victoria Police Centre with another detective from the now obsolete PPD. No gold watch, no pat on the back, no fanfare: just three men walking in silence. None of us knew what to say.

That was a day I'll never forget; it made me realise everyone had a use-by date. No matter how hard I tried, I knew now that I wasn't going to reach Neil's rank: I would never be able to erase the stigma of being a rat.

I did some soul searching that night. Why was I still in the police force? It definitely wasn't the money. If I had another job I wouldn't have to put up with the intimidation of bent cops or the stares of their dodgy mates. For the first time since I'd joined the Force I stopped and wondered what was driving me.

I had wanted to change the culture. I had tried to achieve everything crooked cops thought I couldn't. When they presented me with hurdles, I sought to jump them — just to prove I could. People talked about how I was winning the fight against corruption by doing this or that, but in the early hours of that morning I realised that I was no longer what Simon Illingworth wanted to be. I was one of the most successful and experienced cops in the Force yet I woke up asking myself, Have I made a difference?

O'Sullivan had successfully prosecuted crooks and corrupt cops all his life, but when I looked at his dejected face I felt as lost and empty as he looked. I reflected on my own career. I felt I was looking into the future, that Neil was a mirror image of me in twenty years' time. But I didn't like what I saw, or the way I saw my future panning out without his guidance.

On the day he left, I carried thirty years of Neil's memories to the carpark in a cardboard box. I turned to Neil and said, 'Boss, if this is the way the police force treats you at your rank, how are they going to treat me and others at my level?' His response was one I'd come to expect from such a tough man: 'Your boots could do with a polish, look at 'em! Take this; I reckon you'll need it.' O'Sullivan took the box I was holding, dipped inside it and handed me five tins of shoe polish and a shoe brush. He was always on my back to keep my shoes clean, but I was always too busy investigating to worry about shiny shoes. He knew what it was like to burn leather during investigations. 'Can you blokes sit around any faster?' he'd say. 'No one ever solved anything seated at a computer all day.'

'Oh yeah,' he added, 'call me Neil from now on, will you?'

'No worries, Boss,' I said automatically.

As Neil drove out of the Victoria Police Centre for the last time, I stood in the dark carpark for a couple of minutes hoping he'd turn around. He didn't. I went back to my desk but I didn't feel like working. I had lost a mate, and rats find real mates hard to come by.

The decision to create Task Force Ceja was a good one, although the disbanding of PPD in order to resource it left many investigators scratching their heads. It was said to be robbing Peter to pay Paul, but the articles about corruption in the papers had increased momentum and the media had the Force on the back foot. The resulting public unrest created a genuine desire for heads on stakes — and, unfortunately, the PPD couldn't deliver fast enough. The corruption prevention part of the unit was cast aside, and a handful of resources were thrown at it in what was seen as a token gesture. This concerned many, who believed that the long-term health of the Victoria Police relied on anti-corruption education and proactive policing methods, not on a short-sighted approach to satisfy the public need for blood.

After Neil left, my investigation into the police documents I'd been given began to centre on a crim heavily involved in the Collingwood and Fitzroy scene. Bill Crane (not his real name) had been brought up in my old stamping ground of Collingwood. Unlike many other crims in the area he didn't cause too many waves, nor did he draw attention to himself while going about his business. He was smart, although apparently not smart enough to avoid being involved in crime.

A few years before I joined the police force, Crane had been charged with shooting two men in a grocer's shop, and later for throwing acid in the face of a witness who had been lured out of his house. Crane had been acquitted of all charges. His case was covered in the newspapers but soon after he was anonymous again. Crane was a shrewd operator, very much aware of the boundaries of our legal system. That's not to say he was unjustly acquitted of anything, but rather, that he was a man you'd expect to heavily contest a charge. Crane knew the law better than many cops did.

My investigation covered a wide range of people, and Crane was caught in the middle of my net. It stretched thousands of kilometres, so it was more than bad luck when I realised that one of the worst criminals involved with Crane lived near me. In fact, he lived less than 400 metres away from my house, if that. This guy arrived at my office and asked to see me; he brought photographs of his dog, which he spread out in front of me. His dog, in front of my house. I handed the photographs back to the crook and pretended I hadn't seen the relevance. But the message was crystal clear.

My investigation of organised criminals had expanded immeasurably to take in not just organised crime, but also massive conspiracy and large-scale bribery. My office was literally covered in my paperwork and copies of exhibits. One of my flowcharts showed a tangled web of crime that stretched 5 metres along the floor. In the end I was in charge of several corruption investigations. It was like juggling four or five moving chainsaws. Despite the dramatic escalation of work, resources were not forthcoming. I was forced to work (for the most part) on my own, on a conspiracy inquiry involving violent drug traffickers who had some of the worst criminal reputations in Melbourne, at least one of whom lived near me. This was a case of cat v. mouse or David v. Goliath. I felt I was a taskforce of one, and every night I came home to the sight of a house near mine that had been provided as surety to allow one of Bill Crane's criminal associates to obtain bail. I was in more danger at home than I was at work. Soon afterwards I heard from a reliable source that my address was common knowledge among members of the underworld, and I should consider myself vulnerable at best.

My life was in danger and I knew it. I was no longer the hunter, but the hunted. The lack of resources provided to me by the police had created a situation that was irreversible. From that point on no amount of new resources would be enough to give me a life free from intimidation, not any more. But back-pedalling is not in my nature, so I felt I had to take my chances. I decided to forge ahead — and strike back hard.

Crane was a known associate of one of Australia's most notorious killers, Christopher Dale Flannery, alias Rent a Kill. Flannery's was a name synonymous around Australia with organised crime, murder and corruption. He figured prominently in the ABC television series *Blue Murder*, the drama that portrayed the shooting of an honest Drug Squad detective, Michael Drury. Like mine, Drury's problems had started off relatively small: allegedly, he had refused to water down evidence in a drug investigation in return for a bribe. As a result of his stand, he was shot in front of his children in an ambush at his home — he was lucky to live. Some time later, Flannery's initials mysteriously appeared etched into a wall at the crime scene, and, recalling the words 'Catch and kill your own', Flannery went missing shortly after. He is presumed to have been murdered. His body has never been found.

The lead that brought me into contact with Melbourne's underworld came from one telephone call that encouraged me to concentrate on Bill Crane and his associates. Alarm bells started ringing when I realised that Bill Crane had been busted with eight guns, an amphetamine laboratory, amphetamine product and pseudoephedrine, a highly restricted substance held legally only by chemical companies for legitimate enterprises. It is used by criminals for making illegal amphetamines. The security restrictions on the movement of pseudoephedrine and the limited quantities of the product available make any pseudo on the black market worth its weight in gold.

Crane had a pistol fitted with a silencer and night vision goggles — assassin's equipment in anyone's language. I had to tread carefully: one false move and the flag was up prematurely. No investigator likes to be forced into an arrest without the desired evidence. Underworld criminals don't confess in interviews, some don't even talk at all. I had to be careful.

I decided to approach a young detective I'll call Dave, the informant in Crane's previous drug manufacturing charge. Dave had been a prime witness against Crane and had worked hard to lock him up for possession of large quantities of amphetamines and guns. We met in the Docklands area, near the Yarra. Dave, who was good-looking, quick-witted and fresh-faced, was wary about talking to me. His passion for locking up crooks matched mine, and his attitude reinvigorated me, but Dave was a realist; he knew this was going to be a slow, uphill battle. I asked him whether he knew of any criminals who could have conspired to get Crane out of jail. The blood drained from his face. 'You're joking, aren't you?' he asked.

'No, mate, it's game on,' I told him.

Since Crane had been remanded on the commercial drug trafficking charges brought by Dave, he was temporarily out of the underworld system, but jailing a drug manufacturer affects many people along the criminal food chain. These were the crims who had appeared on my radar as they conspired to pay a bribe and rig Crane's bail hearing.

From that day on, Dave and I worked as a team, investigating the motives and the truth or otherwise of the evidence presented to Court 12 at the Melbourne Magistrates' Court in March 2001. This case was known as the Bill Vincent Crane bail application, later 'the case'. Such court hearings are normally routine affairs; the evidence against an accused is presented and the reasons for declining bail are given by the police informant. The defence often presents the accused as a person who will appear at court and not commit further offences while on bail.

The only difference between a routine case and Crane's was the fact that the quantity of white powder was alleged by the informant to be large enough to put Crane into a reverse onus of proof: Crane was obliged to give reasons as to why he should get bail. Dave also claimed that Crane had trafficked so much pseudoephedrine and so many amphetamines that he had little chance of getting bail anyway. But things didn't go as Dave had hoped, and Crane was granted bail.

On the day we met, as Dave and I stood on the dock watching the Yarra River rushing out to sea, I realised we were on the same side of the fence — we both wanted to lock up criminals who conspired to bribe police.

I carefully dug around for evidence, backstopping everything I did so as not to alert the criminals or anyone else who might have been involved. I sifted through almost 9000 intercepted telephone calls. Thankfully, some were short or misdials. I logged the evidentiary calls one by one, listened to tape recordings and made a meticulous chronology of events. After teaching myself the specialist computer programs used by experienced analysts I then logged them on a chart.

'A picture is worth a thousand words' — nothing is truer than that in court. A graphic display of evidence carries far more weight with a jury than verbal evidence. So I created a number of diagrams that portrayed nexuses between the accused people and the evidence I had collected.

Many of the tasks I performed are not normally the role of an investigator, but owing to my lack of assistance — I could hardly remember what it was like to have a team of colleagues — I was forced to teach myself how to utilise the analysts' programs to present the evidence in the best possible way.

I took the opportunity to ask for help along the way, but mostly my requests fell on deaf ears, and, in the end, I was given too little too late. Other professional corruption investigators were under pressure, although none had tasted the kind of personal threats and dangers I had, nor did many of their investigations involve the underworld, as mine did. One of the suspects of my conspiracy investigation was Detective Black, who was overseas, so I figured it was as good a time as any to begin arresting the criminals. It takes a great deal of patience to ignore the urge to jump early. I'd waited long enough, and was confident I'd gathered enough evidence to present the matter before the courts for conspiracy. [Black was found not guilty.] Long-term investigation is like cooking; it takes skill to know when something is ready to take out of the oven. An amateur chef often does this too early or too late. I talked to a detective who was running a simultaneous investigation upstairs. We discussed the timing and agreed: it was the time to move.

The criminals were released into the community pending being charged. I felt very vulnerable at this stage because they knew charges were coming; they also knew I'd been working on my own for most of the investigation. It was at this point I was told they knew my address. The love I had for the house eroded rapidly and we soon sold it. It was passed in at auction but we accepted a later offer straight away, even though it was significantly less than what I really wanted for it.

My feeling of vulnerability intensified when Bill Crane began to frequent my local pub. Crane arrived with a colourful racing identity, a man I also believed to be a criminal. This man was rumoured to have fired bullets through the front windows of a nearby hotel. My pub was 60 kilometres from Crane's home address, so the likelihood of it being a coincidence was as likely as the belief that a hooker would be a virgin. It was a fluke, however, that I worked late the night he walked in; I was normally propping up the bar after a hard day's work.

A warning bell rang. My life was far too structured, my habits too predictable. I had to change my *modus operandi* — including varying the time I came to and from home or went for a drink. So I rescheduled my life, remembering the words of Billy 'The Texan' Longley when he spoke to a reporter about being an underworld target: 'If you drink, you can be got. If you're known to hang around in pubs frequently, you're an easy target. If somebody wants to kill you, he'll get you while you're talking to the paper [having a crap], if they really want you.'

Crane and his friend stayed at the pub and offered to buy some of the locals a drink, then a ride home. My mobile rang: I received two telephone calls from concerned locals warning me not to attend my usual haunt. One caller simply said, 'Ducks are on the pond', meaning they were out to get me. I knew the voice, enough said. I became less predictable: I put rubbish bins out a day or two early and chose the John Wayne seat whenever I went out (in his movies Wayne always sat facing the doorway to prevent an ambush).

12

Pot luck

On 17 December 2002 I spoke briefly with a good friend from the Australian Federal Police who suggested a Christmas drink at an inner-city hotel. Chris and I hadn't seen each other for a while, and I explained that I had almost completely stopped socialising because of the ongoing threats I'd endured. But I agreed to catch up for a drink. I figured I was safe meeting him for a beer because it was a spur of the moment decision and I didn't go to that hotel regularly.

I finished work a few minutes early and dropped off some paperwork on the way to the pub. When I arrived, Chris handed me a pint, which I gratefully accepted. I was looking forward to a few drinks and a good yarn with a mate. I could let my guard down with Chris, I trusted him with my life and I wanted to talk through a few issues with another honest cop.

As I settled in, I noticed a few lawyers and a handful of off-duty police standing at the bar. There were some other people milling around having a beer, but I was surprised there weren't more people around, considering the time of year. After thirty or forty minutes, I was finding it hard to settle down to a decent conversation because I was receiving a fair bit of optical attention from one of the lawyers and a cop. This concerned me, although not enough to leave.

But at 5.43pm I saw danger signals. A suspect in my investigation, the suspended Detective Black, swaggered through the hotel. He was dressed in old work shorts, work boots and a scruffy polo top. One pace behind him was a close associate, a well-known mobster who was heavily involved in the illicit drug trade, among other things. Black swaggered past me, shoulders back, chest puffed out and arms held as if he were carrying a sandbag under each armpit. His evil mate, who was wearing a baseball cap, looked me up and down as if he needed to take my measurements for a new suit. The stare lasted a long time, and he also swivelled his head as he walked outside staring fixedly at me until he moved on.

I held my ground but to say I felt extremely vulnerable would be an understatement. *What do I do now? How do I leave the pub? Do I leave now? Do I wait until it gets dark? I don't have a car to get home. What do I do?* I was really angry, too, not at the suspended cop and the gangland crook who had intimidated and threatened me with his mannerisms, but at Victoria Police. How can someone be put in this situation?

It was proved on 17 December 2002 at 5.43pm that police and organised criminals were associating with each other. You could have cut the air with a knife. It was like the music stopping in a Wild West movie, it was like everything was in slow motion. I thought I was going to be killed. I told Chris I had to go. Chris had not seen the interruption to our Christmas catch-up; he had been busy buying another couple of beers. I phoned the office and asked for a supervisor; I was desperately in need of advice. The question of whether Black and his mate knew I intended to go to that hotel could be answered later.

I could have saved myself the cost of the call. Apparently, nobody else saw this happen. How could two men move through a hotel, one stand there and intimidate an off-duty corruption investigator and no one else switch onto it? The frustration made me shake my head and look at the floor. The only person I could really trust in the hotel, Chris, hadn't seen what happened. I was on my own, again. 'That whingeing bastard says he was intimidated by …' Who was going to believe me anyway?

I telephoned Tracy and arranged for her to pick me up a few blocks away from the pub. Then I left, careful to adopt anti-surveillance tactics before and after I was picked up at our designated meeting point. I got behind the wheel of my car and drove through two red lights on the way home.

Once we arrived home, we sat down and I washed down the night's events with a few too many bourbons. Tracy and I didn't talk about it much; I was fed up with talk. In hindsight, I probably owed Tracy a better explanation than, 'Those fucking arseholes are playing the game again. This is bullshit! I could have been knocked tonight. I am so vulnerable. It's only a matter of time now.'

No investigation was initiated into this off-duty nightmare I was living, so I decided to make a few enquiries myself. I knew what I had seen and I was going to prove it. The next day I went back to the pub and asked if they had any security cameras. It was a long shot but I had seen a number of poker machines in a side room and figured it might be worth a go. To my surprise, not only did they have a camera viewing the doorway, but after a brief view of the scanned material, I realised that I might also find a digital image of the incident, frame by frame. I checked my mobile telephone call records to ascertain the time I put in my distress call, so I would have an idea when the incident occurred. I then viewed the footage leading up to that point.

I found it! It was an image of one of Melbourne's more notorious gangland criminals and a suspended cop who was being investigated by me for corruption taken on 17 December 2002 at 5.43pm and 43 seconds. This image wasn't innuendo — it was proof that they were associating with each other, proof in beautiful colour images. The surveillance camera had captured both men nicely in the same shot. No doubt it was a surveillance shot no one, including myself, had expected to have existed.

Before I left the pub I asked the manager for a copy of the evidence. He handed me a 50-cent floppy disk that, unbeknown to him, held the images that proved the battle lines between some cops and the crims were blurred. This put Melbourne police in a very murky light. The picture smudged even my understanding of policing and the underworld. To me, it was now in your face organised crime because it was now happening overtly in public areas. Underworld shootings were occurring in Melbourne hotels and other public places more regularly by now, yet there was little acknowledgment of the problem. But there was a problem, and I knew it. I also knew my computer disk could shed some light on a situation that nobody apparently wanted to admit existed.

Eighteen months later, on 3 June 2004, this potent image exploded onto the front page of Melbourne's *Herald-Sun*. The headline screamed 'Crim and the cop — caught on film'. It couldn't have come at a worse time for some. I'll explain why later.

As I've said, a picture tells a thousand words. For legal reasons this one had very little explanation attached to it at the time, but it didn't need any explanation. That headline eroded a number of people's reputations for honesty and transparency, which had nothing to do with any of the people in the picture. I loathe poker machines in pubs, I can never get used to the jingle-jangle and I hate watching elderly people pumping their grandchildren's future education into them, but without the poker machines at that pub, there would have been no video surveillance and these images were the best jackpot anyone ever got as far as I was concerned. It was corruption's smoking gun in one of its purest forms, association. I went back to work, printed off ten copies and downloaded the images onto the computer's database. All of that plus the original computer image ensured that too many copies now existed for them all to be destroyed.

A few months after the Christmas drink incident, Black's mate — the crim who had given me the death stare — rose to the surface. He was charged with the shooting murder of another criminal. This was yet another killing in an alleged string of crook-shoots-crook killings, but this one was particularly gruesome. This victim was blasted from the face of the planet with five shotgun blasts. As in many other killings in Melbourne at this time many bystanders were able to flee unscathed as shots rang out from behind them. They were lucky enough to live and tell the tale. Not that many ever do tell the tale, even if they live, not in court anyway. Escaping a gruesome death once is enough for most people.

I told Tracy of the connection between the Christmas drink intimidation and the man being sought for one of Melbourne's gangland killings, but tried to downplay its seriousness. Easier said than done, because at the same time I began building a fence around the perimeter of the house and fitted security doors, locks and 360-degree security lights. The Police Technical Unit fitted other security measures. I also carried a loaded gun twenty-four hours a day. The ultimate intrusion in our lives was that I slept with a gun. Tracy and I knew I was in trouble, and our lives would never be the same. I began to realise I hated myself for getting into us into this shit.

My investigation had hotted up. I'd had enough. It was time to strike back and I was ready to bring a few crooks to justice. I arrested Crane and his chief criminal associates and charged them with serious corruption offences. If convicted, they faced lengthy sentences. My dogged pursuit of justice had borne fruit; I arrested three crims at this stage. Whatever happened after that was entirely in the hands of the court and the civilians chosen at random from the jury pool.

This was to be my only glimpse of a reward. The effort needed to receive it was the equivalent of a gold miner shovelling through 20 tonnes of shale for one small nugget of pure gold. If this achievement was measured against the liberties I had lost and was to lose in the future, it would turn out to be far from the monumental win a few of my colleagues and friends had talked about. But along with this subtle sense of achievement was a bitterness I knew well. There were many other avenues of investigation I'd uncovered over three years that remained unexplored, untouched, unprobed and, therefore, unsubstantiated, ultimately buried as 'intelligence'. This couldn't be considered a win either, except by those who like to hide, deflect and camouflage the problems of the police force.

But a glimpse of light appeared at the end of the tunnel. Crane and Stanton were temporarily behind bars so I thought everything would settle down for me. How wrong I was.

One Sunday night Tracy and I went to bed, only to be awoken by a persistent knock at the door. Ours was a quiet street, especially at night on a Sunday, so I grabbed my loaded revolver as I walked up to the door. I quickly realised that whoever it was this wasn't a friend. I heard whispering and the security light failed. There was a man at the door, and another deliberately standing out of view of the doorway. I left the door closed and figured out the options — at worst, a crook wanted me to open the door to take me out, or at best, it was a burglar checking to see if anyone was home. What sort of situation had I been put in? I hoped that the unknown people wandering around the front of my house were burglars and not gangsters.

As one forced his face against the stained glass window in an attempt to look into the house for occupants or something to steal, he was completely unaware that a loaded .38 revolver was less than 2 centimetres from his head on the other side of the stained glass. I broke the silence by yelling, 'Fuck off!' The peering face quickly withdrew from the coloured glass. They ran off and jumped my 6 foot front fence as Tracy called 000 emergency. Minutes later, two police cars skidded out the front of the house, but the crooks had disappeared into the darkness. Perhaps his eyes managed to focus at the black cylinder on the other side of the stained glass as I explained the other option available to him. We'll never know.

I was drowning in paperwork, one arrest after another. After the first three well-known criminals, the next to be charged was Detective Black. I explained to him that I would be vigorously contesting his application for bail in the Magistrates' Court. Black's lawyer forcefully requested that his client be shown into court via the front public entrance, not from the private entrance underneath, as was normal. I agreed to the request without a second thought.

A detective who had been assisting me in compiling evidence drove the unmarked police car from the Corruption Office and I sat beside Detective Black in the back seat. We pulled up at the front steps of the Magistrates' Court and were instantly besieged by a huge gallery of press reporters and television cameramen. As I opened the car door the camera flashes dazzled me. We stood on the footpath temporarily to recover our wits; Detective Black was the quickest to recover from the shock of all the press. His intimidating height towered over everyone in the vicinity and the cameramen backed off and left an opening towards the court. Black lifted his head, puffed out his chest and was about to make his way towards the court unattended. Instinctively, I told him to stop and hooked my fingers into his belt. Any experienced police officer or criminal knows that an investigator can't allow an accused man to wander into court on his own then expect to be taken seriously in a contested bail application, especially one fought on the grounds that the accused is an unacceptable risk.

Perhaps Black didn't know the protocol or he too was surprised by the size of the press gallery. Either way, snatching a belt is an action that detectives normally reserve for murderers, rapists and armed robbers, not accused police officers. But this was not a standard case, and the usual cool climate in Melbourne had become tropical, to say the least, and whether this detective was guilty or innocent meant little to me. I knew that, while off duty, he'd associated with at least two members of the underworld: one accused of a recent gangland killing, the other a man known to offer bribes to facilitate drug trafficking.

The moment wasn't missed by the media — close ups of my grip of Black's belt were shown on every news channel. They seized on this defining cop arrests cop scenario. Afterwards I was tactfully told by a few coppers that my holding Black by the belt had upset many police, some high up in the Force, too. That hadn't been my intention, but so be it.

Black was granted bail at the Melbourne Magistrates' Court.

A well-known television reporter contacted me after court and told me I was doing a good job, I'd met her a few years before. She didn't want a story; she just wanted to say, 'Good on you.' I appreciated that.

Once charges are laid against an accused the legal clock starts ticking. As a matter of fairness, Victorian courts have set timeframes for the briefs of evidence to be served on people charged with offences. Normally, these timeframes are achievable but the complexity of these particular briefs meant that even a team would struggle to piece the evidence together, index it and meticulously log exhibits and witness statements in order. The paperwork for these briefs of evidence filled four empty workstations around me. I joked that a small Pacific island probably had no more trees.

I managed to get everything done, but with only hours to spare. I only managed it because of the assistance I received from a newcomer to the Corruption Office. Mark is one of life's true gentlemen, a top investigator and a great bloke. The first day he came down to help me I told him, 'I'm fucked.' And I meant it. Unfazed, Mark was able to grasp the technical aspects of the investigation in a short time, which proved to be invaluable later down the track, particularly during the court hearings. As good as it was, Mark's help came too late. I was running on empty, my nerves weren't what they used to be and my hardened facade was gone. I was spent, and I knew it.

Mark and I compiled the master brief and had it paginated. Then, we copied each individual brief five times. This was a monumental task for two people, a task that required extraordinarily clear thinking, something I was normally very good at, but my confidence in my clear thinking and judgment had taken a very big hit and was at an all-time low. It was a very hard slog, but Mark got the paperwork in order with as much assistance from me as I could give, which, unfortunately, wasn't much.

Most civilians read about notable investigations and arrests in newspapers or see them on TV, but (understandably) fail to comprehend how much time and labour are involved after the arrest in getting the evidence prepared, organising witnesses, briefing prosecutors, selecting, checking and double checking telephone interceptions, listening devices and (once secret) recordings, not to mention learning page upon page of evidence for committal hearings and trials. It's a nightmare. Perhaps less understandable is that some high-ranking officers suffer from the same mindset, so once you've got someone remanded in the pen, the boss wants to hand you on some more work.

Seasoned investigators know that once a crook has felt the cold steel of a pair of handcuffs, has a fist full of blueys (charges) and gets a whiff of prison food you're soon battling a well-paid barrister looking for loopholes, deficiencies in an incomplete brief or, the old favourite, the likelihood of an excessive court delay. I've had many crims let out on bail who, in my opinion, are unacceptable risks to the community — and the reason given is the likelihood of an excessive court delay. Bureaucratic red tape, bungling and inefficiency have enabled some vile criminals awaiting trial to see the light of day. It's not the judiciary's fault, but trust me, sometimes even cops don't want to be witnesses, especially when the only thing standing between a gangster and his future freedom is you.

Just to add fuel to an already raging fire, I was continually called to appear at bail hearings for Bill Crane. These hearings were extremely spiteful and grotesque exchanges. In one such hearing, Crane's barrister called me a 'Scotch poofter' across the courtroom, a reference to Scotch College. I laughed it off but the comment annoyed me, to say the least. This same barrister questioned me about my bashing, a number of years before, at the hands of the thug ex-cop, and all the death threats I had suffered at the hands of corrupt police. At the time I couldn't understand how anyone could draw a nexus between those incidents and whether or not Bill Crane should be allowed out on bail. This barrister's comment spurred me on to ensure that my evidence in chief was given as eloquently as possible, which would no doubt have delighted my Scotch College English teachers.

I believed Crane posed enough of a threat to me even without the assistance of any bent police who could siphon off intelligence about my movements for him. Crane had appeared uninvited to places I frequented off duty, so I'd been through it all before, but it seemed improbable that these attacks were ever going to end. Events like these make you acutely aware of your surroundings, particularly when you're alone. My past — the kicking, punching and death threats — I saw, were never going to end.

As I stood in the witness box under cross-examination I realised my head had dropped. For the first time in my career, I looked down at the floor while giving evidence. Then I noticed, puzzled, that my shirt was wet. Crane's barrister continued to scream louder and louder, smashing my spirit with statements and questions about my bashing by the former cop. 'Liar! Perjurer!' he screamed. I couldn't answer. His words were screamed so loudly that I had trouble comprehending them, and they came like bullets. Crane checked around the court briefly, then interrupted his innocent schoolboy facial expression to puff out his chest and look down his nose at me from the dock. Crane gave an evil smirk. I realised he had seen my head drop. He smiled again, clearly enjoying the moment.

I raised my head in defiance of Crane's barrister. *I am not a liar, nor a perjurer. I am part of the reason why blokes like him can be free to walk the streets or drive a car without being stopped by corrupt police hungry for a bribe.* As I stood in the witness box I breathed in and focused again on the magistrate. Then I saw the clerk of courts move to the front of the witness box and fill a foam cup with water. That was when I realised why my shirt was wet: I had been weeping. Crane's smirk wasn't just because my head had dropped; it was because he had broken me. Like it or not, Crane had won.

Crane's barrister didn't relent either; he continued to ask questions. He screamed at me to admit I had been 'belted up' and that police were behind it. I agreed, but this wasn't a newsflash as far as I was concerned. His glee at having found a weak link in my armour cut right through me — the mental scar of my bashing had all but healed in my mind, but now it was well and truly open again. I began getting flashbacks of my bashing, the women's screams, the blood taste in my mouth and the sense of confused vulnerability that only someone severely bashed from behind would understand.

The magistrate finally stepped in. He, like me, wondered where Crane's barrister was going with this apparently unrelated line of questioning. He was suggesting I should be more concerned for my safety from corrupt police than from criminals such as Bill Crane. I disagreed with the proposition, although, in hindsight, I should have fired a question back at him rather than an answer. I should have asked: 'How can I judge who is more dangerous or what their intent is? The combination of corrupt police and criminals is my biggest nightmare.' But I was too slow off the mark.

Then the penny dropped. The lawyer was suggesting that Detective Black was behind my cowardly bashing. There was no link. But it dawned on me that the lawyer was setting the scene for their defence —alleging that I had twisted the evidence against the accused. The defence would be that I was motivated to convict Black, and in doing so, had to convict his client, Bill Crane, and some of the other so-called innocent bystanders, his criminal co-accused. But Black was just a number to me, the fifth cop I'd given evidence against. Convicting him wasn't my job; that was for the court.

Revenge? This seemed a ridiculous defence to me, but I didn't care any more. I was so angry about being put in danger by my employer that I was almost keen for jail myself. I was thankful that there were no press reporters in that courtroom. They were all buzzing around another court situated only 10 metres away, where a former Australian football champion was appearing. The footballer's nickname during his playing days had been 'God'. On this occasion God was on my side, as he legitimately took the heat off me when I desperately needed it. I left the court a broken man; the empty foam cup sat on the edge of the witness box. Crane cursed as the magistrate ordered him back to the slammer.

My conspiracy investigation was a complex one because Crane used go-betweens, one of whom was an experienced criminal I'll call Ben Stanton. After Stanton was charged he also appeared in court a number of times. He confessed to living a life of crime and admitted he had racked up over 100 convictions and considered himself criminally unsuccessful. Stanton was a prolific drug trafficker, an occupation he didn't see as wrong or even immoral; he believed it was a necessity for our community. An interesting assertion, but there was more — he suggested that it was best that he performed this community service of drug trafficking because he had worthwhile values that the other dodgy drug dealers didn't.

Stanton wouldn't sell to children or non-junkies (ordinary, non-illicit drug-taking citizens) whom he referred to as squareheads, nor would he sell drugs on Christmas Day or Good Friday. I noticed he did sell drugs and smoke bongs in front of his teenage daughter, though — a bit of parental example I'm glad I hadn't experienced myself. Outside his self-imposed rules he saw the community as fair game, something to be plundered.

Jail didn't worry him — Stanton was tough. He'd been bashed by cops in a notorious inner-city suburb on two occasions, once in the cells and once on the street. He reportedly told one cop who was laying into him that he 'punched like a girl'. Stanton drove a Ford Fairlane with a bullet hole in the pillar behind the driver's head rest. He assured me that the bullet hadn't passed through anything human before it lodged in the car. 'The gun went off during a fucked-up robbery. No big deal.' I imagined it in the *Trading Post*: 'Car for sale, driven at excessive speeds through red lights, bullet lodged in door pillar, low kilometres, price negotiable.'

His good mate Bill Crane didn't give up easily either. He was still on remand, so he arranged for another bail application, this time with a new barrister. Crane, like most drug manufacturers, liked being free. This bail application had to be made in the Supreme Court, possibly the most beautiful and impressive building in the state of Victoria. It was in one of these majestic hallways that Crane's new barrister approached me and recited my former home address to me. I was dumbstruck. If this was an implied threat, a way of making me go soft on a drug manufacturer, Crane and his barrister were out of luck. I said no to bail, and Crane withdrew his application, I knew my address was known in the underworld but hearing Crane's barrister say it rattled me.

I made my way home and grabbed a pick and shovel. Hard manual labour was my answer to letting off steam. I dug up a large garden bed and threw down a few hundred seeds I'd collected from some of the beautiful mauve poppies that had miraculously sprouted next to my fence at my previous address.

A few weeks later I had a forensic science laboratory training update and saw my poppies during a drug awareness lecture. 'Fucking hell!' I said. The class roared with laughter when I told them that the slide looked like my front garden, and again when I told them how the poppies had become popular with my elderly neighbours who hadn't seen that type of beautiful poppy before. I drove straight home from the lab and spent hours pulling the poppies out, trying to think what low-life might have thrown opium poppy seed into my garden in the first place. It was a little embarrassing to explain to my elderly neighbours that they too had to remove their lovely poppies as well.

The concerns I had about my home address being known were particularly worrying because one of my best mates looks quite similar to me. Should he ever come to or from my house at times other than in blinding sunlight, this put him in danger of being the victim of mistaken identity. Crimes involving mistaken identity are not uncommon in the underworld. Professional killers and thugs don't often have the ability to do surveillance of a target, so they often act on sketchy verbal descriptions of people.

Early in 2003 my life and marriage took another turn for the worse. As my investigation probe deepened I identified another criminal, another of Victoria's former most wanted who was an armed robber. He had offered the police a $20 000 bribe to alter the course of another of

Bill Crane's previous court hearings. It makes you wonder how much potential money is out there for a bent cop, doesn't it? But this time the crook hit a stone wall; honest cops refused the offer. However, no sooner had I identified a new player in my investigation than I realised that this particular criminal lived less than 300 metres away from my new house. What are the odds of that happening? I hadn't moved from the stove into the fire; this was a move from the fire into an incinerator. This crim was virtually a neighbour.

A bit of leadership from my bosses would have been more than welcome. My daily life became a delicate ballet. In the morning I would be greeted by my most-wanted neighbour wearing his trademark bib and brace overalls as he walked past my home to buy his morning paper. Fortunately, he was still unaware that I was a cop, let alone one on his way to work as a corruption investigator — investigating him. It took me some time to tell Tracy of our nearby threat. I was given permission to carry a firearm all the time and spent days finishing off high-security fences around the perimeter of the house to protect myself and Tracy. While I was working I often wept silently, seeing my life collapse around me. At this time I felt ill — I hadn't slept — and, after breaking down at work, I went to see my doctor. He diagnosed acute stress and gave me a month off. I managed to talk him into reducing it to two weeks because no one else could finish my investigation; it was too complex. It was now mid 2003: I'd started that investigation early in 2001.

This wasn't the only reason I was stressed. My marriage was virtually over. I'd been able to keep our relationship civil enough for Tracy to have been surprised when I told her I was leaving. I was confused, I didn't want to be married any more. I was a worthless rat, crushed by the actions of many people over many years. Tracy blamed me for the breakup, and she was right, it was my fault for many reasons. I wasn't thinking straight, I had become isolated and my actions had let our relationship become irretrievable a long time before the actual split. I didn't know who I was any more.

If I was married to anything, it was to my belief that I was going to win against the corrupt bastards who had plagued my police force for so long, but the harder I worked at Internal Affairs the worse it looked.

Some of my colleagues also knew the Force was being eroded by criminals masquerading as cops, and the more we probed the quicker we found ourselves in white-hot danger. As time went by New South Wales, Queensland and Western Australia got their acts into gear with crime and corruption commissions, while Victoria Police looked more and more unprofessional in the way it attempted to tackle corruption. I heard the public downplaying of corruption in this state by many people who knew better. I wasn't the only person seething over these lies.

As with any marriage breakup there were emotional outbursts of love and frustration between Tracy and me. We each took our personal belongings out of our home; I went into a rented house far away and Tracy went elsewhere. I had never felt particularly safe at that house, and my senses told me that the secrecy of that address had been compromised anyway. As it turned out I was right. Criminals had identified that address too, despite my best attempts at keeping it secret. I wondered again whether my visitors that night had really been burglars, or something more sinister. I'll never know.

I wanted to move to a place where no one knew where I was living. I had lost 16 kilograms in less than two months, joking to a police mate that I should write an article about weight loss for the *Australian Women's Weekly*. Something like: 'All you need do is leave home, put up with death threats and assault and intimidation from underworld criminals and the weight just falls off you. It's easy!'

Tracy's final comment was that I had changed. As I drove to the house I had rented, I thought about it. Tracy was right; I had changed. I trusted no one. I understood what I was feeling, but for the first time in my life I asked, 'Why?' I'm not a religious man, but I thought there must be some reason behind all this. For the first time in years I was on my own. I had no cash, Tracy and I had divvied up our possessions and I had rented a house in a foreign suburb. I didn't even know where the local shop was (I needed cigarettes, not food).

I walked to the kitchen and noticed the washing machine had overflowed. I left it and grabbed a magnum-size bottle of red wine and sat at the top of the stairs at the front of the house. Quietly weeping, I drank it and followed it with a second bottle. Next morning as the sun rose, I awoke to find myself lying at the front door with a dry mouth and a headache, realising one thing — that house was to have been my oasis, but the sudden isolation would have killed me: it just wasn't meant to be.

At about 6.30 that morning I packed everything back into the boxes and carried them down the stairs and into the trailer, including a stainless steel refrigerator which I only dropped once. The scar from the fall is still prominent on my fridge. I put all my belongings into a city storage warehouse and drove away. My muscles were killing me. I hadn't eaten, yet I wasn't hungry.

With me I had an armful of clothes, a sleeping bag and half a packet of cigarettes. I didn't know where to go, so I drove aimlessly around the city before stopping in the carpark of the boathouse at Fairfield, 5 kilometres from the CBD. I was low on fuel in many ways. The boathouse was a special place for me, a place of love. Every minute I had spent there was etched in my memory. I didn't want to get out of the car as tears had begun to run down my face. This was the lowest point in my life. I was broke, my marriage had failed, I had nowhere permanent to live and I was being intimidated and tracked by underworld criminals.

I walked down to the river. The brown Yarra water flowed past, winding and twisting as it made its way to the sea. I contemplated life, love and death. A broken foam cup floated by. I turned and headed back to the car, leaving the cup to swirl in circles. I drove to a mate's house and stopped there for a while.

I then spent a few months investigating some of Victoria Police's worst corruption while sleeping at friends' houses and using my brother's spare car as a wardrobe. I was cash strapped; I'd spent almost $3500 for two days' accommodation in my rented house, including the bond and one month's rent in advance. But I was used to living that sort of life from my childhood at Scotch and then camping with my old man — from one extreme to another. I laughed with my mates that I was the only bloke driving a Mercedes who had his clothes and a sleeping bag in the back of it.

Friends were really good to me in very difficult times. They had their own lives to think about, families, businesses and jobs, without my intimidation and misery being brought into their homes. As Melbourne's gangland killings and corruption crisis worsened they read about it in the newspapers, but none of them asked me what was going on. They told me I could stay as long as I wanted. I will never forget their generosity. I soon realised that this was not one man standing; I had underground support. One good thing came from my current situation: if I didn't know where I was going to live on any given week, the criminals didn't either. I was momentarily safe although I couldn't settle down. My personal disaster had made me safer from further intimidation or violence, yet psychologically I was so low that I was in far more danger from myself than from anyone else.

I was being eaten from the inside out. I had no prospect of a future as a policeman and, no matter how many people surrounded me at any given time, I felt isolated. I gave up the idea of getting promoted within the police force. I even tried to move into a training role, to take stock of my life, but I was told I didn't have the operational experience for the role and didn't even get an interview. What a joke: I'd worked at Homicide and Task Force Lorimer. They just didn't want a rat.

I hit rock bottom, but there was something I had to promise myself. I had to make sure I did everything in my power to ensure that this situation would never happen to anyone else. My goal was to ensure that the notoriously poor treatment of whistleblowers and corruption investigators would stop — enough was enough. I knew it wasn't enough just to tell the story; I had to make a splash and ensure that its ripple caused some positive energy and, hopefully, a cure. I wanted to cut some new ground and open the door for any others who felt betrayed by the brotherhood for merely choosing to do the right thing.

13

Change of heart

Once more I went down to the river and stood at its edge, reflecting on my life. My miserable pondering was interrupted by a fresh-faced young woman who smiled sweetly and spoke to me. I responded, but I was too startled by her fair hair, blue eyes and innocent, cheeky smile to recall what she'd said. Nor did I have the slightest clue whether my reply was appropriate.

I was sure she could sense that I was having a bad time of it. She did most of the talking, telling me about her job in helping victims of crime, which she loved. I was attracted to her positive, can-do attitude; she wasn't bitter or resentful as were so many in policing. But I recall little of the conversation. She was very attractive, with an attitude that life was good. In policing, bitterness is a symptom of good people consistently seeing others in traumatic situations and feeling they are unable to help. I had always hoped to leave the police force before I became bitter. I'm at a loss as to how such a feeling can be addressed. Maybe it can't. I remembered little of that impromptu chat, but I did remember that the gorgeous girl's name was Sarah, and she was going to send me an email inviting me out for a drink after work.

Sure enough she did, but I had to decline the invitation — it was not the sort of function a rat or someone from the filth would attend without a death wish or suitable body armour. It was a function held by a particular squad. It wasn't Sarah's fault. She didn't understand where I worked or what I'd done and she didn't have a clue about the downside of the police brotherhood. She simply did her job in the Police Victims' Unit, helping victims of homicides and rapes, and went home.

I saw Sarah again and asked her out for a drink as a return favour. It wasn't what you'd call romantic, though; we were to meet the lads from my old CIB. Sarah agreed and I picked her up in my brother's car. She noticed that my clothes filled the back seats but said nothing. We met the lads; she enjoyed herself, loved a joke and held her own. I felt something special for this young girl but I had no heart left — the last of it had been shattered a few weeks before and I wasn't about to allow that to happen again.

We met again at work and decided to have dinner. We met in Camberwell, a pleasant suburb of Melbourne, and stopped at a little bar and restaurant. It was a hot night and we decided to sit outside. We sat down, ordered drinks and started talking about how to save the world. I felt comfortable being myself among civilians, but Sarah wasn't a civilian. I had to tell her my story so she knew what she was getting into. I wasn't presumptuous enough to think of a relationship with her, but she needed to know as a friend.

Sarah listened intently to my life in a nutshell, beginning with how my life had changed for the worse after I had made some tough decisions sixteen years ago. I told her I was sleeping on the floor at a mate's house, had little money to speak of, was separated from my wife, lived in fear, carried a gun and that my ongoing job prospects were minimal because I was considering telling my story on television. I explained why I drove a borrowed Mercedes that had a sleeping bag and my clothes on the back seat.

As we spoke the clouds above us got darker and darker, the wind had stopped and, although there was no sign of the sun, it was still hot. Then a drop of rain the size of a 20-cent piece hit the road next to our table, and seconds later down came the rain. It was Melbourne's first big storm after almost a decade of drought.

We sat in temporary silence under our umbrella as the rain grew heavier. An umbrella has one obvious function apart from advertising coffee: unfortunately, ours did not fulfil it. We rushed inside the cafe and found another table. I was curious why a large bucket was placed next to it, and found out when water gushed onto me. The roof leaked. Sarah laughed, but not for long: there were two holes in the roof.

We spoke for hours that night, not small talk but important things, real issues and how we thought things could change. I'd told Sarah about my past for her sake, not mine. I knew she was likely to come in for some unwanted attention for merely associating with me. I asked her to keep to herself what I had said. But she wasn't one to hide the truth so she was ostracised by some people she'd previously considered her friends. It's a fickle world.

I had told Sarah I was going to speak out and I braced myself for the worst; it was realistic to assume that the bent cops I spoke about might seek revenge. Then I had to consider the possibility of saying something that could put me in contempt of court. So I prepared myself for the possibility of jail, still a possibility although I had no intention of saying anything contemptuous, stupid or defamatory. No serving police officer had ever considered going to the media like this so I knew I could be sacked, post haste. An interesting prospect when one has no money.

I forced myself to focus on a solution to the problem of corruption. I had spent months creating a document for the future direction of a super anti-crime and corruption agency, three years sourcing documents, records and notes from around the world. I put together all the details I'd collected while studying corruption, culture and ethics, both interstate and overseas, where I had spoken to as many people as I could: ordinary Australians, Chinese, Brits and Malaysians, but I found a defeatist attitude — 'You'll never change it', 'It's too rampant' or, 'It's already out of control.' Unfortunately, most of them suggested the nineteenth-century solution — long jail sentences and corporal punishment. I have my doubts.

Perhaps history does hold the answer. In 1881, a US Federal District Court judge looked down at a convicted murderer in New Mexico and said: 'Jose Manuel Xavier Gonzales, in a few short weeks it will be spring, the snows of winter will flee away, the ice will vanish and the air will become soft and balmy. In short, Jose Manuel Xavier Gonzales, the annual miracle of the years will awaken and come to pass. But you won't be there …' The judge commanded the local sheriff to swing Gonzales by the neck from 'a knotting bough of a sturdy oak tree . . . And then, Jose Manuel Xavier Gonzales, I further command the Sheriff to retire quickly from your dangling corpse, so that vultures may descend from the heavens upon your filthy body, until nothing shall remain but the bare bleached bones of a cold-blooded, bloodthirsty, throat-cutting, chilli-eating, sheep-herding, murdering, son-of-a-bitch.'

While the judge made damn sure Gonzales never reoffended, it is interesting to observe that the places that still execute people remain some of the most corrupt countries in the world today. China, for instance, has had a chequered history of executing public officials found to be corrupt, yet their corruption is said to be so bad that it can be measured as a percentage of GDP.

I decided to combine my ethical leadership ideas with proven international anti-corruption strategies. Over a period of time I created a master plan involving both reward and punishment. It took in the perspectives of philosophical ethicists, pragmatic investigators, the lawmakers and a marketing strategy, an unprecedented combination. I believe that the answer to our problems lay in an independent commission against corruption. New South Wales had one, but I wanted to incorporate marketing, ethics and prevention as much as investigation and punishment.

Before the gangland wars really took hold, I had spoken to a member of the state Labor government. Having assessed Victoria's situation and believing things were about to explode, I sat down with this politician and carefully explained my experiences and background, as well as telling him that the state appeared to be heading for a monumental crime and corruption crisis. I explained my international experiences and how corruption could fuel gangland warfare. I told him, more or less, that 'The result of a void in the underworld is a vicious vacuum, culminating in the most violent criminals fighting over vacated territory and power. Some don't even know why they are fighting. But the leaders rarely get their hands dirty; they often hand out pathetically small amounts of cash to desperadoes who are willing to do their dirty deeds for them. This ensures a long and bloody war: in the world of a crime boss, both cash and desperadoes are easy to come by.

'There comes a day when some criminals want out. They desperately need to know who the good cops are, most importantly, the good cops who are capable of doggedly collecting evidence and are highly proficient at investigating organised crime, who can present the best case possible on their behalf. They also need one who won't welsh on a deal after conviction or, in the worst case scenario, an acquittal.

Once they've opened their mouth and broken the *omerta*, the code of silence, 'these crims need good cops far more than any law-abiding citizen because often their life depends on it. It should come as no surprise that when many of these crims want to cleanse their souls and turn police informer the jungle drums start beating for them. Here is the problem. When there are allegations of police corruption, these criminals aren't confident they can trust anyone, especially the police. So when they're cornered they figure their best defence is attack. Their reasoning goes that you may be a danger to me, so I'll kill you first. This is the worst possible scenario.'

Understandably, the MP was a little sceptical about what I had said and he probably thought I was exaggerating. Nevertheless, I pushed hard, and insisted that something had to be done. His response at the end of our conversation was an honest one — he thought I was too close to it all. He might as well have said he believed I was suffering from clouded judgment. I'd been at the sharp end of the spear for a long time, I couldn't deny that, but I knew I was right — things were going to get worse.

I was too close to the action, I knew that very well indeed, but it could also be said that I was the only person in this mess that didn't have an agenda. I had no other motive than to get the system fixed, and for fixing it I would receive nothing. Everyone else could be said to have a motive for their action or inaction.

I guess my story did sound fanciful, but unfortunately, I was right: the situation got worse. Melbourne's underworld soon came up from the underground and dark alleyways and onto the streets. Since 1998 there had been twenty-five underworld killings, at least a dozen of which were believed to be related. The situation became so bad that

Melbourne's crime wave was being reported overseas. Criminals began killing each other on the streets in broad daylight and police were being ferried into court charged with allegations of involvement in organised crime.

Despite my reservations, I knew I had to do something. I promised myself this would be the last time I put my head in the lion's jaws. I simply resigned myself to the fact that I was a dead man walking, and my attitude changed. Every day after that has been a bonus. I needed to take the risk, I had to tell my story; it was the last hope I had of ever feeling truly free. As the gangland death count kept rising into the twenties I knew it was time to tell my story publicly, despite the risks.

If I was going to speak out, I had to juggle the legalities of what I said, how I said it and to whom I said it. I also had to voice a solution, a real solution; mine, not some bolt-on stopgap measure.

One day I stood up among the empty workstations around me, switched off the lights and walked out of the corruption building alone, carrying a cardboard box, as my former boss Neil O'Sullivan had done. My box, like his, contained a range of personal awards, including two awards presented by the governor of Victoria, a Royal Humane Society Award, the Sir Vincent Fairfax glass trophy, a chief commissioner's commendation and numerous other commendations. Each of them related to incidents involving homicides, life-threatening fires, investigative leadership and the arrest of armed and dangerous criminals — seventeen years' worth.

I went to see my doctor. This was a man who had seen me through many of my worst policing incidents. He had left his surgery to help me deal with the fallout of almost killing someone in a wild brawl after two attempted murders. He had treated me after I was bashed at the Hellfire Club and reluctantly put stitches in my face even though his advice had been to see a specialist. The possibility of scarring worried him more than it did me. The doc had also been around when I was stewing over my address being given to criminals, among other things.

He diagnosed post-traumatic stress reaction, looked me in the eyes and respectfully said, 'It's over, Simon.' With the stroke of a pen it was all over. Not in the blaze of glory I had expected, but in a small room not dissimilar to the one in which my initial recruitment interview had taken place. I hadn't expected my police career to end like that, but then someone once said that 'The pen was mightier than the sword'. It certainly didn't hurt any less.

I took my medical certificate and drove off in my brother's car. I didn't contact the office; the people who cared knew what was going on. I never went back. It took eleven days for a supervisor to realise I was no longer coming in to work. Obviously no one back at the office had bothered to check on me for almost two weeks. Just as well I hadn't had a heart attack at my desk.

I had to get my story out without the help of a PR expert. I wanted to ensure that the fallout was to be positive for the good police and bad for the corrupt. The vast majority of the Force is made up of decent, hardworking people and I didn't want the public to think otherwise. On the whole, I was proud of Victoria Police, despite it being the same organisation that had crushed my spirit.

My decision to speak out had been a tough one, but now another tough decision awaited me. How was I going to tell my story? I had thought about going to commercial television, but a number of things concerned me. The maximum time allotted for my story on *60 Minutes* would be twelve to fourteen minutes I liked the program but twelve minutes was too short; likewise the time for stories shown on *A Current Affair* or *Today Tonight*. On the other hand, those programs were very popular, so the story would be televised nationally and to huge audiences. But I didn't believe that the amount of time I would be allotted could do the story justice. Besides, I would be at the mercy of an interviewer, and therefore not the master of my own story. My story couldn't be told that way. It wasn't an isolated incident; it was a long-running saga.

I didn't want to sensationalise my life's story. I knew it was unique and I knew it stood on its own merits. Being broke, I thought long and hard about payment. Despite my lack of cash I decided not to be paid. I was doing this because the system needed to be changed, a culture needed to be reflected upon and, whether they liked it or not, Australians needed to hear about it. I'd long passed worrying about my own wellbeing; I figured I had nothing left to lose. That fact alone made me the most dangerous person the Victoria Police employed.

I knew the time had come to call my mate in Queensland, Damien 'Dib' Morgan, or 'Damo' as I call him. We had met and worked together during the Sir Vincent Fairfax Fellowship days. Damo always had his finger on the pulse. Being based in Queensland, he had seen the Fitzgerald Inquiry on Police Corruption in 1989 that had led to the downfall of the Bjelke-Petersen government and the jailing of the chief commissioner of police. Damo knew the stakes.

Damo said, 'Gov, it's up to you mate, bloody hell, it's a big call. Ethics was meant to be warm and fuzzy, it wasn't meant to be like this.' We laughed. 'I'll back you all the way, but it's bloody heavy.'

I'm not one to go back on a decision, so once I made it I knew I'd stick to it. Then, in a moment of absolute clarity, I knew what I had to do. I was the most danger that corruption faced, the flashpoints in my life and the tough decisions I'd made, for better or worse had made me strong. As they say, what doesn't kill you makes you stronger. I knew who I was and what I stood for. Yes I was an underdog, but I was powerful. This situation was magnified in my case because I had nothing left to lose, I'd been cornered and my back was against the wall. I was ready to rumble.

I told Damo: 'I'm doing this program as me — no pixilation, no blacked-out face, no actor and no voice change. I am doing it, as me, my head, my voice and my fucking neck on the line. If anything happens to me, it is not your fault. Now, can you please tell me what program I should go on?'

Damo knew I had made up my mind. He said, 'The ABC's the place I reckon. *Four Corners* is a good show, but you don't want to throw a grenade at the police force. I think *Australian Story* is the go. Think about it — you'll get twenty-eight minutes of prime time, no ads, and you tell your story, your way. But you'll need a handful of people to go on it with you!'

Damo arranged for me to meet Mara Blazic from *Australian Story*, who introduced me to producer Belinda Hawkins. I made a list of friends and associates who would have something to say about my experiences and would be willing to say it on national television.

My mother and my sister Binny were both willing, though reluctant. I asked my former boss, the newly retired Neil O'Sullivan, if he would be prepared to go on with me. (I still had the tins of Nugget shoe polish he had given me. I hadn't used any since he'd gone.) He also agreed. For an old-school cop such as Neil, speaking on television was completely foreign; it was for Mum, too, because she hated speaking in front of even a handful of people, let alone a national television audience. Everyone on the program had their own personal reasons for doing the show but it came down to loyalty, honesty, truth and the greater good.

Two of my very good mates, who work in the corporate sector, also put their hands up to go on the program, despite my warnings of possible retribution. Both are very strong individuals and committed to doing the right thing. Damo also offered. A few days later I had enough people to do the program, though none of the participants really wanted to do it, including me. I told everyone to take time to think about their decision. No one committed immediately, but each of us had our own personal reasons for wanting to do their bit.

I first met producer Belinda Hawkins in a coffee shop. She was an attractive woman in her late thirties or early forties, and very well spoken. I didn't trust her and I daresay she didn't trust me. Building trust between cops and journos takes time, a luxury that unfortunately neither of us had. I hated that fact. Our approach to language was totally different. I had spent my police career trying to express complex issues in simple terms, using a lot of analogies, as cops do. Most people I'd dealt with in my career understood what the 'giggle' was, 'an earn', 'a dirty 30' or what 'pro' or 'anti' meant. But even when I used everyday comments, such as 'cat and mouse' or 'crushing bugs with sledgehammers', I couldn't win. Hawkins wanted it straight, but this was part of my everyday vocabulary, that's just the way I talked now. It was years since I had been a student at Scotch College and even then I didn't listen very intently. The last person I knew who used the King's English was my grandmother. On the street, these phrases don't need explanation: they are part of the culture; everyone uses them. But Belinda was unfamiliar with street culture and used English differently.

At times she used four- or five-syllable words that took me time to understand. My usual response to Belinda's highbrow lingo was, 'Oh, come on, spare me, will you?' To which she would reply, 'Oh, sorry, I'll drop it down to gutter level for you.' We often duelled, but ended up having a laugh despite the pressure. Our lives were also very different. I lived a brutal challenge from day to day, yet Belinda's challenge was to temporarily live other people's lives. It took quite some time for Belinda to understand the way I lived.

It took me a short time to realise that Belinda was a career journalist of a high calibre, winner of a prestigious Walkley Award. Early on our relationship was cautious until I broke down on camera. Up until then I constantly reminded myself that Belinda was a journo, not a mate. This became impossible after I'd told her things I hadn't even told my mother. I had only one request — that Belinda finish the story in a positive light. I might have an opportunity to teach once I had been sacked from the Force for appearing.

At times throughout the filming and interview process I felt I was being pushed unnecessarily hard in some aspects of the story in order to get a fiery or animated response. Sometimes I felt betrayed because the rules I had set did not include my breaking down on camera. One of my requests was that no one was named in the program except for willing participants, including people already convicted in court. A conviction made these people fair game for the media but I argued at length with Belinda, telling her it was my story, not theirs. I also believed that everyone should be given a second chance, bent cops included — it is up to them whether they take it. But most of all, the story was about the need for change.

The first day of filming I was surfing at Port Campbell. Ron Ekkle, the ABC cameraman assigned to the story, said that, according to the surf report, Torquay's world famous Bells Beach had only half-metre waves. He was right, Bells was small, but then he drew the wrong conclusion when he went on to say that Port Campbell would be the same.

Before we left Melbourne Belinda told me she needed some driving footage. I liked getting away from the city so she figured we first needed some shots of the environment in which I'd worked. I drove around the CBD as Ron Ekkle rolled the film for the first time. Then, apparently, we needed a change of angle, so Ron strapped the camera to the bonnet of my car. It was like a bloody beacon as I drove along the most populated streets in Melbourne. The angle picked up my face in the windscreen with the city buildings reflected on the glass.

People on the street stopped and pointed, and I heard a woman say, 'That guy's being filmed! Who is he?' The answer from her friend was, 'Ah, nah, he's no one.' I desperately hoped that this no one wouldn't drive past a someone who knew him, especially a someone of the police variety.

After the city footage had been shot, we made our way down to Port Campbell and arrived in mid afternoon to the raw might of a 3-metre sea. So much for Bells as a predictor. Swirling water and a roaring sea inspire me, and even though I knew I would not make it out to the really big waves, I said I'd give it a go anyway, because I wanted to get wet. Thirty minutes later, I was being rapidly pushed closer and closer to one of the Twelve Apostles by a fierce rip. I picked one of the smaller waves to ride into shore to avoid one of the large rock formations I was rapidly approaching. This was about self-preservation rather than high-quality wave choice.

Ron rolled the film and captured the ride for the program. The next day he filmed my lunatic attempt — on my own at dawn — at surfing 4-metre Massacre Reef near Peterborough. I sat upright on my board, relaxed and began looking to relaunch my big wave career that had petered out a few years before. As I peered over the top of a monstrous swell my reincarnation was put permanently on hold as I saw and then felt the bone-crushing action of a Peterborough freak set. I'd seen these waves many years before. They literally appear from nowhere. Even the local surfers get caught by these sets and here I was, at the age of thirty-six, caught in the wrong place at the wrong time with an ABC camera crew filming from the clifftop. I was pounded by huge waves of cold, unforgiving southern juice. My body felt as if it had been involved in eight individual car crashes, each followed by a washing machine spin cycle in Antarctica. The one major difference was, years ago, I could have held my breath for at least thirty seconds because I didn't smoke like a petrol refinery. Thankfully, I made it onto dry land and over the jagged rocks with my bare feet without too much more damage having been done. My head popped up through a rock cave in front of Belinda and the camera crew. 'Can we go now?' I pleaded.

'No, just a little bit more filming,' Belinda said. Those seven words were starting to annoy the shit out of me already, but there were plenty more times I'd hear them. We headed for the township of Port Campbell. As we entered civilisation for the first time in twenty-four hours we came across the local newsagent with the front page poster displayed out the front. 'Action on bent cops', the headline screamed.

Just moments before, I'd been surfing 4-metre waves in the middle of nowhere, on my own, but my tough exterior immediately broke down. Could it all be over? After all this time? The camera rolled as I read the headline. The article said the chief commissioner appeared to be sanctioning an independent commission against corruption.

My head shook, I couldn't believe it. Wow, common sense was going to prevail. Then, as Ron was filming me reading the paper, I verbally backed the chief's reported call for a commission, feeling that everything I had fought for hadn't been in vain. I fought back tears of relief. It was too good to be true, I thought. Spontaneously, I said, 'I always thought good would defeat evil. Here we go.' The *Herald Sun* had given me a glimmer of hope.

It was too good to be true. A short time later the chief commissioner either backed down on her call for a corruption commission, or had been misrepresented in her support for one. It mattered little, because clearly I was supporting one. And I had locked in my opinion. I was well aware that I would be the first serving police officer ever to publicly push a government to establish a crime and corruption commission. It was a stand I was happy with, I'd done the research on it. Nevertheless, I'd have preferred to have the chief commissioner's support on the issue. But by this stage I was beyond caring about backup.

I went home exhausted. Belinda warned me that the interview process was next. I was worried about the interview, because every person I'd seen on *Australian Story* was reflecting on a historical event, something they could put up on a shelf afterwards. My position was dramatically different — I was still living it. It was raw, happening now. I worried for the safety of many people.

Soon after our flooded dinner engagement Sarah and I had become romantically involved. She was incredibly supportive, but being with me made her vulnerable. Despite this, Sarah moved into my mate's house with me. It was not ideal; I was sleeping on the floor with a gun and a clock radio. My clothes were still on the back seat of my brother's spare car.

I knew I couldn't forgive myself if something happened to Sarah. I was already duelling with my conscience knowing that she was being treated differently by some people in the police force. Ignoring my advice, she made no secret of our relationship. It was a brave move, considering she knew I was about to blow the lid off some of the murky elements of Victoria Police.

Then something happened that rocked my foundations. On the morning of Monday, 17 May 2004, Sarah and I were woken by the 6 o'clock radio news. I only heard the sentence: 'Two corruption witnesses have been murdered in the latest twist in Melbourne's gangland crisis.' We'd heard enough. We walked to the back porch, puffed on our first cigarettes for the day and watched the sunrise.

A career criminal named Terrence Hodson and his wife Christine, who lived in the wealthy suburb of Kew and who were heavily protected, had been assassinated in their home by an unknown gunman or gunmen prior to Hodson's appearance in court. They lived 2 kilometres from where I had been living months before. They were both shot in the head at close range. Terrence Hodson had been waiting to be dealt with in the Supreme Court after indicating he would give evidence against police. He and two police detectives had been charged with drug-related offences. Unfortunately, the detectives were from Victoria Police's freshly named Major Drug Investigation Division, a highly embarrassing situation for some, even if one of the police had had charges withdrawn after Hodson's murder. Originally, the three men faced charges over an alleged conspiracy to burgle a house in East Oakleigh and the theft of drugs reported to be worth $1.3 million.

The Hodsons had been offered protection but allegedly knocked it back. I knew the feeling: the more security measures you wanted meant the more people and cops knew who you were and where you lived. It was a Catch-22, particularly when you don't trust many cops. For me it was a day for soul searching as the press gathered around the scene of yet another grisly crime and shot footage of the victims' bodies being taken away in body bags.

It was obvious that my appearance on *Australian Story* would be too late for many people and that Melbourne's underworld situation had well and truly hit a new flashpoint. My prediction had become a reality — this was crime's perfect storm.

Belinda Hawkins's original concern that I wouldn't follow through with the filming intensified after the Hodson assassinations. My television interview lasted five hours. Tape after tape, hour after hour, I spoke about my life and corruption. It was hard, really, really hard. Finishing the interview was a real kick in the guts; I no longer had control of the end product. I was a wreck that night and soon went from being a social smoker to a Marlboro man. I also found alcohol to be a good substitute for food and used it to wash down my new pack-a-day cigarette habit.

Belinda also began smoking. She was worried about what was happening in Victoria's criminal world and, in particular, what would happen after the story went to air. She told me she was under immense pressure from me, the ABC and those who didn't want the story told. She became acutely aware that in becoming involved with me, in telling my story, she had put herself at risk, a warning she had shrugged off early in the filming process. Belinda told me that she had begun receiving crank calls: the scum on the other end of the line had decided that the messenger was fair game. As we stopped talking and sat reflecting on what a mess we were in, Belinda's phone rang. I watched as her face went pale. It was, she told me when she'd hung up, the same voice as before, asking cryptically, 'Have you checked your security system?'

'Everything will be all right' are very easy words to say when it's someone else putting their neck on the line, but it's different when it becomes personal. I felt compassion for Belinda when she admitted how many rogue calls like that she had had — she was new to the subtleties of threat.

On the evening after my long interview, I hit the proverbial wall. It was the first time I had realised how much I had been through. When things had gotten tough, time and time again, I always told myself, 'It'll be all right tomorrow.' But I'd always looked at my misfortune in an incident by incident form, never holistically as I had been forced to do over the five hours of the interviews.

A sobering thought entered my mind. I had narrated my story without repetition, spoken for five hours, incident after incident, detail after detail, year by year. I stood on my mate's back porch with my beautiful Sarah and realised I was no longer confident that there would be a tomorrow, not a good one anyway. I always believed that good would defeat evil but for the first time I started to think it was a hoax. I was still the main witness for four court cases that involved a number of notorious criminals, no matter what happened on *Australian Story*. Everything indicated that the stakes had risen to a new level, but I hadn't read the telltale warning signs of pending danger.

Occasionally, Sarah and I flirted with the idea of taking off somewhere to have a break from Melbourne before *Australian Story* went to air, but I knew in my heart that I had to stay in Victoria and stick it out. Besides, it just wasn't in me to flee something. I'd seen what being on the lam did for crims — they always said it was worse than jail — so we set ourselves to tough it out.

Herald Sun

THURSDAY, APRIL 8, 2004 — NEWS PICTORIAL

ACTION ON BENT COPS

New powers due in war on corruption

John Ferguson, Nick Papps and Shelley Hodgson

ROGUE police will be rooted out under sweeping anti-corruption powers to be introduced by Premier Steve Bracks.

The Ombudsman's office — Victoria's official watchdog of police and government affairs — is to be handed greater powers, possibly to mirror a royal commission.

Corrupt police could be forced to give evidence for investigations by the Ombudsman, who could also instigate independent inquiries without a complaint.

Premier Bracks met the new Ombudsman, George Brouwer, yesterday when giving him more muscle was discussed.

An announcement on the police anti-corruption package could be made today following allegations of police corruption in Victoria.

The moves come as Police Chief Commissioner Christine Nixon interrupted her holidays to suggest a state crime commission to end corruption — a call unlikely to be backed by the Premier.

"If that's what we need, it would deal not only with criminals, it would deal with police officers who are criminals as well," she said.

It is believed the Government is examining further measures to tackle the gangland war, in which 23 people have been murdered in five years.

It's also believed to be considering measures including:

FORCING police officers to declare all their financial interests, including houses, shares and other assets.

OFFICERS could be made to learn more about ethics in policing amid allegations of corruption.

Continued Page 4

One of the many headlines suggesting that government was about to tackle police corruption. Like other announcements, nothing came of this. COURTESY NEWS LTD

Herald Sun

www.heraldsun.com.au

WEDNESDAY, APRIL 7, 2004 — NEWS PICTORIAL — CITY: BECOMING FINE. MAX: 19. PAGE 64 — $1* (Incl. GST)

FOOTY CARDS $1.50 WITH TOKEN — COMPLETE THE SET — P2

7-DAY TV GUIDE
LABOUR OF LOVE
GOOD FRIDAY APPEAL

Policeman gave me a gun – criminal

DETECTIVE ACCUSED

Lewis Moran

Moran's simple farewell

ABOUT 200 people paid their respects to murdered crime family head Lewis Moran at a simple funeral service yesterday.

Estranged wife Judy Moran walked behind the coffin as it was carried from St Therese's Catholic Church, Essendon.

Mrs Moran has now laid to rest her two criminal sons Mark and Jason and both of their fathers — all killed in underworld executions.

Lewis Moran's partner of eight years, Virginia Strazdas, sat in the front row during the service.

Reports, Pages 4-5

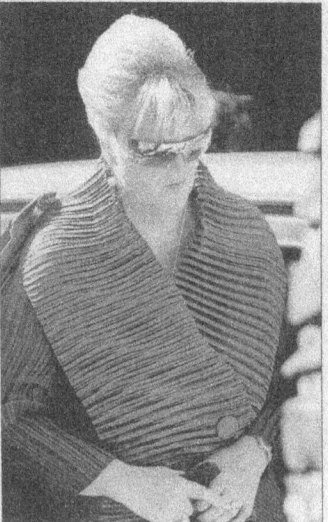

All gone: Judy Moran was a lonely figure at her former partner's funeral yesterday. Picture: JON HARGEST

Jeremy Kelly

A SUSPENDED police officer has been named as the provider of the murder weapon in one of Melbourne's gangland killings.

It is the first direct link between alleged police corruption and Melbourne's underworld killings, which have claimed 23 lives since 1998.

Senior Victorian police sources confirmed the allegation was made.

They say a career criminal had told police a detective gave him a gun that was later used in one of the more recent gangland killings.

Suppression orders and pending court cases prevent the Herald Sun from identifying the criminal, the victim, and the policeman.

While the criminal has named the policeman he says provided the weapon, it is not known whether the gun was handed over with the knowledge it was to be used in the murder.

The criminal, who is in jail awaiting trial on serious offences, made the claim late last year.

The detective has been charged with separate corruption offences, and is suspended.

Pressure is now expected to grow on the State Government for a judicial inquiry into alleged police corruption.

Ethical Standards Department Acting Assistant Commissioner Stephen Fontana would not comment on specific allegations last night.

"There are a number of allegations made from time to time, and we are investigating those as a matter of course," he said.

GANGLAND KILLINGS

"Victoria Police will not comment on ongoing investigations or specific allegations until the matter has concluded. The Ethical Standards Department continues to investigate a number of issues."

As the allegation was revealed: **AUTHORITIES** moved to seize more than $1 million in property and bank accounts held by murdered criminal Lewis Moran, 58, who was unemployed when he was shot dead in Brunswick last week.

ACCUSED drug trafficker Carl Williams withdrew an application to vary his bail so he could travel overseas.

Mr Williams, who faces charges of trafficking $20 million in amphetamines and threatening to kill a detective, applied to the County Court to alter the places and times he has to report to police while on bail.

Continued Page 4

Lloyd out two

ESSENDON'S Matthew Lloyd was banned for two matches at the AFL tribunal last night after being found guilty of striking St Kilda's Nick Dal Santo.

Report, Page 92

A reporter warned me that this referred to the detective I'd seen 'associating' with the underworld identity in a city hotel; the criminal was now accusing him of supplying a gun.
COURTESY NEWS LTD

Police shields

Call for cop bodyguards

Evonne Barry and Laeta Antonysen

Police whose lives were threatened while investigating corrupt cops should be given bodyguards, the Opposition said this morning.

Victoria Police admitted today at least three threats had been made against members of its anti-corruption taskforce, Ceja.

They included one investigator being sent two bullets, etched with his and his wife's names, last month. The wife and child of another were followed to a kindergarten about a year ago.

Opposition police spokesman Kim Wells warned this morning the lives of officers and their families were at risk.

He claimed the threatened officers had been offered only burglar alarms and home security.

"If it means that these men need a minder then that's what should happen, but the security offered to these men has been absolutely pathetic," Wells said.

"Once they leave their homes, my understanding is that these guys are on their own."

Police Minister Andre Haermeyer branded Wells' comments "ill-informed and reckless".

Deputy Commissioner Peter Nancarrow echoed those sentiments, saying public speculation about security only lessened its impact.

Nancarrow, Ceja's chairman, said "adequate action" had been taken to secure at-risk officers.

He would not elaborate on security measures, but said the member who found bullets in his private mailbox had since taken time off.

Police refused to confirm whether the bullets were police-issue, but Nancarrow said those who sent them would be dealt with harshly.

"They will be caught. Those found will be subject to the full force of the law."

Nancarrow said one policeman had already been charged with threatening a Ceja taskforce member 12 months ago. That member's wife and child were later followed.

But Nancarrow said that neither Ceja member had left the taskforce.

Police Association head Paul Mullett said internal disputes should be resolved "through sensible dialogue".

"You don't go and conduct what is a very weak and gutless act of this type," he told 3AW.

Three days before my Australian Story program went to air, in May 2004, there was a call for corruption investigators to be protected. COURTESY NEWS LTD

Inquiry on leak of addresses

CARLY CRAWFORD

VICTORIA Police is investigating how the home addresses of three corruption investigators were leaked to the underworld.

The probe comes as more disturbing details emerge about threats against the police who are trying to weed out bent cops.

It is understood at least one officer has moved home four times in a year. Another has been intimidated by a notorious gangland criminal.

The Ceja taskforce investigators involved are believed to be among the three whose home addresses have been leaked to criminals.

Opposition police spokesman Kim Wells revealed the developments yesterday.

"We know this is of concern to Victoria Police because they are investigating how these leaks happened," he said.

Mr Wells said one corruption investigator who was subjected to threats had moved house four times in 12 months.

One officer was confronted by an underworld figure accompanied by a detective who he was investigating. The confrontation involved a criminal who is now in custody and the encounter took place in the city.

But that investigator's address is understood to be one of the three leaked. Another address belonged to the officer who received two bullets in the mailbox inscribed with his and his wife's name.

The other leaked address belonged to the officer whose wife and child were followed to a kindergarten and watched.

The revelations came amid rumours that surveillance cameras at the home of slain informer Terrence Hodson had no tape in them at the time of his execution.

Hodson was to give evidence against two detectives, David Miechel and Paul Dale, suspended over their alleged involvement in a $1.3 million drug rip-off.

Police Minister Andre Haermeyer would not comment on speculation surrounding the Hodson shooting, which happened in Kew last Sunday.

Asked whether there was a need for an independent investigation into police corruption, Mr Haermeyer said: "These are operational matters. I have full confidence in the integrity of the police conducting these investigations."

The State Opposition has decided to back moves towards a permanent police integrity commission. Until this week, it had supported the State Government's resistance to the push for an independent probe.

The Government has strengthened the Ombudsman's office with additional powers and $1 million.

The Ombudsman and internal police investigators within the Ethical Standards Department are the only authorities responsible for keeping corruption in check.

Monash criminologist Associate Professor Colleen Lewis believes the only way to restore public confidence in the force is to establish a permanent and independent police corruption watchdog.

"We are just hearing too much of this and you're getting this drip, drip, drip effect," she said.

COPS IN CRISIS

I wasn't the only person feeling the heat, but after suffering years of it responsibility fell on me to do something. COURTESY NEWS LTD

The investigators had to cope with the threats, not the police media spokesman. The bullets weren't in his mailbox. COURTESY NEWS LTD

Herald Sun

TUESDAY, MAY 25, 2004 — NEWS PICTORIAL

I fear for my life, says whistleblower
COP BASHED CRIMEBUSTER

Geoff Wilkinson

A FRIGHTENED crimebuster said last night he had been bashed, threatened and intimidated by other police while battling corruption in Victoria Police.

Det-Sgt Simon Illingworth called for an independent commission to fight corruption.

He wept as he revealed how he was king-hit by a policeman in a Carlton hotel.

"I fell down to my knees and I was kicked in the head a number of times," he said.

"I got on to my hands and knees and stood up. I wanted to show that a whistleblower had what it took, and then I fell head first into the floor.

"But I am still here."

Det-Sgt Illingworth said that he had been forced to move house three or four times in the past few months, had sold his home, and carried a firearm.

The corruption investigator said his life and his family's lives had been put at risk by someone in the Victoria Police who leaked his home address to criminals.

He told of the pressure that he faced from within the force.

"You don't know whether you are going to turn a corner and get a handshake or a bullet," he said.

Det-Sgt Illingworth, 36, is on stress-related sick leave from his job in the force's ethical standards department.

He worked in the department's corruption investigation division, which handles the most serious cases of police corruption.

Det-Sgt Illingworth said six people he had charged were now before the courts, and he could not elaborate on what he had uncovered.

But he said one of the targets of his investigation had intimidated him in a hotel with a man accused of one of Melbourne's underworld killings.

"I've got this underworld figure staring at me and I'm thinking, 'How vulnerable am I?' " he said.

Senior police admitted last night there had been continued attempts to intimidate Det-Sgt Illingworth.

Acting Assistant Commissioner Steve Fontana said Det-Sgt Illingworth was a dedicated investigator.

Continued Page 4

CORRUPTION CRISIS

- Crime figure refuses to testify against accused detective
  — Report: Page 4

- Corruption commission needed to fix Victoria, urges former top cop
  — Report: Page 18

At the end of May 2004, things were really difficult for me.
COURTESY NEWS LTD

Herald Sun

www.heraldsun.com.au

THURSDAY, JUNE 3, 2004 — NEWS PICTORIAL — CITY: SHOWERS. MAX: 15 PAGE 81 — $1* (Incl. GST)

OUR MISS UNIVERSE PAGES 3, 23

OLYMPIC TORCH RELAY 8-PAGE GUIDE

PLUS Hit MOVIES & MUSIC — PLUS MZURI AT 20 SOUVENIR POSTER

EXCLUSIVE: Caught on film
CRIM AND THE COP

Together: a detective and an underworld figure pictured leaving a Melbourne club.

Geoff Wilkinson and Jeremy Kelly

A DETECTIVE facing criminal charges and an accused gangland murderer have been caught together on camera in dramatic evidence of Victoria's worsening web of police corruption.

Closed circuit TV pictures obtained by the Herald Sun show the suspended detective leaving a city club with the known underworld figure.

The pair, who cannot be identified for legal reasons, allegedly went to the club to intimidate a police corruption investigator who was drinking there.

Both face charges, and details cannot be published on legal advice.

Opposition Leader Robert Doyle last night described the photographs, taken in December 2002, as "the smoking gun" that should force the State Government's hand on corruption.

Photographs of the detective and the accused killer became public for the first time as it was revealed that:

POLICE have confirmed the authenticity of a secret police report published in yesterday's Herald Sun.

THE detective who wrote the report declared his innocence of any connection with the murder of a police informer and his wife.

THE State Government has trebled the Ombudsman's budget and authorised new powers, including the use of

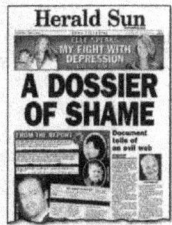

Genuine: police have confirmed the authenticity of a dossier detailed in yesterday's Herald Sun.

sting operations, undercover agents and telephone intercepts.

A LAWYER accused in the police information report of paying bribes to police also proclaimed his innocence.

AN informer who fled overseas is reconsidering his decision to return to Australia to give evidence in a high-profile drugs hearing after being named in the secret report.

THE second interim report by the State Ombudsman on the Ceja taskforce's investigation of drug-related corruption in the former drug squad will be tabled in Parliament today.

Continued Page 4

PM'S DEPARTMENT KNEW ABOUT IRAQI TORTURE – P3

Herald Sun

SATURDAY EDITION

www.heraldsun.com.au
November 13, 2004 $1.30 (incl GST)

Whistleblower turns down $250,000

YOU CAN'T GAG ME

Simon Illingworth

EXCLUSIVE
Jeremy Kelly

A POLICE corruption investigator terrorised by bent cops and criminals has refused a $250,000 payout because it would stop him criticising Christine Nixon and the force.

Detective Sergeant Simon Illingworth refused the compensation after Victoria Police demanded he never speak ill of the force or Chief Commissioner Nixon on any matter.

"They are not going to buy me," Det-Sgt Illingworth, 37, yesterday told the *Herald Sun*.

"I am not for sale. What they have tried to do is put a complete hush on me. To shut me up.

"I thought this stuff only happened in tobacco or asbestos companies."

The ethical standards department investigator went public in May about what he says is a lack of support for anti-corruption detectives. He said he had been bashed and threatened by other police and accused underworld killers.

Det-Sgt Illingworth, who is on stress leave, sought compensation from the force, accusing it of not providing a safe work environment. He said his position was untenable.

Last week he rejected a settlement offer of $250,000 to leave the force and refrain from making statements likely to harm Victoria Police.

He said he declined because of the gag clause.

Det-Sgt Illingworth gave the *Herald Sun* the offer, sent to his lawyers, Arnold, Thomas & Becker.

"Your client is not to make, or induce anyone else to make, any statement or statements which are likely to harm the interests of (Christine Nixon) or the Force generally," the letter says.

The offer has other clauses, including that he quit the force and a requirement he keep confidential information discovered in his duties as a police officer.

Continued Page 8

November 2004: turning down $250,000 never felt so good.   COURTESY NEWS LTD

Herald Sun, Tuesday, November 16, 2004

Chief, I can't sign

Simon Illingworth

DEAR Chief Commissioner Nixon: As a young man who was spending far too much time surfing and not enough time at university, I realised I was wasting my life.

I had accepted the freedom this country offers without a second thought.

Then I decided to do something about it, so I joined the Victoria Police.

I relied on the way I was brought up, the values passed down by my school and family to me to help me make life's choices.

These values and principles didn't allow me to ignore the corruption that was thrust in my face all those years ago. I never wanted to be the subject of newspaper headlines.

I didn't choose this life; it chose me.

Investigating police corruption backed me into a corner. It challenged me. So did the recent gag clause your office wanted, stopping me commenting on police matters in return for paying me compensation when I leave the force.

I agreed to speak to the Herald Sun last week as a cry for help, out of sheer frustration. I would like to explain why I can't sign your gag clause.

When things went haywire years ago my social life went from being a person liked by all, to being hated by most.

I was once comfortable in crowds; now I hate it. I used to like a bit of time to myself; now I crave it. I have become isolated, and very afraid. Not paranoid — justifiably afraid.

I've felt numb for a long time. I didn't let anyone in. I had relationships, but I kept my sorrow inside. I didn't share the burden because I felt it was my problem. But I was wrong.

It isn't my problem. It's our problem. That is, all of us.

Every person in this country who enjoys the freedom of living here has a responsibility to stand up and be counted despite the possibility of personal detriment. Our freedom relies on it.

Aussie mateship was always based on mutual trust and loyalty. That loyalty is based on solid values like honesty, transparency and integrity.

People who assume positions of power accept the esteem, perks and status that come with their positions. Rightfully so, but these positions come with a catch. They come with a greater responsibility to be transparent, open and honest.

Every police officer, chief executive, company director, politician and others have to take that responsibility as part of the deal.

It should come as no surprise to you that my previous relationships failed. Not because of any fundamental flaw, but because I couldn't love anyone, including myself.

I HATED myself (as did many other people), so loving anyone else was going to be difficult, if not impossible. Nevertheless, I now have a wonderful girlfriend who has helped me to love.

It helps to talk with her about my experiences.

This is not just dealing with post-traumatic stress — it is dealing with a continuing crisis every day, wondering what is going to happen next.

We still live in fear of normal, everyday situations. The stress of this life is taking its toll.

I explained from the outset I wanted this financial settlement cleared up quickly so I could focus on the pending court cases. But months passed and I was continually asked to sign a reworded silence clause.

I became desperate and rang your assistant directly a few weeks ago. I pleaded for the matter to be concluded one way or another and explained that my girlfriend was losing her hair because of the stress.

I again explained my position on the hush clause.

There is no denying the fact that at times I feel hatred towards the corrupt police who have taken my innocence away from me. But I am not bitter, nor vengeful.

I wish that one day I can be another face in the crowd, one of the boys, a fellow who likes a laugh, a surf, a game of cricket or footy and a few beers after.

That's Australian freedom. I yearn to feel free again.

I loathe the spotlight and always have. But all those years ago I knew I had a responsibility not to give up, to stand up and be counted despite being in very unfamiliar territory.

I did, but unfortunately my situation snowballed and I've had to repeatedly put my neck on the line.

I identified organised criminals allegedly working in harmony with corrupt police. I know it and you know it.

But I can't help any more — I've done my bit openly, honestly and transparently. Clearly, it is time for me to go and do something else.

Whether you settle my claim or not is a matter for you. I will not sign a hush clause, ever.

I will remain true to myself and the people I promised to serve. But unfortunately I expect to confront extreme financial difficulty as a price. So be it.

I have lost many liberties in recent times but no one will ever take away my free speech.

For the record, I like this state and I like Victoria Police.

It is a wonderful organisation with many thousands of hard working, trustworthy, intelligent people in it. I will not speak against those individuals — you have my word.

Once my superannuation is sorted out, I will resign as you wanted. I will do my duty and appear in court as a witness in the remaining corruption matter, as I had promised you.

I will appear as a civilian.

**Yours Sincerely,
Simon Illingworth**

The author is a detective-sergeant with the police ethical standards department, presently on sick leave.

My letter to Chief Commissioner Christine Nixon in the Herald Sun, 16 November 2004.
COURTESY NEWS LTD

I loved surfing the treacherous waves around Port Campbell: one of the few times when danger was exhilarating.

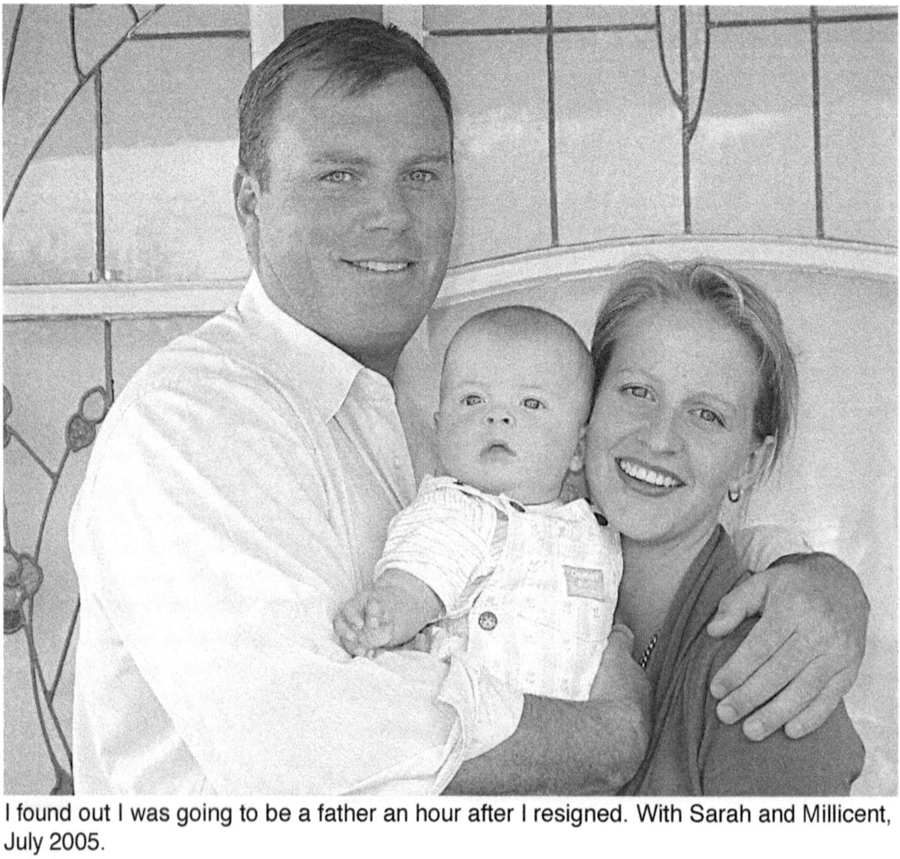

I found out I was going to be a father an hour after I resigned. With Sarah and Millicent, July 2005.

14

Collecting the mail

The extortion of other corruption investigators had begun to spread like wildfire. They, too, became the hunted. One corruption investigator received a special home delivery in his letterbox: two .38 calibre hollow point bullets. My colleague's name and that of his partner had been etched into the bullets. The bloodthirsty message was clear: 'Pull up or else'. But for a cop who's juggling a number of investigations, as many of us were, you don't even know what it is you're being told to turn a blind eye. Maybe you've unwittingly stumbled across evidence, a witness, or found something that someone else doesn't want you to. Perhaps the threat is more generalised. It's no coincidence that the anti-corruption detectives who receive threats are the most professional investigators, which is what makes them a threat.

The Ceja taskforce had clearly made some ground; they had charged thirteen detectives. But on 21 May 2004, less than three days before my *Australian Story* was to air, the *Australian* newspaper reported that Victoria's corruption was taking a toll on others when it broke the exclusive bullets story mentioned above. 'Two bullets in the mail for police corruption investigator' screamed the headline. The *Australian* then quoted a colleague of the bullet recipient: 'Is it going to take the murder of an internal investigator before [government and police command] acknowledge that there is a major problem within the organisation, and stop resisting calls for a full independent inquiry?'

The newspaper wasn't quoting me but I suspect I would know the person who made the statement. Nevertheless, I agree with it. Then another top corruption investigator, who allegedly received a threat to kill from another detective, became aware that a person close to him was possibly under surveillance. It was intimidation, nothing new, other than the fact that these mongrels had apparently hit an all-time low.

Soon after that I was told that a private investigator was checking into my past, asking questions and harassing people who knew me to make derogatory statements about me. Apparently, the statements claimed that I had some sort of vendetta against the people I had investigated. I don't know whether he got anyone to sign one, nor do I know who paid for this private investigator, but I have my suspicions.

I reminded myself of why I was driving this campaign: it was to create an environment for future generations of police where 'the bad cop feared the good cop and not the reverse'. These words were first uttered by Frank Serpico, formerly of the New York Police Department. Serpico was an honest cop in a bribe-infested police department (he was shot in the face). Having decided that enough was enough, he led from the front in an anti-corruption campaign. New York City administrators stepped in and stopped the situation in their city in the 1950s, almost six decades ago, yet the world's most livable city in the lucky country was yet to properly address its problems. Strong leadership, a rare quality often promised, was overdue in this state. It was obvious to me that it didn't matter where you were in the world: anti-corruption bodies needed to be set up, resourced and given independence. I'd seen independent corruption commissions operating overseas, in places previously nobbled by a culture of corruption. These bodies had put the corrupt on notice and had held out a hand to the most vulnerable people in their communities — those people had paid in more ways than one.

Months had passed. I naively continued to hope that the worsening crisis would force changes to the way Melbourne's organised crime was being tackled, lasting changes that one would expect to put pressure on the criminals to toe the line before any more innocent or not so innocent people were killed. But radio and newspaper articles brought back a sharp taste of reality. It wasn't to be.

I'd hoped for some hard-hitting decisions to be made now rather than later. I believed in the need for, at the very least, a stopgap measure that involved an injection of expert human resources, equipment, technology and cars where they were needed most, in the investigative squads, witness security, Police Corruption Division and Ceja Task Force. I had expected that broadcasting my story would create an opportunity for the public to see Melbourne's underbelly and the pressure within which some investigators had been forced to work. I confidently assumed that the public outrage would cause the government to act. I hoped that Melbourne's conservative and silent majority would stand up and push for change, ensuring a new and unfamiliar sense of vulnerability in the underworld, that the sheer weight of numbers would force the crooks onto the back foot.

To the inexperienced eye it seemed that carrying out underworld murders was the core function of Melbourne's mobsters. This wasn't the situation in Melbourne and rarely is anywhere else; murder is a by-product, a show of strength or a symptom of business in the underworld. Organised crime's core function is feeding insatiable greed, not murdering people.

Unfortunately, the extraordinarily large number of macabre gangland murders had whipped the media into an understandable frenzy, but it seemed to me that most people were missing the point. Tit-for-tat murder meant that many of the suspected killers were indeed shot dead themselves, so the investigating detectives were destined to spend much of their time as coroners' clerks posthumously investigating the crimes of dead crooks, rather than filling jails with live scumbags still involved in the highly lucrative organised crime business. I'd explained many times to my superior officers and colleagues that this frenzied situation would only be brought back into order when someone looked beyond the next murder victim and refocused on what I see as the core function of policing — stopping organised crime. It is easier said than done to look beyond a person lying dead on the street with spent cartridges or a sawn-off shotgun lying nearby, but history shows that the only lasting inroads ever made into entrenched organised crime are made by targeting racketeering, illegal gaming, taxation, money trails and the illicit drug trade, not murder. Solving a murder in the process should be considered a bonus. Investigators need to target the foundation upon which organised crime stands — greed.

A homicide taskforce named Purana had been created and immediately pumped with manpower and other resources, but the intricate nature of murder investigation, coupled with the need for clear and professionally gathered intelligence, takes time, especially when one has admitted to having one's eye off the intelligence ball for such a long time. But time, as I've stated before, was a luxury very few people seemed to have during this period.

Those selected for the Purana Task Force were seasoned officers who went about their task methodically and proactively, a smart move that allowed them to jump ahead of the pack and not get dragged down in reactive (after the event) policing. A number of significant arrests indicate that this philosophy may have paid dividends; time will tell.

The Purana Task Force was a perfect example of how resourcing detectives to tackle crime pays off. But the Victorian Crime Squads need more, specifically in respect to the long-term infiltration and investigation of organised crime. Fortunately, criminal enterprises can't operate effectively without leaving identifiable trails. Paper and money trails, banks, betting and taxation paperwork leave evidence often far more credible than any found at a grisly murder scene.

I am well aware from my own experience that the investigative process is not over when a mobster is arrested and remanded (refused bail) in jail and that the court process is fraught with risk. Court processes can be incredibly unrewarding for detectives. This is particularly true when detectives begin to rely heavily on the evidence of notoriously unreliable witnesses (often criminals themselves) who are expected to tell the truth. Many such witnesses backflip at the last minute, the worst possible time for any prosecution case, and can often alter the outcome.

These risks are so well known that the extra resources immediately pumped into trying to solve Melbourne's mob killings in the short term could have been better spent in specific targeting of criminals involved in activities such as narcotics, gambling, prostitution, extortion, debt collection and labour racketeering. Those investigators specifically target the wealth and possessions generated from these activities.

But that isn't the only reason why homicide shouldn't be the primary focus of extra resourcing. Organised crime isn't about individuals, it's about culture, a culture of greed and illegitimate power, power that's based on violence. If creating long-term wealth through crime continues to be a risk worth taking, the void left by one gangster's untimely death or incarceration will be quickly filled by another, and so on. Misdirecting the extra resources into the investigation of murder, which is a symptom of organised crime, ensures that a police force is likely to be chasing its tail for a long time.

The Al Capone method of catching mobsters, favoured by my old boss Neil O'Sullivan, rose once again, this time in its purest form. The Australian Taxation Office was going to join the fight. On 31 May 2004 Federal Treasurer Peter Costello announced a crackdown on the drug barons who held Victoria in a state of fear. He was going to try to tax them out of existence. If targeting taxation evasion and fraud was the answer to cracking the underworld's power, that's what we'd do. It was not as sexy as murder investigation but history had proved it would work.

A few days prior to the screening of *Australian Story*, I was contacted by the leader of the state Liberal Party, Robert Doyle, who asked me to meet with him and his assistants. Doyle had received a copy of a document entitled 'Victoria's Anti-Corruption Strategy'. I knew it well, because I'd written it.

At our meeting I laid everything out in confronting terms. My voice rose at times as I spoke passionately about the frustrations I had endured; I swore throughout. I showed no respect for anyone's political status in the room, as requested by Doyle. He asked for it — warts and all — and that's exactly what he got. Speaking to the leader of the Opposition was a bit strange at first, as if I had gone behind someone's back, but I reminded myself that I had spoken to a representative of the government about twelve months before. The city morgue had been working overtime since then and corruption scandals were now making headlines on a weekly basis.

My exchange with the Hon Robert Doyle included a blow-by-blow explanation of my anti-corruption strategy. I was confident he would approve of its proactive and educational features, as he was formerly a teacher. I was right: Doyle liked my plan. He liked it a lot. I also told him that I would be appearing on *Australian Story* as an anti-corruption investigator and whistleblower. I didn't tell him what was going to be on the program, nor did he ask. I wouldn't tell him what was to be shown on the program, because I didn't want to be unfair to the government. But I couldn't have told him anyway, because I didn't even know myself.

We parted company with a sense of nervous expectation. Doyle's last words to me were: 'Look after yourself, Simon, you've done your bit. You can call me twenty-four hours a day. I won't rest until this is fixed.' I told him I expected a smear campaign afterwards, but I was willing to walk away with a tarnished reputation, as long as I had a guarantee that the Liberal Party would fight to get this mess sorted out once and for all. Doyle gave me his word.

I knew my story rested in the hands of a journalist, Belinda Hawkins. On Saturday, 22 May 2004, at midday the ABC began running promotional material for my *Australian Story*, which was going to air a week earlier than originally scheduled. The ABC laid it on thick — the promotion described how my address had been given out to criminals and my life was in danger. The commercial channels were quick to pick up that a big story was about to break and by Monday they had grabbed the ABC's promotional material and run segments of it on their news broadcasts. By 7pm on Monday, 24 May, an hour before broadcast time, all commercial news broadcasts around the country had earmarked *Australian Story* as compulsory viewing, despite it being shown on a rival network. I knew the audience was going to be bigger than expected.

By 8pm that night, thousands of sets all over Australia were tuned in to the ABC's *Australian Story*. Sarah, my sister Belinda and I, sitting in my mate's old weatherboard shack among unpacked and unmarked cardboard boxes full of my possessions, nervously waited for the show to start. Then, as the show began, the anxiety completely stopped. I sat back and found for the first time for many years that a sense of freedom came over me. I paused for a minute, put my arm around Sarah, kissed her and looked across at my sister and smiled. I was so proud of Binny's courage in going on the program; she'd done it without blinking an eyelid. We watched the program on my mate's shonky TV set that, under normal circumstances, would have found its way to the rubbish dump long ago. Nevertheless, the TV provided perfect audio, although the picture quality was similar to light snow falling. It didn't matter, the program wasn't for us.

A few kilometres away Neil O'Sullivan, who was at home, couldn't bring himself to watch, so, in the middle of winter, he sat on a deckchair on his back porch next to his blue heeler pup before his wife coaxed him in as the program began.

A transcript of the program appears at the end of this book.

In that half hour my life changed forever. I saw my seventeen-year policing career finish in a blaze of controversy. I knew I ran the real risk of being charged with offences against the Police Regulations Act, an Act I knew better than most in the Force, but it was a risk I was more than willing to take. I knew if I'd been charged, my lawyer would have used the case to open a can of worms few others wanted to see hit the light of day. I felt a sense of pride that I'd actually accomplished something, despite breaking a few rules doing the *Australian Story*. I'd done it for the right reasons. It was a relief, the wait was over. Belinda Hawkins had done an incredible job in piecing the story together and the footage was testament to Ron Ekkles's experience as a cameraman. It was a win for the ABC, a win for free speech and a win for democracy. Personally, though, I had risked my life, broken a number of regulations, lost a job and my privacy all in the space of thirty minutes. It was a cold winter in Melbourne as I walked outside and sparked up a smoke. Sarah joined me. 'Belinda did a good job didn't she?' I said, as fog came from my mouth. 'You did a good job, Sime, I'm so proud of you.'

'What now?' I mused.

'I don't know . . . I don't know.'

I hadn't envisaged the size of the media wave that followed; it rivalled some of the fierce waves of the deep Southern Ocean. While I was proficient at tackling the ocean with a surfboard, I was in completely unfamiliar territory now. I awoke the morning after and walked down to the local shop. The Asian shopkeeper smiled widely as I purchased a couple of extra copies of the *Herald Sun*. The front-page headline gave an indication that the program had made an impact — 'Cop bashed crimebuster' (referring to the coward who had belted me that night at the Hellfire Club).

Having been a detective and investigator for a number of years, unlike most whistleblowers, I knew how to manage and assess risk, was highly proficient at strategic planning and knew how to research the probabilities of responses, with consideration of the people involved. I had accepted the possibility of three responses from the police force after my story had been aired on national television. First was the inevitable downplaying of the events that had taken place — the 'he's exaggerating' factor. Second was the possibility of being attacked on minor, personal or work-related rule or policy breeches — the 'he's broken many (technical) rules, laws or policies' factor. Last, and perhaps most intimidating, was the need to brace myself for a personal smear campaign that would almost certainly include some comment about my mental stability or relationship breakdown situation and therefore undermine the real truthfulness and impact of the release — the 'he's unwell/unstable' factor.

As it happened, the Force command didn't have time to brace itself. The first they knew about the *Australian Story* program going to air was on the Saturday, two days before it aired. I have no doubt they would have been whipped up into a frenzied state: 'What is he going to say on TV?' But most importantly: 'Who is in charge of him?'

On the afternoon before the program went to air, a meeting reportedly took place between Chief Commissioner Nixon and government representatives. What did they talk about? The media were told by the government's spokesperson that the conversation was about gangland killings rather than police corruption. Whether this was true or not, an increasingly cynical and pessimistic media and general public weren't likely to believe it.

The morning after the program was broadcast, the newspapers quoted the chief commissioner's statement that I would not be disciplined. That was a relief, but it would have been ironic if I had. What could I have been charged with? Telling the truth? At that stage

I was coming around to the idea of making my own charges and spending days giving evidence about corruption, lies and poor risk management, among other things.

The chief said, 'He's done a terrific job, but you might want to also notice the people who threatened him were charged and in fact convicted.' True, but only because I had the courage to stand up to bent cops, time and time again: there was certainly no reason for the police force to pat itself on the back. The police culture had allowed me to be ostracised, threatened and bashed, not for doing the wrong thing, but because I'd done my duty. You, the public, asked me to swear an oath. I assume upholding people's rights was meant to mean something. How many honest cops have quit the Force when confronted with a similar situation? Since *Australian Story*, I have learnt of many, and not just from Victoria. These people sent me their best wishes. At least one fled overseas, and it was with much heartache that I recently learnt that this person took his own life. He was one of many decent people, their names are unknown to the public, who have paid the ultimate price for doing the right thing. I'd be the last person to judge him for his final action. Being considered a rat, a snitch or a whistleblower is very isolating and at times depressing.

Is an organisation's reputation worth one good person's life? I would hope not.

At least one prominent school headmaster joined the fray. The headmaster of Melbourne Grammar School, Paul Sheahan, wrote in the school bulletin:

> In the face of potential brutality and possible death at someone else's hands, Simon Illingworth has shown incredible courage in doing what he thinks is right (and what the rest of the community would agree is right, I'm sure). Clearly this is intimidation of the most brutal kind, designed to silence this man who has uncovered corruption amongst his work colleagues and cannot live with it. It is rather instructive that Illingworth now finds himself as a 'one-man band' in the Ethical Standards Unit, too. The code of silence permeates many organisations but, in the police force, the stakes are very high; yet Illingworth still believes that defence of the principles of honesty and

integrity in the organisation that is designed to protect the community and uphold the law is paramount.

Since the time of the Ancient Greeks, the compelling question has been: 'Who guards the guardians?' Interestingly, also, the motto of the Victoria Police is not 'Uphold the Law' but 'Uphold the Right'. Illingworth is doing that *par excellence*, even in the face of retribution that few in the community ever have to contemplate.

Premier Steve Bracks congratulated me on my courage in helping bring corrupt officers to justice, but went on to say that he hadn't been advised of any direct link between the underworld and police. I put this down to a lack of understanding of the necessary elements for a bent cop to actually be corrupt; crims and bent cops go hand in glove. Cops don't bribe cops — that is a ludicrous suggestion. Corruption almost always involves inappropriate associations with organised criminals.

It didn't take long for the *Herald Sun* to provide the premier with a direct association between police and the underworld. They showed a picture of my interrupted night out at a city hotel where a man accused of an underworld killing, in the company of a suspended police detective, had glared at me. The newspaper's headline, 'The crim and the cop' made sure that everyone knew what the picture showed; the leader of the Opposition called the picture 'the smoking gun'.

Unfortunately, people like me aren't considered courageous or valued until we're about to appear on television. Why hadn't anyone ever told me or the other men and women dealing with crime and corruption that we are valued by the Force? Why do we have to work ten hour plus shifts and do more with less? Why hadn't anyone recognised the courage of the people affected by undermanned or under-resourced investigations? Because these are the things we don't talk about.

It's quite simple: I was not rewarded for my work because my success in weeding out corruption had tainted the image and reputation of the very organisation for which I fought.

Robert Doyle had previously tried to work with the state government's idea of boosting the ombudsman's office but now he whipped up a storm of controversy when the Opposition took a very different position on it: mine. When I first met Doyle and explained the state's crisis, he was bloody angry; the information flow to the Opposition is always notoriously slow and they had been consistently playing catch-up. But the tables were turned once *Australian Story* went to air and Doyle began landing telling blows on a previously unperturbed government that, since the election of 20 November 2002, held a huge majority in the Lower House and also controlled the Upper House. The gloves had come off.

The day after *Australian Story* aired, a key prosecution witness, a crim, announced to the court that he was no longer willing to provide evidence in an upcoming corruption trial. He gave scant details as to the reason for withdrawing his promise, but made it clear that his decision had been made with the knowledge that his original discounted sentence would be reassessed and increased for non-compliance. He was also aware he would be immediately charged with contempt of court, which carried additional penalty. Incredibly, the perceived lack of protection for witnesses and investigators in Victoria had taken another blow. The criminal had chosen jail ahead of giving evidence.

In state parliament that same day, Robert Doyle opened the debate on his anti-corruption and crime strategy. The strategy, research and ideas were mine, but Doyle had done a lot of work himself. It was clear he'd read and checked the accuracy of the material, an exactness that was a legacy of his early teaching days, but I was far more confident with my material now than I had ever been back at school (unless, of course, I'd copied it from a textbook). Moments before Doyle walked into parliament he contacted me and said he'd read it more than fifteen times. He asked me a few extra questions — tough ones. He just wanted to get every fine detail right. He knew it as well as I did.

It was a proud moment for me. I'd always promised myself I'd try to be part of the cure, not part of the disease, despite many of the problems I'd faced. Robert Doyle spoke with passion and conviction equal to mine. He finished by saying: 'Let me repeat Simon's closing remarks: "I have always thought good would defeat evil. Here we go!" We in this parliament must prove him right when he says, "Here we go!" Let's go together.'

I hadn't envisaged how many people would be affected by the program. A week later, Sarah and I went for a walk through the Botanic Gardens in Melbourne. As we walked aimlessly through the lush gardens an elderly woman walked up to us and asked if I was Simon Illingworth. I admitted I was. She hugged us both and thanked me for making a difference. She turned to Sarah and thanked her.

Then the emails and letters flowed in, bags of them, more than a thousand in the end. It was overwhelming. I couldn't possibly write back to everyone. I replied to one letter from a man called Ivan, a quadriplegic; he'd signed his letter with his mouth. Ivan brought back all the reasons why it was worth pushing on; happiness is a positive state of mind. We read every letter and each one inspired us to keep going. They made me realise it was all worthwhile. Then, two strangers offered Sarah and me a place to stay, somewhere interstate, in an isolated rental house among forests of nut trees. It was off the beaten track, at least 20 kilometres from the nearest corner store. Initially, we declined and then, as the pressure built with the articles in the newspapers and radio talkback segments, we agreed to take a break.

Sarah and I made our way to the airport. I was flustered getting everything together and when we'd arrived there I had that sickly feeling as we waited in the queue — I'd left my photo identification at my mate's house. I had no identification with me at all. But that catastrophe was soon sorted out when Sarah suggested I use the morning *Herald Sun* as identification.

Reluctantly, I agreed, breathed deeply, told the check-in staff that my wallet was at home and explained my alternative. My anonymous exit from the state was completely shot down as I stood in the airport terminal in Melbourne, embarrassed, holding a colour newspaper photograph of me weeping under the headline 'Living a nightmare', which Sarah pulled out of her carry bag.

The check-in lady asked, 'Is that really you?' I answered her question with another question. 'Do you think anyone else would admit to being me?' She thought for a minute, agreed and handed me a boarding pass.

As we waited for our flight, an off-duty policewoman walked over to me and introduced herself. 'Well done.' She didn't have to say anything else — her comment meant far more to me than she could have realised.

Sarah and I hired a car and drove to the rental house to spend a few days before returning refreshed to my mate's house in Melbourne. We'd ventured out of the house a few times to surf and sit on an empty beach. It was great, just the two of us in the sunshine on the beach — or so we thought.

When Sarah and I returned to Melbourne we moved house again, hoping this would be the last move for some time. Settlement on my previous house went through smoothly, as did the separation documents with Tracy. We had found a house to live that was in good condition yet needed a little TLC. Despite the odd jobs that needed doing, the first job I did didn't involve a paintbrush or a garden shovel — it involved putting security measures in place. This was a lifestyle I was now becoming accustomed to. Fortunately, the Police Force assisted us by financing those arrangements.

Four months later, Robert Doyle contacted me. He'd received a not too subtle message directed for me — a photocopy of our guest book entry at the remote interstate hideaway and some confidential police documents had been sent to him. The magnitude of this message was one only we could truly understand. It made us feel more vulnerable than we'd ever imagined. We soon conceded that, regardless of how vigilant I'd been about the secrecy of our movements, we could be found wherever we went. The thought of permanently relocating interstate was no longer an option; irrespective, this nightmare would follow us everywhere.

After *Australian Story* I had to get a lawyer. I first met Lee Flanagan from Arnold, Thomas and Becker in his office. Lee wasn't well known, but a barrister friend suggested I see him. 'Are you sure?' I asked. 'I've never even heard of him.'

I knew the chances of my life hitting the headlines again were similar to the odds my old man's nags had of winning at a picnic race. But Lee specialised in personal injury and he needed to know what to do when it mattered. 'He's the one,' my mate said firmly. I needed an all-rounder because I didn't know where my life would take me and I knew I couldn't afford to change lawyers midway. I told Lee the situation. He'd obviously heard some horror stories in his time but he had trouble hiding his surprise at some of my revelations.

By the next meeting we had, Lee had done his research. He'd gone through the Acts of parliament, checking the legislation and case law before giving me a legal prognosis. 'It's going to be tough. This case doesn't seem to fit into any of the current laws. But we won't give up.'

When we went to see the chief of police, Lee was nervous. In hindsight that was probably because I had told him I'd do the talking. Lee was a surfer, so we talked about surfing until we walked into the chief's office. It wasn't the first time we'd met. I told her that I didn't want a golden handshake or a pension; I wanted to work again. As Lee and I left that meeting we were confident things would progress with the Force lawyers, but months passed without agreement. In the meantime, I was on WorkCover, which I hated: it ate away at my conscience. I knew I could do something; I was considering sweeping the streets while I waited for a short-term resolution. Then, an old mate called me. He worked at a school in the inner western suburbs of Melbourne and asked me to speak to the kids there. I readily agreed. The challenge was to get the kids to reflect on their own lives by talking about mine. That might alter their future.

Up until that moment, my feeling of being a non-contributor had made me contemplate forcing myself to go back to the police — something I knew would be catastrophic. But this short-term situation was becoming a long-term one. Sarah was a tower of strength during this time, but she too concerned me; the strain of everything was causing her hair to fall out. I decided I would try my hand at speaking engagements. I knew I could speak about ethics, leadership and making decisions; I'd proved that. But would it pay the bills? I didn't know (at the time of writing I do appear to be forging a successful career in it).

I arrived at the school and smiled as my mate handed me a coffee in a styrofoam cup. The kids filed in, perhaps fifty of them. The western suburbs of Melbourne are populated by many groups of unskilled migrants, and the children at this school and many others in the area were often the first generation of Australian-born kids. It was a tough life for some. They lived in two separate cultures, one at school and the other at home. They alternated between languages. This was different to the luxury I had had at Scotch College, where most of us were from white-collar, middle- to upper-class families. By this stage, though, I was used to the rough and tumble of the west, having been a cop for seventeen years.

The kids sat quietly for almost two hours and asked question after question. We talked about happiness, wealth and how to make a difference. Then, as I finished, the kids clapped, really loudly. It was such rousing applause that I felt lost for words. It was a defining moment. My passion and strength returned. I knew those kids would be my toughest audience and likewise the best judges of my ability to speak, pass on a message and (hopefully) be able to make a living from it. There was no middle ground with them; I was either a champ or a chump. This was judgment day; no one else knew how much weight I had put on that lecture.

As the kids filed out, I too packed up and began walking out, leaving the empty cup on the table. But I stopped, picked up the cup, crushed it and put it in the bin. I knew where my life was going from that moment on.

In late October 2004, despite being on stress leave, I appeared in the County Court to give evidence against Bill Crane and another crook I had charged with being involved in a conspiracy to bribe Detective Black. Bill Crane, the worse of the two and the greater threat to me, was also facing charges of drug manufacturing and multiple gun possession charges. I knew I was likely to be standing in the witness box for anything up to two weeks. My witness statement was over twenty pages long, a daunting prospect for anyone. I chatted to a couple of reporters to fill in the time, only to be surprised by a freelance photographer taking multiple shots of me as I walked from the court after an adjournment. I asked Katie Lapthorn, a young, experienced court reporter, why she thought I'd been photographed.

She hesitated at first. 'I shouldn't say this, but . . . it's just in case you end up dead,' she told me. I hadn't had it put to me as bluntly as that before, but I was used to Katie's brutal honesty and I like people like that. We paused for a moment and laughed.

As the trial continued one of the crooks walked into court and said that he didn't 'gamble with his freedom'. What was that meant to mean? While we were still scratching our heads, his co-accused found words somewhat less cryptic when, a few days later, he called me a 'fucking maggot' as he walked from the courtroom. Seconds after this comment the trial was aborted; the jury had been excused. We had to start again with a new jury.

The police took my mobile phone back so I was unaware people were trying to warn me during the trial. Once I purchased a new mobile phone I got an anonymous call: 'Ducks are back on the pond.' I knew what the caller meant — I'd heard the phrase before. Word filtered back that Crane, the man who'd been caught with silencers, night vision goggles and eight guns, was frequenting places I was known to go. Then I put two and two together: 'I don't gamble with my freedom.'

As the second jury was sworn in, Crane and his criminal mate, who I'll call Nowise, sat in the dock. They looked like two old men; butter wouldn't melt in their mouths. Crane perfected an innocent look; his eyebrows were permanently raised in a surprised state as if some incredible injustice had been served on him.

As the case started again, my private lawyer Lee, my barrister Sandy Robertson and I went to finalise my resignation and settlement with the police to break a deadlock that had been going for months. Crane and Nowise's court delay meant that my financial settlement was going to take place during a lunch break in my stressful conspiracy evidence. Everything I had achieved, suffered, fought for and tolerated in my police life was now to be attached to a financial figure, a dollar value. I told my lawyers that I would not sign any contract that had anything I considered to be a hush clause, no matter how much money was offered.

During the court lunch interval I walked away from an offer of $250 000 compensation from Victoria Police because I refused to accept the following three lines as part of the deal: 'Mr Illingworth is not to make, or induce anyone else to make, any statement or statements which are likely to harm the interests of the (Chief Commissioner) or (Victoria Police) generally.' The chief commissioner said she did not at any stage have any intention of silencing me, and the clause was regarded by her advisers as a normal term of any commercial settlement. I have no reason to disbelieve her.

I chose to walk away with nothing. I turned to my legal counsel and told them, 'Don't get comfortable, we're leaving.' Lee, Sandy and I walked out of the meeting. It wasn't a ploy or a trick — it was over. Financially, I was left with a great deal less after my marriage breakup and despite the large sum on offer it was a matter of principle to refuse it. I was fed up with my rights being eroded and I was determined not to lose any more.

The three of us got back into the plush lift, we said nothing. Soon we were at the ground floor and stepped into the ostentatious marble foyer of the lawyers' Collins Street building. We had turned up for the meeting wearing similar suits, so three men in dark suits walked in a line past two elegant marble water features, our minds racing. I was determined, yet sick with worry. I'd just bought a house and I knew I would have to sell it because I could no longer pay the mortgage. We walked out into the street and still nothing was said.

We joined the crowd and became three anonymous people again, but we were different to those around us: we shared a secret.

Lee was the first to speak. 'Walking away from $250 000 never felt so good,' he said.

I said, 'We've walked away with something a lot more valuable than that, mate.' Sandy agreed, but suggested we hadn't heard the last of this story.

Lee and Sandy shook my hand, wished me luck and peeled off at their respective offices along the way. They knew I was minutes from resuming in the County Court witness box. I had a few minutes to spare so I lit a cigarette and tried to get my mind ready for giving evidence again. Of course, forgetting that I had no financial security any more made it difficult to concentrate on criminal conspiracies, but I collected my thoughts, climbed back into the witness box and resumed the role of fucking maggot on behalf of Victoria Police, whose lawyers I'd just told where to stick their money.

15

Just the birthday present I wanted

It was 10 November 2004, my thirty-seventh birthday, and I'd been in the witness box for six days. The subpoenas kept coming in, corruption case after case. I expected them but it annoyed me when the police began serving subpoenas on me with conduct money, a small amount of cash given with a subpoena to ensure that a civilian witness has enough money to get to court, which was insulting for a person who was still technically a policeman. It also reeked of someone being worried that the star witness might not appear in court as promised, highlighting poor leadership, for example. By then everyone, including the crims, knew that no one else could give my evidence. I never backed down on my word, and, as I'd promised, I went to court as the conduct money went to the Salvation Army.

I started my birthday in the same way as the days leading up to it: standing in the witness box producing evidence. But something changed midway through that day. I looked at my hands and saw marks from more than twenty surgical stitches, a littering of scars and a few previously broken fingers; I touched another scar next to my right eye that added to a few inside my mouth. My body told the tale.

The trial judge stopped the case temporarily, bringing my mind back to the job at hand. *What now?* I felt tired. The jury was sent out and the barristers duelled. Then came a surprise.

'How do you plead?' the tipstaff asked the accused.

'Guilty, Your Honour,' Crane replied.

'Guilty, Your Honour,' said Nowise.

The weight of the evidence had reached a point where the accused men had decided to plead guilty to the conspiracy. Crane also pleaded guilty to Dave's original Drug Squad charges of manufacturing and trafficking amphetamines, and possession of all the guns.

I was pleased that the case was over, but my joy was soon replaced with a hollow sense of relief rather than any significant personal gain or career achievement. This was meant to be one of the monumental wins that everyone had talked about, the primary reason why I was meant to risk my life, and never give up. But as I walked from court there was no fanfare, no lights and no cameras; just a city street crowded with people going about their lives.

I was joined by the barrister acting for the Office of Public Prosecutions, two solicitors and two police who had stood by me through the trial. Sarah met us at the front of the court and we walked up the road past the Victoria Market and stopped for lunch. The Office of Public Prosecutions had been great throughout my career and I thanked them.

Sarah and I walked out of the restaurant and back to my car. The carpark had cleared out and my car was alone next to the deserted courthouse. We got in and I drove to the exit of the carpark but stopped short. I paused for a few seconds; I didn't know which way to turn. The toll of my life had left me wondering where home was.

Being financially insecure is no one's dream, but the choice between having principles and being rich is easy. I don't wish to comment about the clause I refused to sign, but I will comment about clauses in general.

Some clauses in commercial settlements put forward in contracts by lawyers, organisations and corporations need to be put under the moral microscope. I say this even though they are considered routine, standard or normal in legal corporate culture. However, that does not alter my opinion, even though I know how often such contracts are signed. People shouldn't be allowed to sign away their rights and freedoms as part of a settlement process.

People don't receive compensation unless they have lost some freedom through illness or loss, either temporarily or permanently. If a corporation or organisation is to blame then they should pay the due compensation. Injured people should never be asked to sign away more rights in the form of hush clauses; they do not need to be victims twice over.

How do we expect our work safety issues to improve unless people are allowed to receive compensation and still be able to speak freely? That is an issue that I believe needs legislation. I'm not talking about the secrecy provisions that govern national security — or even Colonel Sanders's eleven secret herbs and spices — I'm talking about attempts to buy damage control to protect a brand name, public perception or a person's ego. Buying someone's silence does not seem ethical to me.

We live a fast life where money, perception and fame have become increasingly important. Would you like a hush clause with that money? It's tempting, but think about it. No matter how we package it, luring a person's silence about poor treatment, racism, sexism or crime in return for compensation sounds wrong. A person who receives compensation for ill treatment has a responsibility to talk about it, for themselves and for others, so it doesn't perpetuate itself.

How much would you have had to pay Nelson Mandela to shut up about apartheid? Some people's ideals aren't for sale.

Unfortunately, many people who contemplate signing such documents are almost always under extreme pressure.

The following article by Jeremy Kelly appeared on the front page of the *Herald Sun* on Saturday, 13 November 2004. It speaks for itself. The headline was 'Whistleblower turns down $250,000 . . . "You can't gag me"'.

> A police corruption investigator terrorized by bent cops and criminals has refused a $250,000 payout because it would stop him criticising Christine Nixon and the Force.
>
> Detective Sergeant Simon Illingworth refused the compensation payout after Victoria Police demanded he never speak ill of the Force or Chief Commissioner Nixon on any matter.

'They are not going to buy me,' Det-Sgt Illingworth told the *Herald Sun*.

'I am not for sale. What they have tried to do is put a complete hush on me. To shut me up.

'I thought this stuff only happened in asbestos or tobacco companies.'

The Ethical Standards Department investigator went public in May about what he says is a lack of support for anti-corruption detectives. He said he'd been bashed and threatened by other police and accused underworld killers.

Det-Sgt Illingworth who is on stress leave, sought compensation from the Force, accusing it of not providing a safe work environment. He said his position was untenable.

Last week he rejected a settlement offer of $250,000 to leave the Force and refrain from making statements likely to harm Victoria Police.

He said he declined because of the gag clause.

Det-Sgt Illingworth gave the *Herald Sun* the offer sent to his lawyers, Arnold Thomas and Becker.

'Your client is not to make, or induce anyone else to make, any statement or statements which are likely to harm the interests of [Christine Nixon] or the Force generally,' the letter says.

The offer has other clauses, including that he quit the Force and a requirement he keep confidential information discovered in his duties as a police officer.

Det- Sgt Illingworth says he is unconcerned by those clauses but the gag order amounted to hush money.

'I don't care if it's 2.5 million; I am not going to sign it. I am not going to sell my soul. It's not for sale. It never has been. Everyone has their price? I don't.

'This is hush money and the cover-up makes it a scandal.'

He said he would resign from the Force after sixteen years' service and be forced to sell his house.

'At least I'll have my soul and feel good about myself,' he said.

'I don't believe hushing up a problem is going to fix the problem.'

He said he would resume negotiations if the gag clause is removed.

'I am not going to come out swinging against the Force.'

Det-Sgt Illingworth said he still had concerns for his safety, as many criminals and police he had charged are still going through the courts.

'Particularly because of the crooks I was involved with,' he said.

One of the criminals he charged was busted with eight guns, a silencer and night vision goggles.

'And he was given my address. [These] are not just criminals; they have the equipment of an assassin.'

Since he knocked back the offer, Det-Sgt Illingworth said he had learned that Police command had started auditing every case he had worked on.

'Going through everything I have had my hands on. I guess they want to know what I might say,' he said.

Asked what the Force feared he might say, he said: 'I don't know, I asked them that and they said "Everything".'

Det-Sgt Illingworth is currently trying to establish a small business giving workshops on ethics and leadership.

Police last night refused to comment.

I waited for three days and heard nothing from the Force, but I did hear from a familiar voice. 'Hang in there, don't give up. I've made half a dozen phone calls and we've already raised $50 000. Whatever happens with this gag thing, you won't be selling your house. Simon, you have no idea how much support you've got. I put the word out, and now they're calling me volunteering to donate money; it's amazing.' The caller was Robert Doyle, the state Liberal leader.

That conversation made Sarah and me feel as if we were going to be OK. But I would never have accepted their money unless we were absolutely desperate. The negotiations appeared to be over as we'd expected, so I approached the *Herald Sun* and asked if I could write an article myself. It was published on 16 November 2004 and headed 'Chief, I can't sign'.

Dear Chief Commissioner Nixon,

As a young man who was spending far too much time surfing and not enough time at University, I realised I was wasting my life.

I had accepted the freedom this country offers without a second thought.

Then I decided to do something about it, so I joined the Victoria Police.

I relied on the way I was brought up, the values passed down by my school and family to me to help me make life's choices.

These values and principles did not allow me to ignore the corruption that was thrust in my face all those years ago. I never wanted to be the subject of newspaper headlines.

I didn't choose this life; it chose me.

Investigating police corruption backed me into a corner. It challenged me. So did the recent gag clause your office wanted, stopping me commenting on police matters in return for paying me compensation when I leave the force.

I agreed to speak to the *Herald Sun* last week as a cry for help, out of sheer frustration. I would like to explain why I can't sign your gag clause.

When things went haywire years ago my social life went from being a person liked by all, to being hated by most.

I was once comfortable in crowds; now I hate it. I used to like a bit of time to myself; now I crave it. I have become isolated and very afraid. Not paranoid — justifiably afraid.

I've felt numb for a long time. I didn't let anyone in. I had relationships, but I kept my sorrow inside. I didn't share the burden because I felt it was my problem. But I was wrong.

It isn't my problem. It's our problem. That is all of us.

Every person in this country who enjoys the freedom of living here has a responsibility to stand up and be counted despite the possibility of personal detriment. Our freedom relies on it.

Aussie mateship was always based on mutual trust and loyalty. That loyalty is based on solid values like honesty, transparency and integrity.

People who assume positions of power accept the esteem, perks and status that comes with their positions. Rightfully so, but these positions come with a catch. They come with a greater responsibility to be transparent, open and honest.

Every police officer, chief executive, company director, politician and others have to take that responsibility as part of the deal.

It should come as no surprise to you that my previous relationships failed. Not because there was any fundamental flaw, but because I couldn't love anyone, including myself.

I hated myself (as did many other people), so loving anyone else was always going to be difficult, if not impossible. Nevertheless, I now have a wonderful girlfriend who has helped me to love.

It helps to talk with her about my experiences.

This is not just dealing with post-traumatic stress — it is dealing with a continuing crisis every day, wondering what is going to happen next.

We still live in fear of normal everyday situations. The stress of this life is taking its toll.

I explained from the outset I wanted this financial settlement cleared up quickly so I could focus on the pending court cases. But months passed and I was continually asked to sign a reworded silence clause.

I became desperate and rang your assistant directly a few weeks ago. I pleaded for the matter to be concluded one way or another and explained that my girlfriend was losing her hair because of the stress.

I again explained my position on the hush clause.

There is no denying the fact that at times I feel hatred towards the corrupt Police who have taken my innocence away from me. But I am not bitter, nor revengeful.

I wish that one day I can be another face in the crowd, one of the boys, a fellow who likes a laugh, a surf, a game of cricket or footy and a few beers after.

That's Australian freedom. I yearn to feel free again.

I loathe the spotlight and always have. But all those years ago I knew I had a responsibility not to give up, quit or cover things up. I knew to stand up and be counted despite being in very unfamiliar territory.

I did, but unfortunately my situation snowballed and I've had to put my neck on the line.

I identified organised criminals allegedly working in harmony with corrupt police. I know it and you know it.

But I can't help any more — I've done my bit, openly, honestly and transparently. Clearly, it is time for me to go and do something else.

Whether you settle my claim or not is a matter for you. I will not sign a hush clause, ever.

I will remain true to myself and the people I promised to serve. But unfortunately I expect to confront extreme financial difficulty as a price. So be it.

I have lost many of my liberties in recent times but no one will ever take away my free speech.

For the record, I like this state and I like Victoria Police.

It is a wonderful organisation with many thousands of hard working, trustworthy intelligent people in it. I will not speak against those individuals — you have my word on that.

Once my superannuation is sorted out, I will resign as you wanted. I will do my duty and appear in court as a witness in the remaining corruption matter as I had promised you.

I will appear as a civilian.

Yours sincerely,

Simon Illingworth

After the article went to print negotiations resumed. The Force's lawyers requested to meet. We were happy to oblige. Jeremy Kelly's article covering that event appeared the next day.

> The Victoria police force has dropped a gag clause that stopped corruption-busting detective Simon Illingworth ever speaking out on police matters.
>
> The backdown came yesterday after Chief Commissioner Christine Nixon intervened to end the deadlock after saying she was unaware of the details of Det-Sgt Illingworth's compensation payout.
>
> The *Herald Sun* revealed last week the police's lawyers had demanded any payout include a clause preventing Det-Sgt Illingworth from ever criticising Ms Nixon or the force.
>
> It stated: '[Det-Sgt Illingworth] is not to make, or induce anyone else to make, any statement or statements which are likely to harm the interests of [Christine Nixon] or the Force generally.'
>
> Ms Nixon yesterday said she had not seen the offer and only became aware of Det-Sgt Illingworth's concerns in Saturday's *Herald*

Sun. 'The lawyers have been dealing with this. I haven't seen the final paperwork,' she said.

Ms Nixon said she had instructed the force's lawyers to resume negotiations with Det-Sgt Illingworth's lawyers to have the matter resolved. Talks were last night continuing as the parties sought a resolution.

Ms Nixon indicated she was willing to drop the clause, which she denied was an attempt to silence him.

'I don't care if Simon criticises me. He's perfectly entitled to do that, as many other people have and will, I imagine, in the future,' she said.

'I certainly don't need to be protected in any way, shape or form — I can defend myself.' The terms of any settlement with Det-Sgt Illingworth will remain confidential but the payout is expected to be $250,000 — the same amount offered to him several weeks ago.

The Ethical Standards Department detective went public in May with chilling tales of being bashed, threatened and intimidated by police and a lack of support offered by the force.

The settlement, in lieu of a severance payout and any WorkCover claim, would still prevent Det-Sgt Illingworth from discussing certain operational matters and ongoing investigations.

The State Opposition yesterday devoted Question Time to the matter.

Opposition police spokesman Kim Wells accused Police Minister Andre Haermeyer of instructing police to 'fix up this mess only because of embarrassing public criticism of the Government and Victoria Police'.

Mr Haermeyer denied the accusation.

Premier Steve Bracks praised Det-Sgt Illingworth in Parliament for his work in tackling corruption within the force.

Opposition Leader Robert Doyle said Det-Sgt Illingworth had been badly treated by the Government and Victoria Police.

'We should be sticking up for blokes like Simon Illingworth,' Mr Doyle said. 'Simon Illingworth is a hero, not a villain.'

I must add here for legal reasons that the chief commissioner does not necessarily accept the truth, accuracy or veracity of the articles written, except where specific reference is made to the specific position of the chief commissioner.

The matter settled on 17 November 2004 after two days of negotiations. I drove home exhilarated, exhausted and saddened. My police career was officially over but I knew it was for the better.

I sent a text message to Sarah: 'I'm coming home, S xxx.' I didn't tell her of the breakthrough in the negotiations because I wanted to get home first. When I arrived I blurted out, 'It's over.'

Sarah looked at me and we hugged each other; a tear rolled down my cheek. After a pause I began to tell her how hard it had been, this happened, that happened, my lawyer did this and that. Eventually, I drew breath only to notice Sarah wasn't drinking her champagne. Sarah was trying to talk.

Finally, she got a word in. She didn't need to speak for long. 'You're going to be a father,' she said.

I sat in stunned silence, laughed, closed my eyes, smiled and looked to the sky — it was the best day of my life.

In the end my career finished with an overwhelming amount of media pressure focused on one of the core functions of government — keeping people safe from crime. But, even in devastation lies opportunity.

The Office of Police Integrity was born, the new name for many of the same punters who had filed in under the police ombudsman's umbrella. It didn't satisfy many at the time, and I won't rest easy until there is a Royal Commission into corruption or an independent crime and corruption commission, but it's a step in the right direction. In the meantime on 21 November 2004 a writer for the *Herald Sun* reported an allegation that one of my corruption colleagues had an underworld contract taken out on his life in 2003. Apparently taking him out was worth $100 000 for any would-be hitman.

Nik 'The Russian' Radev, a vile Melbourne crook, was reported to have been making discreet enquiries about that policeman's whereabouts in 2003. The truth or otherwise of that allegation will never really be known because by April that year Radev himself felt the wrath of another vicious criminal; he was said to have been buried in a gold-plated casket. Radev's funeral was well attended, just like many other underworld funerals in Melbourne over the last few years.

I've read many tributes to murdered criminals in the daily newspapers over the last decade or so. There are often columns of tributes filled with bullshit about integrity, love, generosity, loyalty and honesty. Never any mention of the dear departed having been a thug, a standover man, a rapist, a street fighter, a pimp, a thief, a drug dealer or a hitman. The legacy of such vile people lives on inside their victims; their legacy stays alive long after the time the crim meets his grisly end. Victims can never erase the memory of what these people did to them, whether the crim is dead or alive.

But the motivation of these human vultures was best described by the Victorian National Party leader Peter Ryan on 25 May 2004 in parliament: 'This issue is about money — filthy, rotten lucre. It is about greed and the criminal elements in this state, both individuals and organisations, that are prepared to kill to get the money and keep the money. Worse still, it is about that small element of corrupt police who similarly want money. They are also about greed, and corruption has become their benchmark.'

I thought the government should have cleaned up this underworld mess by creating something that would last into the future. It should never come to the point where an honest cop loses his or her life before a real Victorian crime and corruption body is created. If I were to be murdered tomorrow, say, who would investigate it? Is a person's ego, an organisation's brand name or a political leader's reputation worth one good person's life? I think not. Is Australia's freedom worth a crime and corruption investigator's life? You decide. At the time of writing, the Office of Police Integrity had only recently attained the power to use telephone interceptions. It's a mess. The OPI still relies on the police force (which it is meant to investigate) to provide it with assistance to achieve this.

Soldiers know the risks they take and many have lost their lives fighting for our freedom. Are crime and corruption investigators the same? The short answer is yes, only because there is the possibility of a freak event such as a shootout or mistake occurring during a raid. Crime and corruption investigators aren't meant to go to war, nor are they equipped for it; but crime and corruption in Melbourne became a filthy war.

The safety and success of corruption investigators can be greatly increased by having the right strategy and resources available to them. But there's a reward for not being fair dinkum about corruption: limited strategy and minimal resources means corruption won't be uncovered. This of course means fewer embarrassing scandals in the short term, but what will this inaction create in the future? As organised crime continues to gain pace in Victoria there will come a day when we won't need to look overseas to see a culture of corruption emerging.

The way ahead is strong, ethical leadership and the intelligent use of resources dedicated to eradicating organised crime and corruption, not just what affects the crime statistics. And that includes ethics education programs and anti-corruption prevention strategies, coupled with a wide-ranging ethical leadership marketing campaign. Not the clever advertising stuff with fancy ponytails to make the force look good, but slogans that challenge our police to be the best they can be and that put the corrupt on notice.

Increased and well-used resources are only part of the solution, however. It is easy to be critical, easy to point out where another has failed or could have done better, but the best leaders are never those who simply hand out more resources and funds to tackle a problem; anyone can do that. History shows us that leaders can change culture, whether it's a team, an organisation, a town or even a country — many have done it. Mostly, good people rise to leadership positions, though sometimes they don't. Leadership has no connection to a university degree, a job title, class or social status, but leaders do have power. They are often people of strong values and principles, but not always. Criminals have values too — many drug cartels, crime empires and mafia organisations around the world have very successful leaders. But that's as far as these people go because they lack the key ingredient for greatness — ethical courage.

Great leaders focus on long-term goals. They guide and coach their people to be wise with their resources. Great leaders teach their people to grow, hunt and collect, rather than provide them with a meal. Leaders take responsibility: they walk the walk, not just talk the talk. They are mentors because it comes with the territory. They are confident of their values and principles and are willing to take the big step into the unknown. It takes courage to step away from the pack. It's easier to go with the flow and drift along the surface, like a foam coffee cup.

US President Theodore Roosevelt said,

> It is not the critic who counts, nor the one who points out how the strong man stumbled, or how the doer of deeds might have done better. The credit belongs to those who are actually in the arena, whose faces are marred with sweat and dust and blood, who strive valiantly, who err and come short again and again, who know the great enthusiasms, the great devotions, and spend themselves in a worthy cause, who at the best know the triumph of high achievement and who, at the worst, if they fail, fail while daring so greatly that their place shall never be with those cold intrepid souls who know neither victory nor defeat.

Very few Australian leaders have ever entered the arena. They move with public opinion and overseas trends. These days there is little respect for people of public status. We judge such people suspiciously because we are often lied to. Many of the people mentioned in this book have been handed power and public status; these people assume themselves to be great leaders. But our generation's leadership will be judged by the next generation, not by us. Some leaders will be found to have used their power well, others to have satisfied their own needs. Some leaders will be judged as weak, others as courageous. Weak leaders will have left the decisions to their propaganda specialists and spin-doctors who cleverly throw up smokescreens to camouflage a problem.

We live in a time of spin, marketing, lies and propaganda. In the 1980s it was said that 'Greed is good'; now it is said that 'Perception is reality'. But greed was never good, and, unless you live on a movie set, perception isn't reality. Almost everyone knows that. While we live for the present we mark time and leave these problems for the next generation. As a corrupt cop once said: 'Some people get on the bus, some run alongside it, [but] very few stand in front of it.'

Welcome to the arena.

APPENDIX I

Glossary of expressions used by
seasoned crims and cops

accelerator an arsonist
aka also known as
armgeographical or illicit drug section of a gang or criminal network
asphalt army traffic police
bad rap a hefty sentence
baggage apprentice crook
beak judge or magistrate
blat shoot at
blow away to shoot dead
bluey (get a) to be charged (reference to the blue-coloured defendant's charge sheets)
boss anyone above yourself in police rank
bower bird a prolific thief and hoarder of stolen property
brick a substantially fabricated brief of evidence 'bricked in'
brief a lawyer
buckled arrested by police
calling card a fingerprint or modus operandi of a crook left at a crime scene
canary, cockatoo a lookout used by illegal gaming rings
cap to kill someone; a small amount of drugs, usually heroin
caves derogatory term meaning 'the slums'
cells police jail
cement shoes any method of ensuring a murder victim's body stays underwater

character adjustment a flogging
choirboy a new constable
cleanskin a person with no prior criminal history
cod a dumb crook who takes the bait every time
contract an offering of money to kill someone
colours patch worn on the back of a leather jacket by motorcycle gang members
corrupter mediator between police and criminals
crayfish, lobster $20 note
crew a gang
crow a prostitute
dab fingerprint
deadbeat a person who borrows money but doesn't pay it back
docket head criminal with extensive prior convictions
dog whistleblower
drink, there's a drink in it you'll be paid for it (generally a bribe)
drop a cheque to pass a dud or stolen cheque
ducks are on the pond a warning to be quiet or careful.
earn (an) something that makes you money
eckies designer drug ecstasy
eyeball have a view of
eyewash capsicum spray or tear gas
fall guy someone willing to take the punishment for everyone else charged or apprehended
filth Internal Affairs
finger, collar to arrest someone for a crime
fit up set up to plant evidence to ensure a conviction
flog to assault
fuckknuckle an idiot who needs to be belted
gopher a person who gets things when instructed
go-between a third person used in underworld negotiations, normally for offering bribes
golden beer voucher, Allan Border $50 note
good crook a highly connected and professional criminal
hand relief service offered by illegal brothels masquerading as massage centres

home duties 900 a police officer's partner
hundred and fifty book police rulebook (every time someone stuffs up, a new rule goes into it)
jury wreckers a jovial term for traffic police, often used by detectives after losing a case (the suggestion being that one of the jurors received a ticket on the way to court which affected the outcome)
in the game involved in crime
jack policeman
key sledgehammer
lagger telltale
Laurie (Nash) cash
liquid gold beer
load up to fabricate evidence against an unsuspecting criminal
mellow, water down to reduce the weight and severity of evidence
mirror someone who's always looking into it
nose candy cocaine
nuffy not up to speed
number a cannabis cigarette, a joint
off crook's term for something being intercepted or being secretly listened to by police (example, 'the phone is off')
palm oil bribe money
playing the game a crook being cooperative with police
pole smoker female prostitute
pro-police will assist in any way
put off to kill someone
pyro pyromaniac
rock spider paedophile
roll over to give evidence against co-accused in return for a lesser or lenient jail sentence
rolled raided or arrested
seagull manager a manager who swoops in, shits on everyone and leaves
shrinkage the theft of a small quantity of something
snip to steal
stocktake to burn down your own premises

Street (the) Fitzroy Street, St Kilda
SG shotgun
scrum a NSW term for police getting their heads together to ensure a conviction
sharp aunty a good-looking woman who is past her prime
sharp uncle a good-looking man who is past his prime
sling to share the proceeds of crime with another person
slot, hole solitary confinement
speedball an often lethal concoction of heroin and cocaine
spliff cannabis cigarette, a joint
squarehead straight, law-abiding citizen
stash (a) hidden item or hiding place for drugs
sting or ripa scam where a third party is given stolen goods or drugs in a setup followed by a request for a bribe; a theft of drugs and/or money from a drug dealer
supergrass informer
throwaway a weapon or drug carried by bent cops to plant on a suspect
TJF the job's fucked — police saying
Warwick Farm druggies' rhyming slang for arm
wedge, coin money
wise guy Mafia gangster

APPENDIX 2

Letter to the *Age* by Simon Illingworth [23 October 1992]

May I address the article in this newspaper on 21/10. It was made apparent in your article that Constable Morgan and I committed perjury. This is simply not correct.

During the course of the bicycle helmet case it was brought to the attention of the Judge and the defendant that Constable Morgan and myself had made a mistake. This mistake was as a result of my reading the corroborator's number incorrectly; this number is written on the bottom of the penalty notice. Unfortunately, this resulted in Constable Morgan being included in the statement and later giving evidence.

This mistake does not amount to perjury. Perjury is a wilful and corrupt action and this mistake was neither. I felt ashamed that I had made such a mistake and I passed on my apologies to the defendant prior to this hearing.

This is not the first time I've appeared in your paper. I was the officer that 'stuck my neck out' and gave evidence against a senior policeman who was charged with inciting to kidnap and other serious charges. This filled in the best part of page three as he received a lengthy jail term.

I was the policeman who received the death threat prior to appearing in the previously mentioned case. This was received from another officer who was later charged with contempt and this case went to the Supreme Court. I, again, had to stand up and be counted. I must say I do not feel proud of these incidents and have received a great deal of on-the-job related problems as a result.

I was the policeman who crashed down the door of a burning building in Franklin Street Melbourne and rescued two semi-conscious kids from the second story. The building was well alight. This again appeared in your paper.

It seems ironic to me that after all these articles it would be the *Age* that would print only half the facts in 'the bicycle helmet case' leaving readers to believe that Constable Morgan and I are anything else but honest.

APPENDIX 3

Transcript of *Australian Story* program
'One Man Standing' broadcast on ABC television
Monday, 24 May 2004

CAROLINE JONES: Tonight, a unique insight into the frightening world of Melbourne's gangland killings and police corruption. Simon Illingworth is a young detective sergeant who's spent the last four years working for Police Internal Affairs in Victoria, weeding out crooked police.

He's been commended for his work and brought successful prosecutions against corrupt officers. But Simon Illingworth says he's been isolated, threatened and bashed — not by crooks, but by other policemen. Now at the end of his tether, he's risking everything to tell his inside story.

SIMON'S MOTHER: Simon seems to be on a journey to nowhere, in a way, at the moment, because I think he doesn't quite know what the future holds for him.

DET. SGT SIMON ILLINGWORTH: The city brings back memories. It does bring back a lot of the bad memories. You turn on the radio; you can't get way from it. There's corruption. Those sorts of things just continually bring back what you're about.

SIMON'S SISTER: For completely unselfish reasons, Simon put his life at risk. He didn't know that it would be as severe as it was, but he didn't do it for himself, yet his entire life has been completely changed as a result of it.

DET. SGT SIMON ILLINGWORTH: I do look back and wonder — if I had my time again, whether or not I would have just taken off, gone interstate and worked interstate, but I love Victoria Police. I like surfing here. I love this place. I didn't want to leave; I didn't want to go somewhere else.

It's not in my nature to flee something, to leave it unfinished, and so I won't.

SIMON'S MOTHER: When Simon first started in the police force, Victoria was thought to be the best police force in the whole of Australia, absolutely no corruption at all.

DET. SGT SIMON ILLINGWORTH: I was nineteen. I'd come straight out of the surf into the academy. Looked pretty naive, I suppose. You know, it was something that was worthwhile. I mean, it sounds corny, but when you get interviewed for a police career, you say, I want to help the community, and I still believe that.

SIMON'S MOTHER: We were really thrilled, we were very proud. We thought it would be just the thing for Simon.

DET. SGT SIMON ILLINGWORTH: I could be an investigator and a detective, and I thought that this was an opportunity for me to live something that was exciting.

There's an element of danger, everyone knows that, but it was just something that gripped me and that's why I thought, this is for me. Up to the first two years, it was everything that I wanted — you know, there was mateship, I was playing in the police football team, I had got information that led to the arrest of one of the top ten, which was just unheard of.

I saved two young kids out of a burning building — it was a dream come true, everything was great. It was the job that everyone should do. Two years in and I ran into corruption.

NEIL O'SULLIVAN — RETIRED DETETECTIVE SUPERINTENDENT: Early in Simon's career, he was rostered on duty with a sergeant who'd been newly promoted from the Armed Robbery Squad, who came to the station with a high profile.

DET. SGT SIMON ILLINGWORTH: We thought, this guy's a legend. He was what I wanted to be. I wanted to become, you know, a gun detective.

He asked me to take him around where the card games and the gambling took place. We went in there, and I started writing everyone's name down and told them to leave the money on the table. All of a sudden, the till's ringing behind me and there's money being stuffed into a pocket. And I didn't want to look back because I knew who it was and I didn't say anything.

The money on the table went into his pocket as well. I was compromised. I didn't even get a choice in it. And I thought, well, what's going to happen now? Is he, he's gonna offer me half. I mean, thankfully, not only was he a thief but he was greedy as well, and he didn't offer me half.

We drove off. We went to the Armed Robbery Squad and he asked me to grab a bag off the lockers. And the bag was really heavy, and I knew — I didn't even have to look in it — I knew there were guns in it — nothing is that heavy. I didn't know what to do.

And then he picks his own nightshift crew, as they do, you know, you pick the people you can trust, no doubt, and, of course, who can he trust? He can trust me. Because I was willing to just . . . passively take part in it . . . which isn't me, because I've always had the strength of character, but I was becoming someone that I wasn't.

We ended up on this nightshift and he'd hatched a plan to kidnap a criminal. He talked about having — put a boiler suit and a balaclava on. He spoke about a quarry, taking him to a quarry, and then I asked him what he was going to do, and he made this, you know, boom.

This was going to be an execution.

SIMON'S MOTHER: He rang me up and said, 'Mum, I've got to disappear for two days.' I had no idea what was going on, and I was worried, and I said, 'Simon, what on earth's the matter?' He said, 'I can't explain now', and that was the end of the conversation.

DET. SGT SIMON ILLINGWORTH: Everything was going through my head. Do I get out of the police force and just pretend that this plan had just never happened?

Or do I stick true to what I said when I was getting into the police force? But what happened then? I went to Internal Affairs and I made a statement.

NEIL O'SULLIVAN: Whistleblower is a tag — it's like mobster, gangster. It's like having a tattoo on your forehead.

All the criminals that you've locked up, all the times where you've put your life on the line for someone, that becomes incidental because you're a dog.

DET. SGT SIMON ILLINGWORTH: I had to go to court for the committal hearing, and I walked to court because I guess the situation was that no one wanted to drive me there. And I walked up and stood there while all the other police, detectives from the squads or places where he'd worked stared at me like I was some sort of a freak. And then one of the police took it to another level and pointed at his forehead and went 'boom' in my face.

SIMON'S MOTHER: From then on, the police force was different for Simon. But he stayed there; he wasn't going to let them win. But he had court case after court case and it was really difficult. One of the barristers for Simon rang us up and said, 'We're so proud of Simon. He was so brave. This will be the worst thing that could ever possibly happen.' But we didn't know what was to come. And, yeah, there were worse things to come.

DET. SGT SIMON ILLINGWORTH: One night, I went out, as we generally did after finishing nightshift. We went to a pub in Carlton. I went to take a drink and I was king hit. I fell down to my knees. I was kicked in the head a number of times. I recognised him. He was a copper. It just takes me back . . . But I got onto my hands and knees and stood up . . . I wanted to show that a whistleblower had what it took. And then I fell. Head first . . . into the floor. But I'm still here. Football and, ultimately, sport were really my escape from the policing problems that I'd had.

SIMON'S SISTER: Once I was standing on the side of the field and all of a sudden Simon goes running off the field. And one of the opposition in the grandstand was screaming out, 'You stupid whistleblower', and I guess it just gets to the point with Simon where the frustration's too much, and he went up to the guy and he said, 'Do you know why you're yelling that out?' And the guy had no idea.

DET. SGT SIMON ILLINGWORTH: It was one of those moments where you just think, Is this gonna follow me into every aspect of my life? I thought if I went into the corruption area, that I could actually do some good. I could hopefully make a difference because of where I had been and where I had travelled.

NEIL O'SULLIVAN: We had a team of men, up to sixteen. We used to conduct integrity testing. It was a new way of policing. It hadn't been done in Australia before and was quite successful. Simon, as a young sergeant, was outstanding in his ability to analyse situations. He was very perceptive and quite focused.

DET. SGT SIMON ILLINGWORTH: Investigating corrupt police is probably the hardest thing that you could ever do, because it's not cat and mouse; it's cat and cat. Both of you have the same skills. They know the loopholes. They know to speak in code. They know to write things down and hand them to each other rather than speaking over a telephone. They know all those things.

NEIL O'SULLIVAN: All internal investigators get names — there's toecutters, dogs. The current name is the filth, which I believe derives from *The Bill*, which is the English term for 'em, so it's a worldwide phenomenon, because you are . . . hated.

ABC NEWS: The ABC has learnt the investigation by the police's Ethical Standards Department isn't confined to the Drug Squad. It's believed out of nearly forty members under investigation, twenty-five are from the Drug Squad but the remainder are members of regional and suburban stations, including Brunswick, Prahran and St Kilda.

NEIL O'SULLIVAN: In 2000, we undertook a search of the St Kilda police complex which yielded a number of exhibits — guns, drugs, other contraband that shouldn't have been found where it was. Simon was responsible for the analysis and review of that material. Once we pulled it together, he was assigned the investigation.

SIMON ILLINGWORTH: Things started to open up. It really — to describe it, it was like finding an octopus that was peeling off everywhere, and you were going down different arms.

ABC NEWS: After years under a cloud, Victoria's drug investigation team is being scrapped with an internal corruption review recommending sweeping changes to clean out the squad. One crooked drug detective has already been jailed, and confidential squad files stolen four years ago have never been found.

CHIEF COMMISSIONER CHRISTINE NIXON — VICTORIA POLICE, ON ABC NEWS: The Ethical Standards Department, though, was involved, and it is in fact their work that has found this officer.

NEIL O'SULLIVAN: We weren't the most loved people in policing, and I think it was a victory for some of these people that we were closed down. The publicity at the time was that police were being given these extra resources to fight corruption. But effectively, what was done was robbing Peter to pay Paul.

DET. SGT SIMON ILLINGWORTH: People ended up going into different areas. Neil, who was a terrific copper and spent years in it — an old-school tough man, but very proactive — I walked him out to the carpark with a cardboard box [with] his possessions in it.

NEIL O'SULLIVAN: It was fairly emotional for all of us. And Simon said to me that night, he said, 'If they treat you like this, at your rank, he said, how are they going to treat me or anybody else at this level?' The system is very carnivorous.

DET. SGT SIMON ILLINGWORTH: This nightmare that I am living with will continue. I am a taskforce of one. My investigation was given to me and me alone. If I'm not here . . . happy days . . . for some.

NEIL O'SULLIVAN: Simon's gone from a close-knit working environment to an area now where it's like a ghost town where he's been plonked amidst all these empty workstations with another person up another end. That in itself tells the story — you've been cast off. You're superfluous to needs.

DET. SGT SIMON ILLINGWORTH: I'm not going to say why this has happened. People can make up their own minds.

ABC NEWS: Ms Nixon has confirmed the Ethical Standards Department is investigating claims that a suspended senior detective gave a criminal a gun that was later used in a gangland killing.

NEIL O'SULLIVAN: In the course of this investigation, there's some intelligence been provided that implicates a lot of prominent criminals, a lot of prominent police.

ABC NEWS: The now disbanded Drug Squad is at the centre of a police corruption investigation focused on two officers accused of drug trafficking.

DET. SGT SIMON ILLINGWORTH: I'm unable to elaborate on what corruption I have found, other than to say that it's now a matter before the court. I've arrested and charged six people. One of the accused has pleaded guilty. The other five are out on bail.

NEIL O'SULLIVAN: I believe Simon has reason to believe that his safety will be in jeopardy. We're playing for high stakes here.

DET. SGT SIMON ILLINGWORTH: You don't know whether you're gonna turn a corner and get a handshake or a bullet, and I don't like that.

ABC NEWS: Police are investigating reports that a man found murdered with his wife in Kew last night was due to give evidence in a drug case against police. It's believed to have been an execution-style murder with gunshots to their heads.

The dead man's lawyer says the killing points to a direct link between the spate of gangland murders and police corruption. There appears to be no sign of a let-up yet to the spate of killings, the likes of which have never been seen before in Australian criminal history.

CHIEF COMMISSIONER CHRISTINE NIXON — VICTORIA POLICE, ON ABC NEWS: It's a very difficult area to work in, police corruption. I think what we're seeing is a whole range of tactics being used both by perhaps the police under investigation, by in some cases their lawyers, I think, and others who perhaps don't want this whole process to continue.

DET. SGT SIMON ILLINGWORTH: I have had a drink with a friend, and I have had the target of my corruption investigation walk through the hotel where I'm at with a person who's now accused of one of the underworld killings.

NEIL O'SULLIVAN: They weren't there for the good beer or the good company. That was a firm message, obviously, to intimidate.

DET. SGT SIMON ILLINGWORTH: I've got this underworld figure staring at me. And I'm thinking, how vulnerable am I?

NEIL O'SULLIVAN: I think it's devastated him. You have this air of invincibility. After a while, that veneer wears thin and the fear and that becomes an ulcer inside you.

DET. SGT SIMON ILLINGWORTH: Someone in the police, I believe, has risked my life and my family's lives, for whatever reason, by handing over my address to criminals.

ABC NEWS: Tonight, bullets in the letterbox as a top cop concedes a link between underworld murders and police corruption. It's alleged the bullets, similar to these, were police-issue, etched with the names of an investigator and his wife and put in their letterbox.

DET. SGT SIMON ILLINGWORTH: I see today . . . the bullets in the mail and all that sort of thing, and I feel — I truly feel for those people.

ABC NEWS: It's understood that one member of the Ceja Task Force has taken stress leave and another may do so. However, police say they do have measures in place to protect their staff.

SIMON'S SISTER: I think the calm exterior that Simon portrays was ruffled with the recent threats — all the things that would run through your mind about, What's going to happen next? What do I have to be aware of? What can I possibly do to ensure my safety?

DET. SGT SIMON ILLINGWORTH: I have had to sell my home. I have had to carry a firearm.

NEIL O'SULLIVAN: He has had electronic and physical surveillance of his house and his being and his family. It becomes a major factor in your life, in your relationship. You don't want to go out — oh, someone might see me.

DET. SGT SIMON ILLINGWORTH: I'm unable to settle in one place and then have to move again. I've probably moved, I don't know, three or four times in the last few months.

SIMON'S MOTHER: It's really difficult for me at the moment, I think, to see him so upset. I just want him to do something else.

DET. SGT SIMON ILLINGWORTH: My dream was always to be a detective. But I've got to a point where I don't think that I'm capable of doing it any more. I don't believe that, physically or mentally, a person can continue being put in the situations that I've been put in.

You know, it's like you've been at war for sixteen years. That's what I feel like. I am not in a position where I can walk out of the police force and wipe my hands. I've got two years of trials, at least, so if I chose to leave, I'd still be called as a witness in those trials anyway, and I'm not about to walk away from three years' work.

NEIL O'SULLIVAN: Simon is a natural leader. It would be a loss for the Victoria Police to see him go. The issue is that he has a lot to offer.

DET SGT SIMON ILLINGWORTH: I have come to realise that I would prefer now to educate many rather than incarcerate a few. It's these small compromises all the way through. We need to prevent that so that they're not falling into this trap of realising one day, Hey, I'm a copper and I'm also a drug dealer.

NEIL O'SULLIVAN: Simon's taking a huge gamble in telling his story. Again, it's a display of his openness and his commitment to the Victoria Police. It's more about the Victoria Police, about it cleansing itself and moving on, and he should be part of the process of moving on.

DET. SGT SIMON ILLINGWORTH: For myself, I have found someone who's just a wonderful person. My dream is to have a family, ultimately, and have a house that has a white picket fence and not something that is to keep people out — it's just to keep children in.

Ultimately, I'd like to live like everyone else does and not as a whistleblower. When people from my work have said to me, 'Don't let them win, don't let them win' — well, the win is over for me.

I think, ultimately, the win is people viewing this and either deciding to change or staying on the right side of the rails and doing the right thing. That would be a win for me.

Things are on their way up, you know. I hope it's just inevitable now that there will be some sort of corruption commission and it will take the weight off people like me.

I've always thought that good will defeat evil . . . here we go.

APPENDIX 4

Hansard, Victorian State Parliament [25 May 2004]

MR DOYLE (Leader of the Opposition) — Some years ago the head of the Royal Canadian Mounted Police (RCMP) spoke at an Interpol conference. In reading some of his remarks, his introduction in particular struck me as analogous to the Victorian situation we now face. He said:

One of the essential components of a just and well-functioning society is an effective, well-disciplined and honest police service in which citizens have implicit trust.

He went on to say:

When corruption takes hold within an organisation whose very existence is based on integrity, that trust is shattered, and our entire society suffers.

I regret to say that that is where we are today with the question of police corruption, which the bill before the house seeks to address. The fact is, as the head of the RCMP said, 'No system is ever ... impervious to corruption'. We know that 'greed and weakness are the root causes' of corruption and we know that 'denial, incompetence and collusion are the reasons institutions fail to overcome corruption'. We have a police corruption problem in Victoria. This is now an undeniable fact that faces the government and this Parliament. For a long time — I think like most Victorians and most members of this house — I did not want to believe this was true, or rather, I believed that if there was police corruption it was limited to one or two incidents.

Until last week I supported the government's proposal to extend the powers of the Ombudsman to deal with police corruption, although I must say I never believed an extra $1 million was anywhere near enough resources to do the job. I conveyed that support to the Premier and to the Ombudsman.

Indeed only last week I wrote to the Premier offering the Liberal Party's support to bring on this legislation at the earliest opportunity. I offered the Liberal Party's guarantee that we would give the bill a speedy passage in both houses of the Parliament. I understand this bill will pass both houses today. I certainly hope that is the case, and I am sure every effort will be made to ensure that that happens.

Late last week, along with the shadow Minister for Police and Emergency Services, the member for Scoresby, I met police who provided us with confidential information that was impossible for us to ignore. The evidence I heard from the police officers is the most chilling I have heard in my time in Parliament. This information has forced me to change my mind. I now believe the additional powers and resources granted to the Ombudsman by the bill before the house are inadequate to deal with the crisis facing Victoria. That does not mean the Liberal Party will oppose the bill.

It should proceed without delay, but it is no longer the solution to a problem that is now much bigger and more serious than we had thought. I agree with former Victorian and Western Australian senior police officer, Bob Falconer, who argues in the *Herald Sun* today that a beefed-up Ombudsman's office, and indeed the police ethical standards unit, have a critical and complementary role to an anticorruption commission.

We heard today of the police chief commissioner being given extra powers. Again that may well be welcome. We do not know what these powers are — and, by the way, neither does the chief commissioner, according to a radio interview she did this morning. Still, these are no replacement for an anticorruption commission. They may be complementary to it, and we are disposed to look favourably upon the extra powers for the chief commissioner, allowing of course for the detail to be put before us.

As I said, I now believe Victoria needs an anticorruption commission with broad-ranging powers to immediately deal with the problem of police corruption and the connections to the recent scourge of gangland killings in Melbourne. I think we have to stop skirting the issue and pretending that they are not connected. Gangland killings and corrupt police are connected.

While speaking on the merits of the bill before the house today I will outline some initial suggestions from the Liberal Party about how such an anticorruption commission could be established and how it could be effective in getting to the bottom of the very real problems we face in the Victorian police force. Such an anticorruption commission could have a number of elements. I will outline five elements worthy of consideration by the government and Parliament.

The first is an operations unit to deal with special projects such as telephone tapping, listening devices and surveillance.

That operations unit should comprise forensic experts, accountants and computer experts who can follow the money trail back to the crime — something the Attorney-General outlined as part of the powers to be given to the chief commissioner in an answer in question time today. We should not underestimate the importance of that expertise.

The second is an investigations unit which could also work with those forensic experts. This unit should be reactive and could involve the existing resources of the Ombudsman's office and the Victoria Police ethical standards unit, similar to the model outlined by former Western Australian police commissioner Bob Falconer. This unit would also need to have a coercive powers team similar to the Australian Crime Commission examiners. This would involve the utilisation of investigators who could plan and execute sophisticated effective responses.

The commission would also need a proactive program of integrity testing — 'stings', if you like — to uncover involvement in corruption. The preventive power in their knowing that stings may be conducted by an anticorruption force cannot be overestimated. Apart from operations and investigations, the commission needs a major arm which has not yet been part of the public discussion but the importance of which I will spend some time today outlining — that is, a prevention and education arm to generate community programs and even advertisements to relay the right messages about police and public corruption to the corporate and public sectors.

The need for a prevention and education arm is one of the reasons I think an anticorruption commission is a better model than the government's Ombudsman model, as outlined in the bill before the house. There needs to be ongoing education, not just of the police but more broadly of the public, about the total unacceptability of corruption and the consequences of involvement in it. We also need a whistleblowers hotline for the commission to obtain the information which is vital to tackling police corruption. That could be complemented by commission web sites inviting and dealing with any public information.

They are the five headline suggestions outlining how an anticorruption commission might be structured and operate, and I will come back to some of them in detail a little later on.

I say at the outset that I am indebted to a number of police officers, especially the senior anticorruption police whose ideas I have based this model and these ideas on. The courage of the many serving officers who wish to rid this state of the stench of corruption is most encouraging. I wish to say also that I do not believe we have a corrupt police force, because that is not the case. By and large our police force is made up of hardworking, ethical and honourable police force members, but unfortunately there is a core of bad cops —

A government member interjects . . .

MR DOYLE — Just relax! It is very important that the issue of police corruption and what to do about it does not become a political football. The strong desire of the Liberal Party is to work with the government to find the right solutions.

I have tried to outline the reasons for my belief that the police ombudsman model before the house does not offer an adequate response. If the government wishes to go back to the drawing board and redesign such an anticorruption commission, we will not turn this into a political dogfight with finger pointing and accusations of blame. We will work with the government and the Victoria Police to get the best model possible for Victoria so we can be confident that we have the weapons to fight the insidious cancer of corruption. Unfortunately, as I have said, I now believe the bill before the house fails to deliver the very best model — and we deserve no less than the very best.

We need a solution to the crisis facing Victoria Police and all other Victorians. While the bill before the house offers some progress towards finding a solution, only the adoption of an anticorruption commission will provide an ongoing and adequate response by the government and the Parliament. I will point out two reasons in particular for that being the case.

Firstly, we need a long-term strategy, and secondly, we need a coordinated approach to an anticorruption strategy.

I listened carefully earlier today to the Premier outlining a range of measures — some of them quite new — which the government proposes to use to tackle this problem. There is, of course, the Ombudsman bill presently before the house, and I understand extra resources will be given to the Director of Public Prosecutions. We were also told today in question time that the chief commissioner will get further powers and that the ethical standards unit will have the resources it needs to police the police. But the point I make is that it is not a coordinated approach to have a number of different agencies charged with partial responsibility. I was not convinced by the Premier's argument, even on the basis that there would be better coordination.

The other reason why this will not work in those institutions, even if we do the very best we can, is that any investigation that is ongoing must be totally independent. That is one of the problems with the police Ethical Standards Department — eventually its members return to general policing. I will come to some of those problems later.

The lack of independence in internal affairs is not a problem in our police force at the moment, partly because of the calibre of officers we have had — people like Noel Perry, Steve Fontana and Simon Illingworth. But it would be unfortunate, given that those police have to return to general policing, if we go to a situation in the future where an officer was faced with having to make an invidious choice between rigorously pursuing corruption and maintaining his career and his principles, based on his knowing that if he were to return to the general policing population he could be intimidated and isolated because of the rigour with which he or she pursued the corrupt. One of the benefits of an anti corruption commission would be that it could provide a career path for officers who wished to go down that track.

They would not have to return to general policing; instead they could make a career involving a diversity of tasks and be promoted within such a commission.

I turn now to a slightly more detailed outline of the five-pronged attack I have suggested. We need education, prevention, reactive investigation, proactive investigation, research and analysis, and that can only be achieved through a commission. Why not have a royal commission?

While at this stage I am not ruling it out as complementing our commission proposal, I note that there are some shortcomings. Royal Commissions are reactive in their investigation and reporting, they are not accountable for future prevention and they do not have ownership in implementing the recommendation. Having said that, I note the success of Royal Commissions in Western Australia and Queensland in pursing corruption.

When I said the Ombudsman's office is not the ideal model that is no reflection on that office. It is just that the information that has come to me suggests that this problem is of a scale and sophistication that is too great for that office, with its very modest budget, to handle.

The point that I make here is that even with this model — the bill before the house — if the Ombudsman is to do it, they have to provide their report to the Chief Commissioner of Police and also to the Minister of Police and Emergency Services. Again, that is a breach of that independence that they need. Why should they report to the very people they are reporting on? We need to make sure that any such investigation is independent and is seen to be independent.

Time under these new rules is somewhat limited, so here are a couple of quick ideas. I wish I could spell them out in more detail.

Firstly, I refer to the education part of our five-pronged attack. We need to initiate culture change, an element of ethics in the internal courses of police and public officials, including an ethical decision-making model, which includes casework and open forums for ethical discussion. We need to increase the sense of moral integrity of the police and public officials through interactive training; this has been proven to work. We would have open discussion groups, for instance, that are not focused on right and wrong decision making, but on those grey area issues, including discussions about the ethical decision-making model. You focus on those grey areas to force independent thought and to create a sense of ownership of the credibility of the department and the police force.

You encourage the reinvention of employees who know they have started the slide into corrupt practice. I point out Simon Illingworth's very honest appraisal of his own policing experience. It can be that corruption has a blind eye turned to it; this is passive corruption. We need to draw a line there and help those people who have started that slide. The chief of the Royal Canadian Mounted Police actually pointed out an example in his own force that started with a drugs officer accepting a couple of free hockey tickets and finished with the suicide of that officer in the early 1990s, because of the slide into corruption.

We need to have a regime that is prospective not retrospective. We need to make sure that we can support those people who do not want to be forced into corrupt practice. We need to engage the public in community ethical standards. We could have a range of ethical slogans on police and government vehicles.

We could have positive ethical engagement through thought-provoking and visible slogans, ensuring ownership of the idea by the police and the government. We could foster area or regional codes of ethics, like the city of Melbourne code of ethics. All of those areas in education are not meant to be prescriptive. They are some ideas to throw out to say, 'This is an area we have not thought of and we are not addressing'.

Prevention is our second big area. We need to provide a systems review process for our police force. If we have an anticorruption commission — if it becomes a reality — it has to be seen to prevent corruption in the first place. It cannot just find out what happened and what went wrong. That is why we cannot just have a royal commission. You need an ongoing view. Although fear is a more powerful motivator, I find it amazing that we do not really reward ethical behaviour. That can be a powerful incentive and motivator.

It is interesting that we reward our sporting heroes, but we are not so good at rewarding those in public life who are slaving out there, day to day, in service of the community. Measuring good work is hard in some occupations. How do you measure good policing? It is rare for people to recognise good work. Sometimes achieving a goal in policing, for instance, is secondary to the mental and physical strength and discipline that is required, in one police officer's words to me, to 'go for it'. It may well be that the court decision goes against you, but that should not detract from the attempt.

Ironically we reward sporting heroes in the same way. We reward winners and not so much those that have made the attempt. I would suggest a formal reward and recognition policy for police. As I have said, it is a surprise that more is not done here considering the way police services rely on integrity for their reputation.

We also need an anonymous telephone service for people requiring assistance so that we can get in to what is happening, and so that we can provide that help. There need to be cross-cultural messages. We know that people arriving from poverty-stricken, failing or corrupt societies, where there are corrupt police forces, are at considerable risk of being manipulated themselves by the corrupt. We need to make sure that we are getting those messages to a range of those communities that come here. They are often the target of the corrupt, and it is well known that in these communities it is rare that they report corruption.

The third area is that we need a reactive investigation division. Current internal affairs bodies separate general complaints and corruption investigation. I do not see that there is a need to separate those two. Both are trying to get the same outcome. Often you find that people who are corrupt have had numerous complaints made against them leading up to the investigation. They can be an excellent gauge of someone's professionalism or an indicator of a slide into corrupt practices. As outlined by Bob Falconer this morning, you can decide which ones go to the commission, which ones are handled by the Ombudsman and which ones are handled by the police ethical standards department.

The Victorian ethical standards department needs to overhaul its current investigative practices. We are told that in practice investigations are given to teams. Simon Illingworth's remarkable bravery last night proved that that is not so — that often complaints go to one person to investigate. One person is easy to target, to isolate, to coerce, to intimidate — not so a team. We need to ensure the resources are there.

After the past few days I do not think it would come as a surprise to people to hear that investigators and their families are at risk. Three investigators whom I have come across are under genuine threat. An anticorruption commission would have to have satisfactory resources and personnel to ensure we protect those who are protecting us.

As I said before, corruption is always about greed. It is always about the receipt of money or a gift, so we need those forensic accountants, those computer experts to trace that money trail back. That is why I was interested in the Attorney-General's proposal today. Although I will look at it with interest, we need the resources to make sure we can track those money trails back to the scene of the crime. From memory, I think there is only one such qualified person working in the Ombudsman's office at the moment.

We need a proactive investigation division.

This is integrity testing, or stings if you like. We need to target specific persons identified by the research unit as being at high risk. One suggestion put to me was that trainees and new employees should be subjected to random integrity tests. The reasons for such tests are quite compelling: police in particular are susceptible to influence early in their careers, and it is therefore of great long-term benefit for trainees to be targeted for integrity testing on a random basis.

This is coming to me from police; it is not something I would have thought of. Random testing of trainees would provide them with a feeling of vulnerability if they were tempted to be corrupt, but it would also give them a legitimate excuse for non-compliance with unethical or corrupt behaviour. As well, it would ensure that any person who was corrupt thought twice before recruiting others, particularly those more junior.

We need a research unit. Again I wish I had more time to spell this out, but unfortunately I do not. We particularly need a research and analysis division.

We need to have random surveys of public opinion regarding police handling of corruption. We need to assess the intelligence that flows in and suggest that members be targeted in proactive investigations. We need an anti corruption web site, as I suggested earlier. There is a Hong Kong example. That commission set up an adult web site and a child and youth web site. The Hong Kong Independent Commission against Corruption adult web site has had 65 million hits, the child and youth web site has had 26 million hits.

We need to research corruption indicators, which are used by some anticorruption bodies to assist in indicating whether a police officer is corrupt or could be tempted into corrupt practices. We need to know whether employees are displaying any of these indicators: sick days; cynicism; resentment, particularly of management; absenteeism from the workstation; excessive use of force in their duties; and financial debt. The use of those indicators seems to me to be the area where we need to do a lot more work.

We need to be particularly careful — and I am not making any suggestion here — because around the world periods of high induction into police forces can relate directly to levels of corruption flowing into police forces. It is believed to be a result of poor background checks and people putting colleagues into the police for obvious purposes.

I do not see why we would not introduce something like a polygraph test for recruits to the police force, like the American Federal Bureau of Investigation does. We could ask them three simple questions: any recent drug use; any contact with criminals or gangs; what criminal history. We need to tightly monitor known corruption-prone areas. We now know about the Drug Squad, but there are other areas where we need that tight monitoring.

Recent news of what I believe to be an inappropriate use of informers requires us to tighten our protocols on informers. We should not accept anybody who has an unsavoury prior history relating specifically to police interaction like bribe offers or assaulting police.

We should not allow informers to be considered to be 'owned' by individual officers rather than the police force. We must have a termination date on those relationships. We cannot have unregistered informers. Where we need to provide assistance to informers, including character evidence, letters and housing assistance, all of those things should be kept in the individual's file, and that file should be checked periodically to ascertain the overall value of the informer to the community. These are five areas which I wish I had more time to outline. I offer them only as initial suggestions. I am not suggesting I have all the received wisdom on how such a commission should be set up.

There are a couple of things we need to consider. Firstly, spot the greed — if you find the greed, you find the corruption, because corruption is all about greed. That is difficult to do because it requires expertise, proactively and reactively, in research, as I suggested before. Secondly, let us understand that corruption is a cancer. One rotten apple does help to spoil the barrel. It might be a small number of police who are corrupt, but do not underestimate the effect those police have on the force as a whole or our society as a whole, as I outlined in my initial comments.

Thirdly — this is something I think we have underestimated — do not underestimate the energy and resources going into corruption, going into making corruption happen. For the crime world this is one of the best investments they can make. Through their expertise they can identify people who could be recruited to corrupt practices. They are very good at managing those recruits and, of course, they are very, very good at benefiting from those recruits. Do not underestimate the resources and the impetus for crime to foster corruption.

This leaves us with a bit of a quandary, something with which we are all struggling today. Do we get it all out in the open? Do we risk the reputation of something as fine as Victoria Police? Or do we deal with it quietly? Do we deal with it internally and not risk ruining the reputation of the police force? My view now is that that second option means that we react rather than actually taking action when a crisis occurs.

Regrettably, I think that is what has happened in the face of allegations of police corruption and this terrible outbreak of gangland killings and violence. That seems to me to be what has happened. We all need courage both inside and outside this place, we all need the courage of someone like a Simon Illingworth. We need to be prepared to stand up and ask the tough questions; we need to be prepared to do the right thing.

Harking back to that chief of the Royal Canadian Mounted Police, it was interesting when he talked about his own police force and what he did to make sure that he prevented, as far as possible, corruption from occurring. He talked about getting the right people. That is obviously critical both for a police force and for any anticorruption commission. Let us not underestimate the difficulty of finding someone to head such a commission and the difficulty of recruiting the quality of staff we are going to need for such a commission to be truly effective.

Equally important is screening out the wrong people. From time to time that has obviously not happened in the Victoria Police. I am not sure that we could have prevented it — but it is one of the things we need a public debate about. We then need to train people properly. Most police training courses are rather like military training — they are told what to do, when to do it and how to do it. I would like to see, particularly in the training of our police, tuition in ethics, behaviour and decision making. How can that be built in? How can we make sure that we give officers all the right habits from the start of their police careers?

Once we do that we then need to oversee and supervise our police force. That is a big question for us. When you think of the workload that many of our senior police carry, particularly our managerial and command police, you wonder how much of it is about pushing paper rather than dealing with people, which is the only way you get to really know what is going on.

If you are just a paper pusher, because that is what your role has relegated you to, how can you get to know those indicators I have talked about before, including the changes of behaviour that can be the early signs of corruption? We need to make sure people are taking care of their staff.

The fourth thing that this chief of police said involved detection. He talked about the difficulties of identifying and dealing with corruption. Again, regrettably, I have no confidence that the Ombudsman model, even with its powers of coercive questioning and initiating inquiries, has the ability to truly detect, identify and deal with corruption. I recognise that that question is in the hands of all the people in the organisation, not just the overseeing body, but nevertheless it is important.

I am not suggesting that these brief suggestions and ideas are the be-all and end-all.

The Chief Commissioner of Police said a little over a week ago that she wished for a public conversation about an anticorruption commission. I hope this is just such a contribution, and I hope we can work together on this. I hope we can develop a model for an anticorruption commission that has the government, the Liberal Party, the Nationals and the Independents — in other words, the Parliament of Victoria — as well as the police, our legal community and the wider community working together to develop a model. We have a real chance to do that. These situations do not come along very often.

The natural reaction of government is to resist suggestions that change direction or tack. I encourage the government to take up the offer, because it is genuinely made. If the government made the decision to change tack, and if it decided to give the chief commissioner the powers that she needs, to give the Ombudsman further powers and to beef up the resources of the Director of Public Prosecutions, I would accept all of it; but if it also said, 'Just to make sure, we will set up an anticorruption commission and not leave anything to chance', it would get our support.

Finally, this is about whether we have the guts, the courage and the political will to do something about the cancer of corruption. That is the real question that every conscience faces in this chamber. I have an optimistic view of members of Parliament, despite what the public might think. I believe members of Parliament, from whatever side, come here because they wish to make a difference to the community they serve.

This is an opportunity that we must not let slip, because it is an opportunity for us to leave a legacy for future generations so they do not have to face the crisis we have faced over the last months and even years.

Ending his amazing and remarkably brave *Australian Story* last night, Simon Illingworth, in what I thought was one of the most compelling programs I have ever seen, said, 'I have always thought good would defeat evil.' He paused for a long minute and then half looked at us as if in a challenge, saying, 'Here we go!' I take that to mean that Simon has put himself out in the open in a way that is remarkably brave and honest. He hopes that this is the beginning of a chain of events that will lead to what he argued for last night — an anticorruption commission. Let me repeat Simon's closing remarks: 'I have always thought good would defeat evil. Here we go!' We in this Parliament must prove him right when he says 'Here we go!' Let's go together.

Doyle was then followed by the Leader of the National Party.

MR RYAN (Leader of the Nationals) — We have had three murders in Victoria in the last two weeks. Last night we saw Detective Sergeant Simon Illingworth speaking on television in a way which took enormous courage on his part, not only in terms of his own welfare, but that of his family. We have had on the front page of today's papers reports of a refusal to answer questions by an individual who has been given favour in the way in which he has been sentenced. He has now adopted an approach where he says that he is prepared to go to jail for a longer term on the basis of contempt charges, rather than answering questions because of risks to his life and to that of his family. Whether that be so or not, that is in fact what he has had to say.

I thought this issue was summed up very neatly by Simon Illingworth last night, as is reflected in the reports today in the newspapers. He said it is not a question of cat and mouse; it is a question of cat and cat. The distinction he was making was it is not a question of two unequal forces here. It is not the usual sort of circumstances where you have skilled and able police officers knowing the way the system works interviewing someone without the talents to know how the system works. Rather it is police officers investigating particular police officers. Those police officers under investigation know well how the system works and they go through the loopholes, they know how to take best advantage of the law as it stands. It is the reason that we are now in a situation in Victoria where whoever chairs this new organisation, which I advocate and which I understand the opposition to be advocating, needs to be someone who has these intrinsic skills which come with practising in this sphere of the law for a long time and in a lot of circumstances.

So I move to what the government should do: I believe it is timely for the government to establish what I term the Victorian corruption and crime commission. I believe this entity should be established under its own act of Parliament.

MR MILDENHALL (Footscray) — The Victorian community will judge the Opposition and the government by results. This skilled police force, with brave and fearless investigators like Simon Illingworth, is getting traction. Victoria Police is producing results, and the government will assist it and get the results.

We will not be distracted by the Opposition wanting to set up its bureaucracy and to divert the whole process into talk fests. We want results, and we will get there.

THE ACTING SPEAKER (Mr Kotsiras) — Order!

MR WELLS (Scoresby) — The Leader of the Opposition outlined very clearly five elements that we think an anticorruption commission should have. We also believe there needs to be a career structure in the anticorruption unit. At the moment it is not working. You cannot have a person in there for three years doing as little as possible because he knows he is going back out into mainstream policing. That is just not fair.

The last point I want to raise is that these anticorruption police officers must, as a priority, have the protection they need to get on and do their job. Of Victorian police, 99.99 per cent are outstanding; we just need to make sure it is kept that way.

Victorian State Parliament, House of Assembly, Tuesday, 25 May 2004, Question Time

MR WELLS (Scoresby) — My question is to the Minister for Police and Emergency Services. I refer the minister to the revelation by Detective Sergeant Simon Illingworth that he was threatened by a corrupt drug squad police officer in the company of a known underworld killer, and I ask: will the minister ensure that photographic evidence of this incident, currently being sought under freedom of information, is released without delay?

MR HAERMEYER (Minister for Police and Emergency Services) — Firstly, I, like many people, am concerned about the issues raised in relation to Detective Sergeant Simon Illingworth, and I reiterate that Victoria Police and the government place the highest priority on the safety and security of police members and their families. The police do a difficult job, and that means they are often coming into contact with some of the most unsavory members of the community. Unfortunately, in a small number of instances, some of those unsavory members happen to be police officers. It is a very difficult job they do, and we understand the stresses they work under. Victoria Police, I understand, will spare no resources in ensuring that its officers are properly protected.

MR DOYLE (Leader of the Opposition) — My question is to the Premier. I refer the Premier to his claim on radio this morning that he was not aware of evidence linking gangland killings to corrupt police. I also refer to the statement by Detective Sergeant Simon Illingworth aired last night that he was threatened by a corrupt drug squad police officer in the company of a known underworld killer. Is this not evidence that police corruption and gangland killings are directly linked? Why do you refuse to acknowledge that connection?

Victorian Parliament, House of Assembly, 2 June 2004

THE DEPUTY SPEAKER — Order! The Speaker has accepted a statement from the member for Malvern proposing the following matter of public importance for discussion: That this house notes the growing allegations of corruption within Victoria Police with links to 27 gangland killings and calls upon the government to establish immediately a permanent and independent crime and anticorruption commission to investigate the crisis of organised crime in Victoria.

MR DOYLE (Leader of the Opposition) — What we are dealing with today is far more serious. We are dealing with police corruption and gangland killings, and we need to be brave enough to say the two are linked. Members of the opposition believe we need a crime and anticorruption commission, and we also believe the government's approach so far to this crisis in Victoria has been wrong, for two reasons. There are two things you must have in order to respond to what we are facing at the moment — independence of response and coherence of response — and on both of those tests the government fails.

Who is going to investigate the Simon Illingworth story as shown on *Australian Story*, including the range of allegations he very bravely put before us? Who is going to investigate the George Williams talkback call — bizarre indeed — of yesterday? Will that take another special investigator? Who is going to investigate the Queensland incident of the attempted murder of a witness protection subject? Will that be another special investigator? Who is going to look at that remarkable case where a criminal refused to give evidence because of his fear for his life and his family's life? All these things are interconnected; all of them are part of the same fabric.

Are we going to have a special investigator for each?

When you add it all up, every 24 hours we get another revelation and another crisis. What do we get from the government each time? Another bolt-on solution, another ad hoc proposal and another bandaid — a bandaid to try to stop Victoria bleeding. Well, it is not staunching the bleeding! It is the politics of panic, and worse still, it is not even being conducted in a way that is appropriate to this Parliament and to our community. It is being conducted through the media.

Mr Mildenhall interjected.

MR SAVAGE (Mildura) — I rise to make a simple contribution to this matter of public importance, and pose the question: what is corruption?

The word 'corruption' is defined as 'lacking integrity, open to or involving bribery, wicked, spoilt by mistakes, altered for the worse, made evil, pervert, bribe, make rotten'.

Like many members in this place I watched *Australian Story* the other day. After having been in the police force for a long time I should not be surprised about revelations, but I was surprised, disturbed and disgusted that the system left Simon Illingworth out to dry and did not support him or treat him properly. That sort of situation should not occur.

We should not have to rely on people who are courageous enough to put their hands up — especially at a junior level, because it is much harder to do it there than it is at a senior level — and say, 'That is wrong. I do not believe in that, and you should not be doing that.' That is very difficult, and there are not too many people around who have the strength of character or the courage to do that. People like that are rare. We should all do some self-analysis, because not every one of us has to face that conflict. It is very difficult. The police force does have difficulty dealing with whistleblowers; there is no doubt about that.

Read more, view video clips and keep updated:
visit www.filthyrat.com.au

www.fontainepress.com

www.ingramcontent.com/pod-product-compliance
Lightning Source LLC
Chambersburg PA
CBHW021146160426
43194CB00007B/711